ROBERT MANNING
STROZIER LIBRARY

MAY 25

Tallahassee, Florida

Improprieties

For Peter,
Jacob, and Luan

Improprieties

Politics and Sexuality in Northern Irish Poetry

CLAIR WILLS

CLARENDON PRESS · OXFORD

1993

Oxford University Press, Walton Street, Oxford OX2 6DP
Oxford New York Toronto
Delhi Bombay Calcutta Madras Karachi
Kuala Lumpur Singapore Hong Kong Tokyo
Nairobi Dar es Salaam Cape Town
Melbourne Auckland Madrid
and associated companies in
Berlin Ibadan

Oxford is a trade mark of Oxford University Press

Published in the United States
by Oxford University Press Inc., New York

British Library Cataloguing in Publication Data
Data available

Library of Congress Cataloging in Publication Data
Wills, Clair.
Improprieties: politics and sexuality in Northern Irish poetry / Clair Wills.
Includes bibliographical references and index.
1. Political poetry, English—Irish authors—Northern Ireland—History and criticism. 2. Women and literature—Northern Ireland—History—20th century. 3. Northern Ireland in literature. 4. Sex in literature. I. Title.
PR8781.P64W55 1993 821'.91409358—dc20 93–13152
ISBN 0–19–811268–8
ISBN 0–19–818239–2 (pbk)

Set by Hope Services (Abingdon) Ltd.
Printed in Great Britain
on acid-free paper by
Biddles Ltd.
Guildford & King's Lynn

Acknowledgements

I AM grateful to Faber and Faber Ltd. for permission to quote from the work of Tom Paulin; to Faber and Faber Ltd. and Wake Forest University Press for permission to quote from the work of Paul Muldoon; and to Carcanet Press and W.W. Norton & Co., Inc. for permission to quote from the work of Eavan Boland. An earlier version of Chapter 2 appeared in Harriet Devine Jump (ed.), *Diverse Voices: Essays on Twentieth-Century Women Writers in English* (Harvester Wheatsheaf, 1991); an earlier version of Chapter 3 appeared in *Oxford Literary Review*, 13 (1991); and an earlier version of part of Chapter 6 was previously published in my 'The Lie of the Land: Language, Trade and Imperialism in Paul Muldoon's *Meeting the British*' in Neil Corcoran (ed.), *The Chosen Ground: Essays on the Contemporary Poetry of Northern Ireland* (Seren Books, 1992).

This book has had a long gestation and seen many forms. I should like to thank the Principal and Fellows of Somerville College, Oxford, for creating a congenial environment in which to work from 1985 to 1988, and for their more practical help in funding research trips to Ireland. Thanks, too, to the Provost and Fellows of Queen's College, Oxford, for their financial and academic support from 1988 to 1990, when I held a Junior Research Fellowship. I am also indebted to Essex University for a term's study leave in 1992 which enabled me to finish the manuscript.

Personal thanks for constructive help and encouragement go to Angela Bourke, John Carey, Paul Hamilton, Anne Jefferson, Elaine Jordan, Siobhán Kilfeather, Angela Livingstone, David Lloyd, Peter Middelton, Stephen Mulhall, Bernard and Heather O'Donoghue, Karen Van Dyck, Robert Young, and Philomena and Bernard Wills. I am particularly grateful to Ken Hirschkop for advice and discussion, for cheerfully taking on his share of the child care, and for preparing the index. A long-distance, enthusiastic, and critical dialogue with Luke Gibbons has sustained and supported me over several years; this book would have been much the poorer without him. Nor could it have been written without the generosity, hospitality, and good-natured co-operation of its subjects, Medbh McGuckian, Paul Muldoon, and Tom Paulin; their contribution is obvious and my very warm thanks go to them. Finally I am deeply indebted to Peter Dews for many disagreements about poetry and philosophy, for his commitment to creating a new balance between work and family life, and for all his support and love.

C. W.

Contents

Introduction

THERE has been much critical interest in contemporary Northern Irish poetry in recent years, whether focusing on the work of a particular writer, or examining the phenomenon of the group of writers as a whole. This study does not attempt to provide an explanation for the wealth and diversity of poetic talent in Northern Ireland over the last thirty years, but focuses instead on the work of three writers: Paul Muldoon, Medbh McGuckian, and Tom Paulin. Despite their many differences, both aesthetic and political, their work reveals a common interest in questions of community, nationality, the legacy of the Enlightenment, and the burden both of nationalist and Romantic tradition. These are concerns they share with their older contemporaries; where they differ (in the broadest terms) is in the interpretative difficulty their poetry affords the reader. Their work tends to be both syntactically complex and hard to disentangle, and increasingly characterized by seemingly arcane references and an obscure and teasing choice of vocabulary. Much of the discussion in this book will be directed towards finding explanations for the formal nature of the work—should it be interpreted as part of a global 'postmodernist' revolution in the nature of poetry and poetic address? Alternatively, can the reasons for the dislocated structure of the poetry be related to the changing nature of the community in Ireland, since it is now no longer possible (if it ever was) to characterize it as a homogeneous and predominantly rural community, but one divided in terms of class, gender, religious affiliation, race, and urban experience? Or perhaps the reasons for the fragmented and self-reflexive forms can be traced to the increasing dominance of philosophical concepts (primarily post-structuralist ones) within literary studies. Certainly any writer who includes references to Kristeva and Derrida (as Muldoon does in 'Madoc—A Mystery'), or discussions of Heidegger and Paul de Man (as in Paulin's *Fivemiletown*) can hardly claim innocence of these ideas and debates. But possibly it is all far more sinister—despite the Irishness of their subject-matter, these writers have been 'colonized' by the dominant cultural forms in Europe and the United States. Inevitably, all these suggestions are in themselves partly accurate, yet this confluence of intellectual currents in itself suggests an interesting conjuncture between 'dominant' and 'marginalized' cultural forms. This is perhaps most obvious in Paulin's use of the universalist ideals of the Enlightenment in order to examine the contours of the historically 'marginalized' community of Ulster Protestants. But the signs of this conjuncture can be seen equally in Muldoon's use in 'Madoc' of the history of Western philosophy as analogue for the failed eighteenth-century revolution in Ireland, and in McGuckian's dialogue with European poets such as Coleridge, Byron, Mandelstam, and Rilke, as a means of exploring women's experience of sexuality in Ireland.

Whatever the larger philosophical arguments brought forth by the union of postmodern form and Irish subject-matter, the initial question raised by this exacting and demanding poetry turns on the nature of the poetic audience. In part the formal and stylistic difficulty of the work can be traced to the final disappearance of the always elusive local reader, and the growth of an institutional audience based on an ideal academic literate reader, cultivated by university and Arts Council readings (although paradoxically the professionalization of poetry and discourse about poetry in the academy also feeds into the postmodern, multicultural emphasis on local cultures). Both Muldoon and McGuckian have spent several years as Writers in Residence at universities in Northern Ireland, England, and the United States, and Paulin is Reader in English Literature at the University of Nottingham. What I will term the characteristic obscurity of reference in their work is inevitably both symptom of, and response to, contact with a poetic audience educated to expect a degree of interpretative difficulty. The question of an audience for the poetry is further complicated by the fact that their work is published simultaneously by British, Irish, and American publishing houses. However, there is a widespread belief (shared by the poets themselves) that their work does not sit happily within the British, Irish, or indeed the American poetic traditions, diverse though these are in themselves. What is their proper place? Uneasiness with the available categories can be overt, as in Paulin's public recognition that 'the Irish writer who publishes in Britain has a neo-colonial identity. And the central question which faces the neo-colonial and post-colonial writer is—whom am I writing for?'[1] Alternatively the suggestion that the poets need to be placed within a Northern Irish poetic tradition may be almost entirely covert, as in Paul Muldoon's choice of poets for inclusion in the *Faber Book of Contemporary Irish Verse*, which sets up a distinctly bounded geographical lineage for the Northern Irish writers stemming from the Belfast poet Louis MacNeice on the one hand and Patrick Kavanagh (from Monaghan) on the other.[2]

However, rather than explore the contours of a specifically Northern Irish tradition into which the poets may fit more properly, this study focuses on the improper and the anomalous. I emphasize the ways in which the poetry refuses to be contained either within the boundaries of nation-states, or in the available aesthetic categories and theoretical paradigms of current literary discourse. Impropriety characterizes not only the sense of place or home offered in the poetry, and the disruption of 'traditional' poetic form, but perhaps more obviously the sexual narratives the poets tell. Sex and sexuality will be important touchstones throughout this book, ranging from McGuckian's complex representations of feminine sexuality, to Muldoon's exploration of the violence of sexual relations (in *Quoof*), and Paulin's investigation of sex, love, and betrayal in *Fivemiletown*. Part of my argument centres on the ways in which forms of sexuality deemed 'improper' or at the very least impolite—maternal sexuality, prostitution, homosexuality, or simply explicit sex, sex for pleasure, and adolescent sex—become ways of questioning the propriety of political processes, nationalist and unionist concepts of community, and the very basis of the idea of home. As I discuss in detail in Chapter 2, since the regulation of sexuality and reproduction (particularly of women's sexuality, as their bodies are all too often treated as a national resource) is one of the principal means by which the national 'family' is both constituted and controlled, representations of alternative and 'improper' forms of sexuality may not only suggest alternatives to the national representations,

[1] Tom Paulin, *Ireland and the English Crisis* (Newcastle upon Tyne: Bloodaxe Books, 1984), 18.

[2] Another progenitor of Northern Irish poetry which Muldoon chose not to include, but other writers might well have argued for (particularly Paulin), is John Hewitt.

but also deflate the debilitating ideal of purity and perfection on which they are built.

But to what extent can this sense of impropriety be described as specific to a group of Northern Irish poets? Many of the stylistic traits identifiable in the work of these three writers are associated with postmodern experimental poetry identified in England with poets such as J. H. Prynne, Eric Mottram, Allen Fisher, and Wendy Mulford, and in the United States above all with the LANGUAGE poets, among them Charles Bernstein and Barrett Watten. Postmodern poetry's stylistic devices have been variously described as the rejection of traditional forms, the use of dislocated narrative, the resistance to personal anecdote, and a cryptic relation between the event described and its public meaning. Given the recurring difficulty of differentiating these devices from purely modernist stylistic experimentation (suggesting that there is far more continuity between so-called modernist and postmodernist literary forms than is often acknowledged), it is surely also necessary to emphasize the interest in local narratives, the elements of parody and pastiche, and the reuse of historical and literary materials in much contemporary poetry. These elements do indeed seem to be innovative, or to be weighted with new significance, in postmodern work. But the discovery of just these formal techniques in poets published by major publishing houses (generally associated with a conservative tradition in British poetry) suggests the need for a reappraisal of the construction of British experimental poetry as an alternative radical tradition, set against the tradition of empirical poetry of the Movement or the Group. Rather than a sum of stylistic devices utilized by a specific radical and innovative fringe, postmodernism needs to be interpreted as a cultural phenomenon affecting in varying degrees a wide spectrum of contemporary writing.

But if it is possible to argue that Muldoon, McGuckian, and Paulin's work has been affected by the postmodern condition as it questions traditional artistic forms (and perhaps more specifically the pretensions to formal coherence and public significance of modernist poetry[3]) this also suggests a need to produce a more nuanced definition of the postmodern as it applies to poetry in particular cultural contexts. More recent crit-

[3] See Alan Robinson, *Instabilities in Contemporary British Poetry* (Basingstoke: Macmillan, 1988), 1–15.

icism, informed by poststructuralist ideas (for example Alan Robinson's discussion of Muldoon, Heaney, Paulin, and McGuckian, or Thomas Docherty's discussion of McGuckian[4]) has been attentive to the connections between the poetry and contemporary philosophical debates, but there is a danger that the general application of post-structuralist literary theory to the work will elide or ignore its genesis in, and reference to, a specific cultural environment. In focusing on the 'impropriety' of the work I hope to be able not only to examine the poetry in the light of theories of stylistic fragmentation and hybridity, theories of the constitution of the public and the political in contemporary society, and feminist theories of sexuality, but also to reveal the limits of those theories.

At issue here is the anomalous position of Ireland as both part of Europe's drive towards progress and civilization, and at the same time Europe's 'other', a land to be both civilized and under-developed in order that Europe's (and principally Britain's) development should progress unhindered. There has been much critical debate over the relation between the postmodern and the post-colonial. On the one hand the argument has been made that both post-structuralism and postmodernism have their historical genesis in an auto-critique of the dominance of the West, an awareness that the ideals of reason and progress that were the mark of the European Enlightenment had as their underside the violent exploitation of Europe's 'others'. In this view postmodernism is interpreted as 'self-consciousness about a culture's own historical relativity', characterized by a 'sense of loss of European history and culture as History and Culture, the loss of their unquestioned place at the centre of the world'.[5] If this argument focuses on the crisis of confidence in reason and a sovereign sense of self within Europe, it is clear that the force for this reversal has come from the colonized, and suggests a further relation between postmodernism and post-colonialism, where postmodern fragmented form is deemed to arise not from the

[4] See ibid. and Thomas Docherty, 'Initiations, Tempers, Seductions: Postmodern McGuckian', in Neil Corcoran (ed.), *The Chosen Ground: Essays on the Contemporary Poetry of Northern Ireland* (Bridgend: Seren Books, 1992), 191–210.

[5] Robert Young, *White Mythologies: History, Writing and the West* (London: Routledge, 1990), 19–20.

centre, but from the margins of Europe's civilizing process.[6] In contrast, there have also been attacks on the association between the post-structuralist critiques of agency and subjectivity and post-colonial or minority literature, since this tends towards the incorporation of post-colonial culture within a new (Western) universalist paradigm.[7]

It is clearly not possible to disentangle these vexed relations here (still less to offer a general theory of the relation of both postmodernism and the post-colonial to feminism). What can be said, however, is that Ireland stands in a curious position in relation to these debates. On the one hand the course of Irish history has enforced a tangential relation to the confidence of the Enlightenment in reason and progress, for to a certain extent it experienced the raw end of the Enlightenment project firstly in colonization, and then in unequal union with Britain. As Desmond Bell has argued, 'Irish historical development, like that of other colonised societies, has not been intelligible within the universal and foundational thought of metropolitan Europe'. He notes the theoretical paradigms of bourgeois political economy, democratic revolution, and the philosophy of reason and history which were developed to fit the historical experiences of the advanced capitalist societies, England, France, and Germany. And he argues that each of these intellectual traditions and forms of knowledge

> encouraged Europe to imagine itself as harbinger of the modern and to conceive of its sociological experience as universal and as providing a basis for understanding patterns of social and historical development throughout the world. Within a Europe dominated by these

[6] See e.g. arguments about the relation between post-colonialism and minority discourse, in 'The Nature and Context of Minority Discourse', *Cultural Critique*, 6 and 7 (1987).

[7] See Barbara Christian, 'The Race for Theory', in Linda Kauffman (ed.), *Gender and Theory: Dialogues in Feminist Criticism* (New York: Blackwell, 1989), 225–37. However, as Bill Ashcroft, Gareth Griffiths, and Helen Tiffin argue, despite the dangers of a new form of theoretical imperialism, there is a two-way relationship between the postmodern and the post-colonial. 'Conversely, it is arguable that dominant European movements, such as postmodernism, which have sought in recent times to reabsorb post-colonial writing into an international postmodern discourse, may themselves, in fact, be more endebted to the cultural effects of the material practice of colonization and its aftermath than is usually acknowledged' (*The Empire Writes Back: Theory and Practice in Post-Colonial Literatures* (London: Routledge, 1989), 156).

enlightenment propositions Irish historical experience, like that of other peripheral regions subject to colonialism and a subsequent pattern of uneven capitalist development, has often appeared unintelligible.[8]

The crucial historical fact to support this argument is the famine of the 1840s, an occurrence surely unthinkable in Britain, France, Germany, or indeed America in the nineteenth century.[9] But the foundations for the failure of classical ideas of political economy within Ireland were laid far earlier. For under colonialism, and later under the union with Britain, Ireland was prevented from developing an indigenous 'public sphere' or forum for liberal political debate, without which the ideals of individualism and autonomy (requirements for the Enlightenment model of progress and development) could hardly thrive.

However, Ireland can not simply be described as 'other' to Europe; at a very obvious level it is part of Europe, and, as Carol Coulter has argued, it lies to some extent 'between First and Third worlds'.[10] The case for the inclusion of Irish history and culture within the 'grand narrative' of the Enlightenment is particularly strong in the North of Ireland, home of a vibrant bourgeois entrepreneurial class, and of eighteenth-century optimism in the values of democracy and citizenship (albeit that the planned rebellion of 1798 failed, and degenerated into sectarianism). Moreover, as Muldoon's poetry consistently (if wryly) asks us to acknowledge, not only was Ulster colonized during the seventeenth-century Plantation, but Ulstermen in turn went on to play a significant part in the violent colonization of America.

Given the complex historical narrative at work here it should come as no surprise that indigenous Irish arguments for postmodernism tend not to associate it with the triumph of the local and particular (concepts all too easily confused with the tribal and with Romantic nationalist ideas of the folk). Instead the heralds of postmodernism see it as displacing the opposition

[8] Desmond Bell, 'Cultural Studies in Ireland and the Postmodernist Debate', *Irish Journal of Sociology*, 1 (1991), 90–1.

[9] See Thomas A. Boylan and Timothy P. Foley, *Political Economy and Colonial Ireland: The Propagation and Ideological Functions of Economic Discourse in the Nineteenth Century* (London: Routledge, 1992). As Muldoon emphasizes, however, the genocide of the American Indians is indeed a parallel, if not more terrible, historical event.

[10] Carol Coulter, *Ireland: Between First and Third Worlds* (Dublin: Attic Press, 1990).

between Romantic and Enlightenment perspectives on Irish culture, and leading to the possibility of overcoming the divisions between the diverse cultural traditions within Ireland. I discuss these ideas in detail in Chapter 1; while I find many of the arguments for a post-nationalist culture, or for a cultural 'fifth province', or indeed for tolerance of diverse cultural traditions, both illuminating and engaging, there is, I believe, a fundamental difficulty with the concept of culture at work in these debates. Underlying all these arguments (to a greater or lesser extent) is an idea of the aesthetic as above or beyond politics, and outside of ideology; art has a socially redemptive role in a society where the political has so far notoriously failed.[11] So, for example, the Cultural Traditions Group (which is generally hostile to what its members view as the dangerous politicization of the aesthetic) stress the increased tolerance of cultural diversity which can be achieved through literary and artistic projects—though their own eschewal of any links between culture and politics is itself a substantial intervention in the public sphere, designed, moreover, to have specific political effects. Similarly defenders of the post-nationalist ideal in Ireland look to a cultural postmodernism as both symptom and cause of the fragmentation of long cherished ideals of the unity of national culture. For Field Day (who are as a group quite happy with a political definition of their project) the political nature of literature lies primarily in the possibility of reconfiguring through culture narrow definitions of Irish cultural tradition, whether nationalist or Unionist. This has been their principal aim in the production of plays and publication of pamphlets, but *The Field Day Anthology of Irish Writing* is their most significant undertaking in this regard.

Given that this book is concerned above all with literary (specifically poetic) representations, the fact that I am concerned to distance myself from such arguments about the value of literary culture may seem strange. However, I do not wish to argue for the disjuncture between literature and politics, but to suggest an alternative to the ways in which the relationship between the

[11] This is an argument also made by Desmond Bell, 'Cultural Studies in Ireland', 85: 'For the contemporary intelligentsia in Ireland, marginalised from active politics, whether of the Left or Right, of Unionism or Republicanism, the garrulous discourse of cultural identity seems to have displaced traditional political concerns.'

two tends to be envisaged. So, for me, the problem with current definitions of cultural politics in Northern Ireland lies in the notion that art has a 'redemptive' role because it offers a 'resolution' of political difficulties in the realm of aesthetics. As an alternative I could turn to the model of 'engaged' literature, or literature which professes a direct political purpose. As we shall see, this is the model which tends to be applied in readings of Tom Paulin's work, to the detriment of an understanding of the ways in which his poetry works at altering definitions of the political. Readers of Muldoon and McGuckian's poetry might well suggest Theodor Adorno's model for understanding the political nature of modernist hermeticism. For Adorno such literature has a political function by virtue of its very refusal of function as a whole; thus while 'committed' literature is in constant danger of degenerating to mere propaganda, the hermetic nature of High Modernism preserves the specificity of the aesthetic.[12] Such an argument, which again emphasizes the 'redemptive' qualities of art, has clear similarities with the forms of cultural politics in Northern Ireland which I have mentioned. What is lacking in all of these models is an understanding of the ways in which literature plays a role in defining the nature of the public and political itself. Throughout this book I shall argue that the poetry has a critical function in so far as it intervenes in, and comments on the construction of the political sphere. In my view the poets I have chosen to discuss are very apt examples of the need to read 'politically', not only because of the clearly political nature of much of their subject-matter, but crucially because the formal nature of their work reconfigures the division between public (political) and private spheres and modes of discourse.

The book is divided into two parts; in the first I discuss some of the general issues raised by reading the poetry: the relation between poetry and politics in contemporary Northern Ireland; the limits of Enlightenment and Romantic perspectives on Northern Irish culture; the role of myth in definitions of the political (with particular reference to the myth of the motherland); the division between public and private spheres of social activity, and the strategies adopted by women poets in order to combat its debilitating effects; the controversy over claims for the

[12] Theodor Adorno, 'Commitment', in Ernst Bloch *et al.*, *Aesthetics and Politics* (London: New Left Books, 1977), 177–95.

specificity of Irish cultural experience embedded in language and dialect; postmodern arguments about the nature of political violence. In the second part I analyse in detail the more recent work of each of the three poets, arguing that the significance of their work, and specifically its formal nature, cannot be understood using established definitions of the relationship between poetry and politics. Thus I view my own work as having a political function, in that I aim to construct an alternative framework through which to read the poetry, and therefore understand the significance of its critique of the contemporary political domain.

Part I

1

The Politics of Poetic Form

> Is it that to refer, however obliquely,
> Is to refer?[1]

In what ways do the formal dynamics of a poem shape its ideology? How do poetic styles have political meanings? We are used to at least two principal arguments about the nature of the relationship between poetry and politics. On the one hand there is the model of 'committed' or 'engaged' literature, or literature with a specific political purpose, which is not usually associated with a distinctively 'literary' poetic form since this sets it apart from the mass of the reading public. On the other hand there is the paradigm of literature whose politics lies precisely in the fact that it is without purpose in the political world. In Northern Ireland these seemingly opposed views are inflected in a very particular manner, partly because of an aesthetic or cultural interpretation of the nature of the political sphere, which leads to an emphasis on cultural politics and on the poet's role in giving voice to, or representing, his or her community. In a certain sense 'engaged' literature is thus deemed to be that which is rooted in a particular community (and therefore authenticated through 'experience'), but also that which, through its formal qualities, refuses to be reduced to the level of propaganda for one side or the other. The opposition between the drive towards poetic 'responsibility' to the political situation, and the desire for poetic 'freedom' lies at the root of almost all discussions of Northern Irish poetry. In *The Government of the Tongue* Seamus Heaney articulates a now well-established tension. He suggests that in choosing to write the poet is 'arrogating to [himself] the right to take refuge in form'.[2] Noting the dangers of solipsism,

[1] Paul Muldoon, *Meeting the British* (London: Faber and Faber, 1987), 50.

[2] Seamus Heaney, *The Government of the Tongue* (London: Faber and Faber, 1988), p. xxii.

Heaney's conscience is none the less allayed by his conviction of the 'redemptive' qualities of art. As he comments in his reappraisal of Kavanagh's work, that quality of 'redemption' arises from the authenticity of the poet's experience as it is captured in poetry and given form:

> I have learned to value this poetry of inner freedom very highly. It is an example of self-conquest, a style discovered to express this poet's unique response to his universal ordinariness, a way of re-establishing the authenticity of personal experience and surviving as a credible being.[3]

Without this quality of authenticity or sincerity the 'private' lyric cannot hope to find a voice beyond its own individual concerns, and the implication is that herein 'irresponsibility' lies.

This ideal of authenticity is undercut in the poetry of Muldoon, McGuckian, and Paulin. In their work private or personal discourse, the discourse of the family and the small community, are associated with the obscure and enigmatic, rather than with truth value and authenticity. Discomfort with the ideal of poetic sincerity is perhaps clearest in Muldoon's work (and this is signalled in his most recent poetry by his interest in Byron, who made a career out of 'insincerity'). Yet I will argue that Muldoon's suspicion of the value of 'experience' is merely one sign of a more general condition in contemporary Northern Irish poetry. For example, despite McGuckian's ostensible commitment to the representation of her personal life, we might note the teasing play with the idea of 'privacy', the double selves, and ever-disappearing centre of her work. So far from 're-establishing the authenticity of personal experience', McGuckian's poetry puts into question the very possibility of knowing, far less of communicating, such experience. Though perhaps less apparent the rejection of the ideal of romantic authenticity and 'rootedness' has also been of fundamental importance in Paulin's more recent work; as I will argue, it is related to his desire to find an alternative to 'traditional' post-Romantic aesthetics, which he sees as bound to a conservative political ideology. For all three poets, the private sphere is not the place of truth and generalizable individual experience, but is continually displaced, found to be empty, or its contents to be of little significance. The idea of poetic form as 'refuge' or 'resolution' is thus totally inadequate to

[3] Seamus Heaney, *The Government of the Tongue*, 14.

an understanding of this work; the private space of the lyric is parodied, through the mechanism of impenetrability, and at the same time instability of poetic reference ensures that the lyric is open to public and political meanings.

In this chapter I will examine in some detail contemporary debates about the relationship between poetry and politics in Ireland, and specifically the perceived function of 'mythic' or 'tribal' thought in political consciousness. I shall argue that obliqueness carries a particular weight in the work of the three poets and that this has to be understood in part in relation to general arguments about postmodern form. However, in the context of Northern Irish culture and politics, such obliqueness and obscurity has a very particular function in questioning the validity of established definitions of the public sphere—how poetry should speak for a community and thus how it can speak to a political situation.

Postmodernism and 'Obscurity'

This study examines the work of a group of contemporary Northern Irish writers whose writing careers have shadowed and been shadowed by the political situation in Northern Ireland during the last twenty or more years. Their work is shadowed too by the debate over the relationship between 'private' lyricism and 'public' and political statement. In this the younger writers differ from poets such as John Montague, Michael Longley, James Simmons, and Seamus Heaney who were established writers before the onset of the recent violence, and it may therefore be possible to discern in their work a different aesthetic and political response to the Troubles and the perceived need for writers to address them. If not an ideology these poets broadly share a common historical experience. Paul Muldoon and Medbh McGuckian were contemporaries at Queen's University, Belfast; they became students at the beginning of the Civil Rights protests in the late 1960s in Northern Ireland. Academically, they followed a similar path, studying English, and, significantly, studying under Seamus Heaney among others, who was at that time a lecturer in English at Queen's.[4] Tom Paulin's biography

[4] Muldoon's link with Heaney at this stage was a very important one. He attended meetings of the poetry Group which had been set up in the early 1960s

differs significantly from that of his contemporaries, and this is the first of many points at which I shall note a contrast in the tradition from which Paulin springs, as well as in his aesthetic and political beliefs—differences which serve to render the similarities between his work and that of his contemporaries all the more striking. Unlike the other poets I focus on, Paulin's background is Protestant; moreover he left Belfast in 1967 to take a degree in English at Hull University, and subsequently a further degree at Oxford, though he has always maintained strong personal and political links with Northern Ireland.

Beyond biographical considerations, however, there are stylistic and formal links between the work of these ostensibly very different poets. Increasingly their poetry is characterized by a certain codedness and obscurity of reference, although the type of interpretative difficulty which the poetry affords also differs in significant ways (and very rarely does the poetry seem to suggest the impossibility or undesirability of critical interpretation—quite the reverse, as I shall argue, it invites it). But does this obscurity or privacy of reference suggest a lack of responsibility towards the larger political situation? On the level of reception it must be conceded that, whereas Paulin's poetry is read (and often condemned) as fiercely committed and public poetry, readers and critics of Muldoon's work, and more particularly of McGuckian's, have often found it hard to disentangle a meaning for the poems which goes beyond private or enigmatic reference. (Responses to Muldoon's work tend to focus not on the obscurity of the public statement, but on the characteristically enigmatic refusal to take up any one public position.)

McGuckian's work in particular has called forth a variety of strategies in critics and readers for attempting to hold the poetry down to a meaning, or to open the meaning out into general significance. The dense syntax of the poems is peppered with seemingly logical grammatical markers which should add up to a narrative. But words such as 'like' and 'as' take on an almost par-

in Belfast by Philip Hobsbaum, then also a lecturer at Queen's, on the lines of the London poetry Group which he had started in the late 1950s with Edward Lucie-Smith, although by the time Muldoon went to Queen's in 1969 Hobsbaum had left. See the *Honest Ulsterman*, 52, for a retrospective by Belfast poets on the Group. The *Honest Ulsterman* itself, which was started by James Simmons in 1968, was an important forum for new writing and literary discussion, as was the Belfast Arts Festival, which helped to consolidate artistic confidence in the region.

odic role as otherwise logical grammatical constructions are undermined by the randomness of the images. Strange shifting metaphors and circular syntax encourage the diffusion of meaning rather than the pursuit of conclusions. This uncertainty with regard to meaning has given rise to denunciations of the poems as nothing more than a metaphorical game, and one reviewer has characterized the technique as one 'which connects nothing with nothing'.[5] This reaction springs in part from the seeming chaos of the images which seem impossible to fix to a particular referent, as in these lines from 'Rowing', which gather together a seemingly capricious and subjective collection of associations:

> Where
> My hand is, there is the pain that wires
> Its sour honey through my flush,
> As an ear-ring grows precocious in the vellum
> Of a head, with all its sutures
> In the offing, or the sand unhindered
> Thickening with marble dust.[6]

This arbitrariness with regard to meaning is deceptive (and this poem in particular is illuminated by a careful reading of the volume *Venus and the Rain* as a whole), but the very resistance to interpretation evokes the desire to crack the code and to lay the matter open. Knowing full well that the scattered fragments of narrative will not add up, the reader still feels compelled to construct a coherent story.[7] That story has been interpreted primarily as a representation of the 'feminine' sphere: the complexities of women's experience of sexuality and childbirth, the opposing claims of the self as woman and the self as writer, and the intricacies of familial relationships. Yet, as I shall argue in Chapter 5, this intimate sphere is never separated from the public, political world, a linkage

[5] Blake Morrison, 'Tropical Storms', rev. of Medbh McGuckian, *Venus and the Rain*, in *London Review of Books* (6–19 Sept. 1984), 22.

[6] Medbh McGuckian, *Venus and the Rain* (Oxford: Oxford University Press, 1984), 33. For a detailed analysis of this poem see Clair Wills, 'The Perfect Mother: Authority in the Poetry of Medbh McGuckian', *Text and Context*, 3 (1988), 91–111.

[7] Martin Mooney notes the incongruity between logical grammatical structures and a seemingly arbitrary selection of images in 'Body Logic: Some Notes on the Poetry of Medbh McGuckian', *Gown Literary Supplement* (1988), 16–18. See for example the poems 'Harem Trousers' and 'Death of a Ceiling', in *On Ballycastle Beach*.

which is drawn formally as well as thematically. Moreover, in tension with this perceived aim to express the inner self of the woman lies McGuckian's sustained exploration of the legacy of post-Romantic poetry. She carries out a formal and symbolic dialogue with (predominantly male) Romantic and modern poets such as Coleridge, Byron, Rilke, Mandelstam, and Tsvetaeva.

In contrast, Muldoon's poems reveal none of the surface syntactical confusion of McGuckian's work. In the main he uses metaphors taken from everyday life: clichés, and the language of the media. But underneath the surface simplicity, as he says of Robert Frost, 'all kinds of complex things are happening'.[8] In contrast to McGuckian, in Muldoon's work it is not the images, but the grammar which will not fit into a coherent narrative. Interpretation is complicated in his poems not by a mass of shifting images, but by riddles, ironies, word play, and a seemingly hermetic system of mythic and symbolic reference. Muldoon's fondness for tracing duplicitous, ambiguous narratives, in which several histories are held in tandem has often been noted. In his early poems Muldoon creates the sense of parallel narratives, or narratives whose significance lies elsewhere than in the evident tale by means of a duplicitous use of tense. So in the poem 'Mules' the contradictory tenses of the final stanza suggest two planes of time, one earthly, one heavenly, on which the events might be taking place:

> We might yet claim that it sprang from earth
> Were it not for the afterbirth
> Trailed like some fine, silk parachute,
> That we would know from what heights it fell.[9]

The uncertainty of reference is created in the longer poems, such as 'The More a Man Has the More a Man Wants', by an extended use of such techniques. The poem switches between styles, languages, places, and story-lines with no warning.[10] The

[8] Paul Muldoon, interview with John Haffenden, in John Haffenden (ed.), *Viewpoints: Poets in Conversation with John Haffenden* (London: Faber and Faber, 1981), 133.

[9] *Mules* (London: Faber and Faber, 1977), 52. On Muldoon's use of tense see Edna Longley, *Poetry in the Wars* (Newcastle upon Tyne: Bloodaxe Books, 1986), 222–4.

[10] Muldoon notes in his interview with John Haffenden his interest in stories that can be juxtaposed against each other, like mirrors, thereby creating new narrative possibilities (Haffenden (ed.), *Viewpoints*, 136).

creation of narrative out of discrete yet interconnecting units, found materials, and quotations from literary and non-literary texts has been the mark of Muldoon's poetry since 'Immram', and in *Madoc—A Mystery* this hybrid eclecticism seems to have reached its apotheosis. The poem has accordingly been read as an exemplary postmodern work: 'in true postmodernist fashion, its aim is to deconstruct our presumptive desire for a grand, unifying "metanarrative".'[11] In part this association of Muldoon's repertoire of styles with postmodernity arises from the poet's own engagement with contemporary literary theory (and in this sense the postmodern does become thematized in the work), an interest, more or less hostile, which he shares with Tom Paulin.

Paulin is well known for his espousal of a public and political poetry, and yet his most recent work reveals an increasing tendency towards hermeticism, and private or enigmatic reference. While Muldoon's concerns about the referential qualities of poetic language remain distanced, mediated through the frame of the poetic and historical characters which populate his poems, Paulin engages with the relation between textual and extra-textual realities directly and personally:

> We'd hid from your tribe
> and disappeared from ourselves
> (I've heard *n'y a pas de hors-texte*
> and guess Universal Man's
> a simple fold in all our knowledge
> *comme un tout petit pli*
> *de lin ou de toile*).[12]

The difficulty of interpreting Paulin's work arises less from the instability of the writerly persona than from the kinds of knowledge the poetry takes for granted, such as, in this poem, an acquaintance with the ideas of Derrida and Paul de Man, as well as a keen ear for verbal play. 'Universal Man' suggests not only Paul the Man, but also the Enlightenment ideals of free and common citizenship. Such techniques are used to almost bewildering effect in 'The Caravans on Lüneberg Heath' which like Muldoon's long poems undermine the traditional expectations of

[11] John Goodby, 'Elephantiasis and Essentialism', *Irish Review*, 10 (1991), 133.
[12] Tom Paulin, 'Mount Stewart', *Fivemiletown* (London: Faber and Faber, 1987), 38.

narrative and story-telling in the constant cutting back and forth between characters, moments of history, and levels of significance.

So how are we to interpret the significance of this aesthetics of the obscure and enigmatic, this elevation of parody and verbal play? Critical responses divide primarily into two groups; those who interpret the poetic techniques in terms of an international (or European and American) postmodern condition, and those who situate the poetry's problematics of address in the context of specifically Irish debates about the nature of community and identity. While each approach enables certain fruitful poetic and political comparisons to be made, neither can fully account for the status or significance of these poetic strategies.

To take the formalist explanation first, it is not difficult to isolate a series of stylistic techniques in the poetry which have become standard markers of the postmodern. Altogether the juxtaposition of different styles and forms, the parodic reintroduction of traditional literary materials, semantic indeterminacy, and enigmatic statement have been heralded as the radical new forms of British poetry. Indeed both 'obliqueness' and 'relativism' were judged by Blake Morrison and Andrew Motion to be the defining characteristics of contemporary poetry in their Penguin anthology.[13] Moreover they suggest that the increasing hegemony of such stylistic devices springs first of all from the turn away from the self-enclosed nature of the Movement lyric which took place in Northern Irish writing, and they instance particularly the Heaney of *North*. The implication is that the traditional lyric is inadequate to a new social and political reality, and that such obliqueness is the only way to deal with the changed situation in the North in the 1970s. Since obliqueness is clearly valorized by the editors it could be interpreted as a positive symptom of the effects of the political on poetry (as opposed, for example, to

[13] Blake Morrison and Andrew Motion (eds.), *The Penguin Book of Contemporary British Poetry* (Harmondsworth: Penguin, 1982). It should be stressed that this anthology deals solely with mainstream poetry, published by major British publishing houses, and consequently ignores the vigorous tradition of experimental and avant-garde poetry in English. However, part of my aim here is to question the sharp division between experimental work such as LANGUAGE writing and the seemingly more traditional forms these poets use. For a recent anthology which does represent the experimental tradition see Gillian Allnutt, Fred D'Aguiar, Ken Edwards, and Eric Mottram (eds.), *The New British Poetry* (London: Collins, 1988).

Fredric Jameson's negative symptomology of LANGUAGE poetry as the cultural logic of late capitalism).[14] But while it may be able to point to reasons for the emergence of a postmodern formalism, such a reading is unable to offer any more cogent analysis of the work's relationship to the political sphere.

The link drawn by Morrison and Motion between 'post-modernist "secrecy"' and the long poem is expanded in an essay on James Fenton and Paul Muldoon by Alan Robinson. Robinson associates the deconstruction of narrative figurative strategies, which frustrate the reader's expectations of formal coherence, with an increased obscurity or privacy of reference which he deems characteristic of postmodern poetry's drive to mock 'the seriousness of the High Modernist rage for order, which desired to elevate the imaginative structures of art to a socially redemptive role in an era of cultural disintegration'.[15] In this reading the difficulty and obscurity of reference appears to preclude a public or political dimension to the poetry, since public statements are veiled behind a system of symbolic correspondences, and references to public events are subordinated almost entirely to the private narrative the poems tell. The function and purpose of the poetic form thus becomes 'delight in deconstructive rationale.' Central to Robinson's thesis is the claim that what he terms 'unrecognized allusions' and hidden sources do not aid the reader in interpreting the poem, indeed that interpretation is rendered obsolete by the poem's style. Yet this ignores the contradictory messages sent by the obscure and enigmatic style. On the one hand the verbal slipperiness seems designed to undermine the referential aspects of language and to suggest that language

[14] See Fredric Jameson, 'Postmodernism, or The Cultural Logic of Late Capitalism,' *New Left Review*, 146 (July–Aug. 1984), 53–92. Another, equally influential, variant of Morrison and Motion's claim is John Kerrigan's argument for the existence of the new narrative, 'Reflexive, aleatory and cornucopian, the New Narrative deploys its fragmented and ramifying fictions to image the unpredictability of life, and its continuous shadowing of What Might Be'. Kerrigan formulated this description in a review of Muldoon's *Quoof* so it is not perhaps surprising that it should so snugly fit poems such as 'The More a Man Has'; however, he draws a further link between postmodern style and the political. In arguing for 'the essential interdependence, of a metaphoric emphasis in poetry and narrative Post-modernism', he makes the case for the style's natural alliance with feminism in that both reject the received structure of myths and narratives. See *London Review of Books* (16–29 Feb. 1984), 22–3.

[15] Alan Robinson, *Instabilities in Contemporary British Poetry* (Basingstoke: Macmillan, 1988), 7.

escapes the control of both writer and reader, and on the other such techniques necessitate considerable work from the reader in uncovering this very message. In many cases it is only by exposing the hidden references, for example to Paul de Man in Paulin's 'Universal Man', that the escape of meaning can be interpreted for what it is, rather than simple meaninglessness. Far from celebrating semantic irreducibility, the poems in fact ask to be unveiled and interpreted in order that the rationale behind the use of a particular style may be understood. And as a corollary to this, control of meaning remains very much in the hands of the writer, at least as far as his or her project is concerned. Robinson implicitly acknowledges this fact when he associates postmodern narrative techniques with privacy and secrecy (in other words with personal ownership, a form of public concealment in which the data may be available but not their meaning).

In part this misinterpretation of the significance of poetic form stems from a structural difficulty related to the question of audience. The poet's public role, his or her ability to make public statements, depends of course on the public's consciousness of those statements. Neither Muldoon nor McGuckian are generally read or critically received as poets who are attempting to engage their audiences in a political manner, and Paulin's political stance is repeatedly caricatured in critical reception. While this may be explained as the poetry's unsuccessful completion of the writer's intention (so one might ask, does a poem work if McGuckian describes it as dealing with a particular historical or political situation but none of her readers are aware of this level of reference?), it also bears on the nature of the contemporary readership. On the one hand the poets write for an audience highly educated in the poetic tradition, alert to the significance of poetic forms and to literary echoes and allusions. Both Muldoon and McGuckian have spent several years as Writers in Residence at universities in Northern Ireland, England, and the United States, and Paulin teaches in a university English department. Clearly much of the success of their styles depends on an academic readership. Yet their work is also directed towards an Irish readership, and situating it within the context of the contemporary Irish community may offer alternative ways of interpreting the significance of its poetic strategies. One study which has profitably addressed this issue is Dillon Johnston's discussion of contemporary work in *Irish Poetry After Joyce*. As Johnston points out, much contemporary poetry reveals in its strategies of address an understanding of the breakdown of any 'unity of culture' of the Irish audience, a breakdown which suggests the inadequacy of traditional modes of public address:

> To the fluidity of the culture itself we can add a second factor to account for the Irish poet's unstable relation to his audience. The Irish audience is itself unstable and fractured synchronically as the tradition is broken diachronically.[16]

The importance of Johnston's argument lies precisely in this linkage between the poet's stance towards tradition, and his or her relation to an audience. Yet strangely this most contextual of interpretations ends by recapitulating the abstract and formalist readings of the significance of linguistic play and obscurity as part of a generalized postmodernism. For the diverse nature of the contemporary Irish audience is associated with what are deemed to be postmodern developments in the social sphere; the heterogeneous nature of the Irish community is interpreted as both symptom and cause of transformations in the structure of society which seem finally to transcend the debilitating division between 'traditional' and 'modern' Ireland. The title of Johnston's essay, 'Toward "A Broader and More Comprehensive Irish Identity"' is taken from the New Ireland Forum Report of 1984, and it reveals the importance to this strand of thinking of recent debates on the nature of tradition and the need to reconfigure notions of Irish identity in the political realm. Journals such as the *Crane Bag* and the *Irish Review* have entertained arguments for both 'tradition' and 'modernity' in the realm of culture, as well as attempts to transcend the antagonism between the two which seems to have stamped discussions of Irish identity.[17] Seamus Deane clearly delineates the major paradigms of these discussions in his article 'Remembering the Irish Future', where

[16] Dillon Johnston, *Irish Poetry After Joyce* (Bloomington, Ind.: University of Notre Dame Press; Mountrath: Dolmen Press, 1985), 250. In fact Johnston rightly intimates that such 'unity of culture' never existed, but was simply claimed as both result and evidence of Ireland's traditional communal identity.

[17] As Liam O'Dowd has noted, perhaps the major stumbling-block for all these positions is that they lack a material or economic dimension of analysis, 'Neglecting the Material Dimension: Irish Intellectuals and the Problem of Identity', *Irish Review*, 3 (1988), 8–17.

he isolates two characteristic modes of figuring and conceptualizing Irish identity which he calls 'Enlightenment' and 'Romantic', or following William James, the 'tough' and 'tender' minded.[18] As we shall see, the perceived need to overcome the division between Enlightened and Romantic formulations of Irish identity (all too often confounded with quite other distinctions, for example between modernity and tradition, or even Protestantism and Catholicism) has adversely determined the shape of discussions of the relationship between literature and politics in Ireland.

Questions about the nature of Irish literary history are fundamentally imbricated with the debates about Irish social and political historiography, and more particularly with the 'school' of historiography known as revisionism.[19] The overcoming of the opposition between tradition and modernity in contemporary literature is read as the aesthetic counterpart of the new-found faith in 'Varieties of Irishness',[20] which, translated from a historical to a political axis, suggests the resistance to both 'orthodox' nationalist and Unionist positions in favour of a new construction of community which is the mark of the New Ireland Forum. It becomes increasingly clear that this emphasis on new configurations of culture and community constitutes a reflection in the Irish political realm of arguments about postmodernism in the realm of 'international' aesthetics. Both rely on a valorization of the dissolution of tradition and its 'pieties', consonant with the

[18] Seamus Deane, 'Remembering the Irish Future', *Crane Bag*, 8:1 (1984), 81–92. Deane's essay is itself an attempt to conceptualize a means of transcending this division, although his work, and that of other politically engaged cultural critics, has been read both as too tender (i.e. nationalist) and as too tough minded (i.e. rationalist), by critics such as Edna Longley and Witoszek and Sheeran respectively. See Edna Longley, 'Poetry and Politics in Northern Ireland', *Crane Bag*, 9:1 (1985), 26–37, and Nina Witoszek and Jo Sheeran, 'From Explanations to Intervention', in the same volume, 83–6.

[19] As the most well known of its current practitioners, Roy Foster, points out, to call it a 'school' is in fact a misnomer, since 'To the Scholars, it is quite simply a desire to eliminate as much as possible of the retrospectively "Whig" view of history which sees every event and process in the light of what followed it rather than what went before'. Yet Foster's consequent insistence that revisionists are not, as a body, hostile to Irish nationalism is somewhat belied by his claim that what they are hostile to is the 'old pieties' which are the mark of the popular understanding of Irish history: 'as regards political history, the old pieties have it their own way and historians tread carefully for fear of the "anti-nationalist" smear' (Roy Foster, 'We Are All Revisionists Now', *Irish Review*, 1 (1986), 2).

[20] See the introduction to Roy Foster's *Modern Ireland, 1600–1972* (Harmondsworth: Penguin, 1988).

breakup of 'unity of culture', and the consequent reconstruction of the past, and its child, the contemporary community. So, for example, the philosopher Richard Kearney argues for a postmodernist re-evaluation of myth with reference to Marcuse's dictum that authentic utopias must be grounded in recollection, which facilitates interpretation of the past as an enabling force for the future. The reconsideration of Irish identity thus involves the reinterpretation of tradition and myth as ambivalent concepts: 'What is required is a radical interrogation of those mythic sedimentations from our *past* and those mythic aspirations for our *future*, which challenge our *present* sense of ourselves, which disclose other possibilities of being'.[21]

Unsurprisingly, given the uncanny mirroring of formalist and contextual interpretations here, there are both political and poetic difficulties with this reading of poetic strategies as a representation of a more 'comprehensive' Irish identity. Naturally I do not wish to question the necessity and importance of the construction of a heterogeneous Irish community in terms of race, religion, class, and gender. However, the emphasis on the need to overcome the division between Enlightenment and Romantic conceptions of identity suggests that such labels are indeed accurate designations of the two forces in Irish history. In this reading nationalist sentiments are rejected as mythic 'pieties', romantic tribal affiliations which, while perhaps necessary or 'natural', require a healthy dose of rationalism in order to be rendered acceptable, while nationalist history is similarly designated both mythic and homogeneous. But such a construction ignores not only the traditional, customary, and mythic elements within Unionism, but also the many diverse and radical strands within the concept of tradition itself. As Luke Gibbons points out, the association of traditional or pre-modern culture with 'stagnation and conservatism' discounts the fractured legacy of Ireland's colonial history, which, in a sense, anticipates the fragmentation of modernism before the fact.[22] Moreover, the assumption that

[21] Richard Kearney, 'Myth and Motherland', *Ireland's Field Day*, ed. Field Day Theatre Company (London: Hutchinson, 1985), 79. Kearney and others have been accused both of valuing Irish tradition only in so far as it contributes to their postmodernist project, and of seeking a purely and genuinely Irish tradition only.

[22] Luke Gibbons, 'Montage, Modernism and the City', *Irish Review*, 10 (1991), 5–6.

modern nationalism is primarily an irrational and atavistic force denies the Enlightenment values of universal citizenship, political legitimacy, representation, and so forth, on which the very concept of the modern nation in part depends.[23] Indeed it is precisely this interpenetration of 'tribal' and 'civic' values which concerns Tom Paulin in *Liberty Tree* and *Fivemiletown*, as he traces the subsequent history in Ireland of the Enlightenment ideals of the French Revolution and the United Irishmen.

Poetically, the difficulty with both the postmodernist and 'Irish identity' readings of the significance of poetic form is that the poetry is thereby reduced either to merely symptomatic or reactive status. The form of the work is deemed to arise out of a particular set of social co-ordinates, but its function is considered to be a reflection in the realm of the aesthetic of an image of future possibilities in the social arena. While I would wish to deny neither the importance of supranational stylistic movements on Irish poetry, nor the fact that contemporary poetry in Ireland is indeed engaged in representing alternative constructions of community and identity, I would argue that the poetry, rather than being simply a symptom or reflection of the social, is actually engaged in an intervention in public or political discourse, in its alteration of the relationship between public and private discourses. I mean the distinction between public and private here to suggest the most basic distinction between the arena of public affairs, civic society and the public communications of the media, and private life as it is most generally understood, i.e those experiences and events which lie outside the knowledge and discussion of the wider community (but which, of course, is also socially constructed). Readings of Muldoon and McGuckian which emphasize the complexity of poetic address fail to account for the genuinely political aspects of their work, interpreting it as a representation of complexities in the public realm. However, both poets refuse the accepted definitions of public and political statement which have governed debates in Northern Ireland, and in so doing they create new ways of linking private life and pub-

[23] On theories of nationalism which question atavistic and irrational interpretations see Ernest Gellner, *Nations and Nationalism* (Oxford: Blackwell, 1983); Benedict Anderson, *Imagined Communities* (London: Verso, 1983); for an analysis of Irish nationalism in this light see Tom Garvin, 'The Return of History: Collective Myths and Modern Nationalisms', *Irish Review*, 9 (1990), 16–30.

lic assertion, despite the fact that neither poet is generally considered to be a writer of political statement. Responses to Paulin's work are reductive in an antithetical way—he is characteristically read as a self-consciously public poet and the ways in which he problematizes conventional notions of the public arena are ignored. But why this felt need to reconfigure the relationship between public and private languages? To answer this question we need to examine in more detail the relationship between politics and myth in contemporary Irish debate.

Myth and Politics in Northern Ireland

> The trouble with this place (Northern Ireland) is that if you don't engage in it, you're an ostrich, (whatever engage in it means). If you do engage in it, you're using it as a kind of—you're on the make almost, cashing in.[24]

Discussion of the relationship between poetry and politics in Northern Ireland has inevitably tended to focus on the question of the writer's responsibility towards the political situation. I shall argue in this section that such responsibility has been interpreted not as direct political intervention, but as the poet's cultural expression of the particular stamp of his or her community, his ability to give voice to its political complexion. Moreover, given the widespread belief that popular political culture in Ireland is filtered through the aesthetic, and through mythic archetypes (rather than 'hard facts'), poetry seems well placed to explore its contours. Thus arguments for and against the political role of literature tend to revolve around the status of mythic thought and mythic paradigms in the community.

Since the early 1970s Irish newspapers and cultural journals, such as the *Crane Bag* and more recently the *Irish Review*, and pamphlets produced by Field Day and Lip, have provided a forum for discussion of cultural and political identity, the relationship between tradition and modernity, and related issues such as the writer's political engagement, and the role of the contemporary Irish intellectual. To a large extent the debate has become trapped within certain well-defined parameters. To simplify a

[24] Paul Muldoon, quoted in Edna Longley, 'A Reply [to Mark Patrick Hederman]', *Crane Bag*, 9:1 (1985), 121.

debate in which no one participant's view precisely coincides with another's, the opinions may be divided into two groups. On the one hand, there is the belief that myth constitutes the means of access to the primitive and 'atavistic' part of the Irish psyche (and therefore also of the Irish community), without which it is impossible to gain a true understanding of the nature of the political situation in the North. On the other there is the view that the use of myth is a corruption of pure poetic imaginative discourse, and an aestheticization of politics which leads inexorably to fascism, or in the Irish context to militant Republicanism. The interesting fact about this second view is that it believes like the first that myth is a door into archaic atavistic tribalism, the only difference is that it would rather that door remained closed. There seems to be fundamental agreement between both sides in viewing the basic structure of popular consciousness as mythic, the population as caught within a seamless web of ideological mystification or 'false consciousness'. For both sides, as I shall argue, the value of art is that it can find a way out of the misrecognition of reality by forging a heightened self-consciousness, a knowing, ironic, or rational stand towards the mystifications of myth. In other words they believe that it is possible to stand outside myth in art. Thus, rather than any more fundamental disagreement on the nature of political consciousness (and therefore over the nature of a poetry which would speak to that consciousness), the debate actually centres on the way that art and literature can achieve an awareness beyond ideological misrecognition. As I shall argue, this concept of poetic form as appeasement, refuge, or resolution does not fit the dislocated, formally improper and deliberately unresolved poetry of the younger Northern Irish writers.

It may be helpful in analysing the contours of the debate on poetry and politics in Northern Ireland to focus on one particular moment: the controversy surrounding the publication of Seamus Heaney's volume *North*, which attempted to deal with violence in Northern Ireland in a more direct way than his previous work.[25] Given the more overtly political content of the volume, reactions to it tended to be polarized into different lines on the acceptability of public statement in poetry. The volume is divided into two

[25] Seamus Heaney, *North* (London: Faber and Faber, 1975).

parts, which were perceived to correspond to the two principles in the poem 'Hercules and Antaeus': rationality and mythic atavism. In an interview with Seamus Deane, Heaney describes the poem as evincing a 'nostalgia' for Antaeus' sense of place, a sense which he connects with a primitive, tribal, and hence bigoted view of the situation in Northern Ireland, while assenting to the rationalism of Hercules. (Importantly Heaney qualifies the poem in the phrase, 'but I think that is wrong now'.[26]) In keeping with this paradigm Conor Cruise O'Brien's review of *North* in the *Listener* focused debate on politics and the relation between atavism and 'rational humanism', and laid down the terms in which the debate has been conducted ever since. For O'Brien, the 'area where literature and politics overlap has to be regarded with much suspicion. It is suffused with romanticism, which in politics tends in the direction of fascism'.[27] In other words the attempt to translate the ideal fictions of the imagination into the real currency of politics must result in some form of totalitarian or fascist dictatorship. O'Brien's views are echoed by Edna Longley in her article on *North*, '"Inner Emigré" or "Artful Voyeur"?', where she objects to the use of mythic archetypes as an expression of a political situation. Longley is surely correct in isolating the difficulty with Heaney's attempt to represent the contemporary situation in terms of mythic archetypes, as that such symbols 'remain above or below argument'.[28] By utilizing myths associated with prehistoric rituals, current conflicts are represented as ahistorical paradigms. In the same vein, Ciaran Carson's review in the *Honest Ulsterman* criticizes the poetry for its 'historical determinism' in the comparison of prehistoric Jutland and present-day Northern Ireland:

> It's as if he is saying, suffering like this is natural; these things have always happened; they happened then, they happen now, and that is sufficient ground for understanding and absolution. It is as if there never

[26] Seamus Heaney, 'Unhappy and at Home', interview with Seamus Deane, *Crane Bag*, 1:1 (1977), 68.

[27] Conor Cruise O'Brien, 'An Unhealthy Intersection', *New Review*, 2:16 (1975), 3–8.

[28] Edna Longley, '"Inner Emigré" or "Artful Voyeur?" Seamus Heaney's *North*', in Tony Curtis (ed.), *The Art of Seamus Heaney* (Bridgend: Poetry Wales Press, 1982), 80.

were and never will be any political consequences of such acts; they have been removed to the realm of sex, death and inevitability.[29]

However, it is not merely the equation of past and present to which Longley objects; her argument is made more explicit in a later article in the *Crane Bag*, 'Poetry and Politics in Northern Ireland', where she objects to propaganda in poems because 'poetry can be political only on behalf of its own values'.[30] Interestingly she chooses Muldoon as an example of a poet who, unlike Tom Paulin, Seamus Deane, and what she regards as the worst of Heaney, subordinates political statement to the demands of the poetic medium: 'Muldoon's methods give the lie to the notion that language can operate politically in Irish poetry only by declaring firm allegiances.'[31] There are two interconnected issues here: first, the question of the poem's stylistic or formal felicity which, she believes, is destroyed by making 'statements', and, secondly, the distortion of the poet's 'imagination': 'Poetry and politics, like Church and State, should be separated. And for the same reasons: mysteries distort the rational processes which ideally prevail in social relations; while ideologies confiscate the poet's special passport to *terra incognita*'.[32] For Longley, poetry is set above and beyond politics, and yet at the same time it has a political role precisely in its separation from the ideologies present in the political sphere. So Longley quotes approvingly Derek Mahon's statement on the connection between poetry and politics, and poetry's role of 'resolution':

The poets themselves have taken no part in political events, but they have contributed to that possible life, or to the possibility of the possible life; for the act of writing is itself political in the fullest sense. A good poem is a paradigm of good politics—of people talking to each other, with honest subtlety, at a profound level'.[33]

This view of art's role in resolving conflicts in the political realm precisely by going beyond them has marked similarities to the celebration by Heaney, Kearney, Hederman, and Deane, (critics who otherwise seem to oppose Longley in stressing the

[29] Ciaran Carson, 'Escaped from the Massacre?', rev. of Seamus Heaney, *North*, in *Honest Ulsterman*, 50 (1975), 184–5.

[30] Longley, 'Poetry and Politics', 27. [31] Ibid. 37. [32] Ibid. 26.

[33] Derek Mahon, 'Poetry in Northern Ireland', *Twentieth Century Studies*, 4 (1970).

necessity for art to take account of the mythic strata of consciousness), of the 'realm of possibilities' opened up by art.[34]

Longley's statements have produced a number of combative responses from critics in both the North and South of Ireland. What is striking about the debate, however, is the extent to which there is fundamental agreement between the participants over what constitutes the political in poetry. So although critics such as Hederman and Kearney contend with Longley's view that when politics enters poetry it necessarily 'coarsens to verse', they agree that the nature of the relationship between poetry and politics offers a way for 'atavistic tribalism' to enter literature. Thus the argument centres on the evaluation of this consequence, rather than on the issue of how poetry may make political statements. Longley's article, 'Poetry and Politics in Northern Ireland', initiated a response in the *Crane Bag*, by Mark Patrick Hederman, 'Poetry and the Fifth Province'.[35] Hederman's argument draws on Jung and Heidegger in maintaining the necessity for poetry to lead the population through the 'psychic hinterland', into the fifth province, an 'other world' which differs from Longley's *terra incognita* in its relationship to the world of Northern Ireland. It is not, he claims, 'a platonic realm irretrievably cut off from the real world in which we live', and he equates it with Heaney's 'Antaean' region: i.e. it is set against rational argumentation: 'The Antaean use of intellect is one whereby this faculty is used, not in its authoritative and autonomous capacity, but as the receiver of something "given". The intellect recuperates for the realm of communicative discourse those instinctive gestures of poetic inspiration which, at the same time, reveal its source'.[36] Therefore it is in touch with the 'primitive' tribal side

[34] The debate has also centred on stylistic issues, particularly the relevance of the Movement lyric or 'well-made poem' to Irish writing; for example, Heaney stated in his 1977 interview with Deane that major poetry will always burst the confines of the 'well-made poem', which tends towards insulated and balanced statement. Major poetry will always therefore be one-sided ('Unhappy and at Home'). Longley objects to the way the statement 'ties in the espousal of a Nationalist attitude with divorce from "English" modes' (*North*, 92). Her argument has by contrast been seen as a form of 'literary unionism'.

[35] Mark Patrick Hederman, 'Poetry and the Fifth Province', *Crane Bag*, 9:1 (1985), 110–19. Hederman had himself earlier written a response in *Crane Bag* to O'Brien which had been picked up on by Longley in her earlier essay on *North*. See also 'Seamus Heaney: The Reluctant Poet', *Crane Bag*, 3:2 (1979), 61–70.

[36] Hederman, 'Fifth Province', 116.

of the Irish psyche. Here Hederman's argument mirrors the editorial to an earlier *Crane Bag* issue, which describes a fissure between civilized and primitive Ireland: 'This schizophrenia may be expressed as humanism versus atavism, rationalism versus archetypical irrationalism, inner versus outer vision.'[37]

This editorial in turn can be read as an expression of Richard Kearney's view of the relationship between myth and poetry. Kearney's theorization is among the most interesting, since it makes explicit assumptions hidden in, for example, Hederman's view. Kearney has been greatly influenced by the writings of Paul Ricoeur on myth and ideology, and in keeping with Ricoeur's work he stresses myth's utopian role in the community. Myth for Kearney is a double-sided symbolism, it harbours both a critical utopian 'forward look' and an ideological 'backward look' (which he argues is the one most often focused on by 'demythologisers' who seek to uncover myth's ideological role as a mystifying false consciousness). In fact, Kearney's argument here rests on a precarious distinction between 'genuine' and 'deviant' myth, the first of which has universalist potential, and the second of which has become reified, caught within the 'abuses of doctrinal prejudice, racist nationalism, class oppression or totalitarianism'.[38] But the importance of Kearney's argument for the discussion here lies in the fact that, despite his more complex theory of the functions of mythic paradigms in society, he repeats the assertion that art lies to a certain extent outside the mythic realm since it fosters a self-conscious, critical attitude to the mystifications of ideology. In *Transitions* he notes how Irish authors have:

> demythologized the insularist clichés of Irish culture in order to remythologize its inherently universalist resonances. Once a myth forgoes its power of ideological dissimulation, once it ceases to be taken literally as a force of domination, it ceases to *mystify*. Myth then no longer serves as a monolithic doctrine to which the citizens of the nation submissively conform; it becomes a symbol bearing a plurality of meanings. It is precisely the *symbolic* nature of a myth's reminiscences and anticipations which commits it to a multitude of interpretations.[39]

He calls this a 'post-modern' understanding of myth, since it goes beyond the traditional dichotomy between a conservatism

[37] Editorial, *Crane Bag*, 1:2 (1978), 6.

[38] Richard Kearney, *Transitions: Narratives in Modern Irish Culture* (Dublin: Wolfhound Press, 1988), 275.

[39] Ibid. 278.

which would value all myths as part of the Irish identity, and a modernism which would reject them as constraining. And yet, in what might seem on the surface to be a contradiction in his argument, Kearney argues that it is poetry's inclusion of mythic archetypes corresponding to those embedded in the Irish psyche (Ricoeur's 'original mythic nucleus') which enables it to fulfil a critical role in society.[40] So despite the fact that myths, in Kearney's view, work ideologically to mask truths, it is possible to use myth 'utopically'—the self-conscious awareness of myth leads to its bearing towards future horizons. However, myth's liberatory qualities must depend on the context in which it is read, a fact which Kearney fails to acknowledge. He analyses the transmission of postmodern myths solely in terms of authorial interpretation, but this intentionalist reading includes no concept of how the new narrative is received; there seems to be nothing intrinsic to the narrative which would preclude its being read in terms of continuity, and confirmation of sameness with the past, rather than postmodern dislocation.[41]

The views I have discussed concur in assuming a fundamental connection between the role of the artist as a spokesperson for his people, and the role of myth in supposedly symbolizing the atavistic thought of those people. Myth is the means by which the poet can approach the timbre of the community, and it is therefore through the harnessing of myth that the poet can speak 'for' his community. The underlying assumption here is that by opening himself up to the psyche of the community, the poet's cultural artefacts will exist in continuity with the desires and beliefs of the community. The political thrust of such poetry thus inheres in its capacity to stand or speak for a tribe. While Kearney argues this in philosophical terms drawing on Ricoeur's theory of the 'mytho-poetic nucleus of a society' which is constitutive of a culture, writers such as Seamus Heaney, Seamus

[40] See Paul Ricoeur, *Lectures on Ideology and Utopia*, ed. George H. Taylor (New York: Columbia University Press, 1986), 17, on Utopia's escapism as the cure of the pathology of ideological thinking. See also Kearney's interview with Ricoeur, *Dialogues with Contemporary Continental Thinkers: The Phenomenological Heritage* (Manchester: Manchester University Press, 1984), 36–45.

[41] The problem of intentionalism in Kearney's theory arises, in turn, because of the link which he draws between an individual writer and the 'cultural imaginary' of the community. For such a continuity to exist there can be no asymmetry between the writer's perception of the effects of his work, and its actual effects.

Deane, and John Montague award the poet a similar role as spokesperson in more strictly poetic and political terms. So the poet's public and political role springs not from direct political statements he may make, but from his ability to articulate a community; in this way Heaney argues that his poetry is consistent with, almost an extension of, the 'mythos' of his community (i.e. it is automatically in the public sphere by virtue of its congruence with a public psyche):

> Poetry is born out of the watermarks and colourings of the self. But that self in some ways takes its spiritual pulse from the inward spiritual structure of the community to which it belongs; and the community to which I belong is Catholic and nationalist . . . I think that poetry and politics are, in different ways, an articulation, an ordering, a giving of form to inchoate pieties, prejudices, world-views, or whatever. And I think that my own poetry is a kind of slow obstinate papish burn, emanating from the ground I was brought up on.[42]

The underlying assumption here is that there is no rupture between the world of literary culture and that of day-to-day life. Heaney claims a surely tenuous continuity between an undeniably English literary style and the act of bearing witness for a dispossessed agricultural Catholic and Irish community.[43]

So it is the issue of community which brings together the question of public or private writing and myth, a connection which is nicely brought out in an early essay by Seamus Deane, 'Irish Poetry and Irish Nationalism'.[44] The essay is significant in that it was written before the publication of Heaney's *North* and the subsequent focusing of the debate on the question of myth, and it is therefore useful in revealing how the connection between the

[42] Heaney, 'Unhappy and at Home'. Heaney has undoubtedly changed his views on the role of myth in poetry since 1977, but this is the position which has formed the response among younger poets which I wish to examine. Moreover, despite the many formal and stylistic changes in Heaney's poetry over the years, as he argues in the Preface to *The Government of the Tongue*, he maintains his commitment to a 'redemptive' understanding of art.

[43] See David Lloyd on the poem 'Digging', which attempts to situate the subject in continuity with a culture he no longer shares, in '"Pap for the Dispossessed": Seamus Heaney and the Poetics of Identity', *Boundary 2* (Winter/Spring, 1985), 319–42, and note Heaney's more recent, explicit attempts at the role of spokesperson, such as 'From the Land of the Unspoken', in *The Haw Lantern* (London: Faber and Faber, 1988), 18.

[44] Seamus Deane, 'Irish Poetry and Irish Nationalism', in Douglas Dunn (ed.), *Two Decades of Irish Writing* (Cheadle Hulme: Carcanet, 1975), 4–22.

use of myth and the political force of poetry was made. Deane suggests that twentieth-century Irish poetry can be divided into four phases, according to the characteristic way in which national feeling has been expressed in the work. His final phase comprises contemporary Northern poets (although from this he excludes Montague who falls into his third phase with Patrick Kavanagh). The writing of the Northern poets is characterized by a separation from national feeling. They are 'more ambitious to redraft the emotional geography of the respective areas in terms, not of history and politics, but of the free personality', creating work which is 'remarkably without political conviction'. Importantly, Deane relates this to the formal dynamics of the poetry. The emphasis on lyric poetry as opposed to epic and narrative is, he argues, a consequence of the poets' lack of interest in articulating a community and its history rather than personal issues of interior freedom, love, faith, and growth: 'The epic bespeaks a culture which is whole; the lyric one which, while broken, is reconstituted in its fullness for the duration of the poem'. And here he associates the lyrical tradition with the celebration of interior freedom, 'It pits an infinite privacy against a finite convention'.[45] Deane goes on to qualify these statements, particularly with reference to John Montague's work, but also regarding Heaney's *Wintering Out* and Mahon's *Lives*.[46] In these works, he maintains, private intimacies are set against public pressures, and in this way the private world is contextualized. A form of engagement is deemed to take place as the private concerns of lyric poetry are opened up to scrutiny by a more 'communal' consciousness. And in a later essay on Heaney, where he describes his work much more as an attempt to give voice to Catholic experience, to develop a space for Irish protest within English poetry, Deane explicitly links the articulation of a community's experience to the use of myth: 'When myth enters the poetry, in *Wintering Out* (1972), the process of politicisation begins.'[47] So, for Deane, myth is the way for Heaney to open up his private

[45] See also Seamus Deane, introduction to *Celtic Revivals* (London: Faber and Faber, 1985), 15, where he argues that Irish nationalism is a moral passion more than a political ideology, evidenced by its sense of past: 'In literature, in place of political ideology we find a whole series of ideologies of writing in which politics is regarded as a threat to artistic integrity.'

[46] Derek Mahon, *Lives* (Oxford: Oxford University Press, 1972).

[47] Deane, *Celtic Revivals*, 179.

exploration into the public, or more particularly 'communal' sphere, since, as previously noted, it gives the poetry access to those 'atavistic' layers of the Irish psyche and the Irish experience without which any understanding of the situation in Northern Ireland remains merely rationalist and therefore ineffectual.[48] Here again, the assumption is that the popular consciousness of the population of Northern Ireland is caught within a mythic or seamlessly ideological view of the world, and it is by tapping that mythic spirit that the poet gains a right to be poet of the community.[49] His usefulness then lies in achieving a poetic resolution ('the appeasement of the achieved poem'), which transcends both mythic and rationalist views of the world and therefore offers his people an alternative 'world of possibility'.

This view of the role of the writer is thrown into question by the writing practices of the younger generation of Irish poets. One might argue that this is unsurprising given the ambivalence of the term 'community', which is generally preceded by adjectives such as 'divided', 'Protestant', or 'Catholic' but rarely suggests the entire population of Northern Ireland. Thus the disruption of continuity between the individual and his or her community might be read as a reflection in poetic form of the complexities of modern Irish society. I have discussed the shortcomings of this interpretation of the significance of form, suggesting that it cannot account for the critical aspects of the work. In relation to the younger writers, I will argue that there is what might be called, following Deane, a fifth phase of Northern Irish poetry which attempts to set up a new relation between public and private worlds, the languages of the media and the history books, and the language of personal experience. The relation between poetry and politics in their work is an oblique one; and it is oblique partly because of their transformation of the relation between public and private modes of discourse. However, the established paradigm of the relation between poetry and politics in Ireland would suggest that the rejection of communal modes of address leaves the writer caught within the limits of the private lyric poem which refuses all wider general significance. More

[48] Deane, *Celtic Revivals*, 180. See also Heaney, 'Unhappy and at Home', 66–72, where Deane again links myth and epic.

[49] Note the similarity here with the revisionist historian's consciousness of himself as warring against the popular understanding of Irish history.

specifically, if the poets reject myth as a means to gain access to their community, what means are they able to use to expand their private narratives into something with public significance?

Private and Public Narratives

In the discussion so far I have delineated the broad outlines of contemporary discussion of the relationship between poetry and politics in Northern Ireland. To a certain extent it seems the writer is required to achieve a precarious balance between the formal pleasures of the lyric (with its dangers of solipsism and 'irresponsibility'), and the broader sweep of public statement. The 'ideal' resolution of this opposition lies in rooting public statement in personal experience, from which it derives its authenticity and hence the authority to speak of more communal concerns. As I have discussed, in much of the poetry and critical discussion of the 1970s, myth was awarded the role of holding together personal and political registers. Moreover, by submitting mythic or popular understanding to the formal rigour of art, the poets were deemed to be able to achieve a resolution beyond both 'rational' and 'atavistic' modes of political understanding.

In order to appreciate the alternative construction of the relation between private and public, or personal and communal discourses, in the work of the younger writers, the 'privacy' of the lyric has to be understood in a different way. Even the most casual reader of Muldoon, McGuckian, and Paulin cannot fail to notice the emphasis in the work on personal events and private narratives. However, the exploration of such experience is presented not as a 'refuge' from the social and political world, but as constituted through it. Despite the coyness and secrecy which surrounds much of this material (for example, McGuckian's representation of the maternal body, or Muldoon's exploration of the failure of personal and sexual relationships), the private world for all three writers is never closed off, but improperly breaches the boundaries of public life, at the same time as it is invaded by it. The issue for these writers is not how to open up the lyric into something with 'communal' significance, but centres on the unstable boundary between public and private spheres.

Perhaps the most telling sign in the poetry of the disruption of the link between personal and communal modes of discourse lies in the refusal in all three writers to accord the 'personal' or 'private' the significance of truth value, authenticity, or sincerity. Despite the ostensible valorization of 'inner freedom' (particularly in McGuckian's and Muldoon's work, but also in Paulin's celebration of the value of imagination), the poetry insists on the arbitrariness, even the 'uselessness' of personal experience, its fundamentally deceptive nature. And in keeping with this rejection of the authentic and the natural the work continually emphasizes the interpenetration of individual experience with the political and social arena. As I argue in Chapter 5, even McGuckian's exploration of the contents of her womb suggests that there is no natural or innocent experience of the body and sexuality before the intervention of culture. It is not merely that the poetry is saying 'the personal is "relevant" to an understanding of the social situation', but that each is constituted by the other.

In order to put some flesh on these assertions I will take just one example of the reconfiguration of public and private registers, Muldoon's short poem 'Bran':

> While he looks into the eyes of women
> Who have let themselves go,
> While they sigh and they moan
> For pure joy.
>
> He weeps for the boy on that small farm
> Who takes an oatmeal labrador
> In his arms
> Who knows all there is of rapture.[50]

The title here seems to refer to the oatmeal-coloured labrador, but when the references to Irish legend are eked out it appears that Bran is not merely the name of the narrator's dog, but Finn MacCool's favourite hound (and his metamorphosed female cousin). Moreover, Bran is also the hero of a voyage saga, *Immram Brain*; Bran's quest, like Oisin's, leads him to an ideal 'Land of Women' from which it is impossible to return. At one level of course the mythic reference is unnecessary to an understanding of the poem in terms of nostalgic longing for the securi-

[50] Paul Muldoon, 'Bran', in *Why Brownlee Left* (London: Faber and Faber, 1980), 12.

ties of childhood.[51] The poem ostensibly sets up a distinction between the unsatisfactory nature of the adult world of casual sexual encounters (in which the poet figures himself as something of a stud), and the experience of true union in the past. The hidden suggestions of entrapment in the 'land of women', and the association of the dog with a metamorphosed woman merely enrich this interpretation. The mythic structure seems to be almost a parody of mythic reference since it is in one sense 'unnecessary' and then it hangs merely on a chance collocation of words. Yet many Irish readers might recognize the reference to the myth, and the poem therefore offers different meanings to different audiences: those equipped with local knowledge, and those (in England or America) without it. The inessential nature of the mythic reference, its subordination to the personal narrative of nostalgic longing for complete contentment, is important for an understanding of Muldoon's project as a whole.

Myth can be used as a complete structure to give coherence to a modern narrative—as famously in *The Waste Land.* Here the myth works syntagmatically—it underlies the complete structure of the work of art, infusing it with its significance as a whole; fragments of the disrupted modern narrative can be set in place and explained by reference to the mythic narrative. Muldoon's 'Immram' and 'The More a Man Has the More a Man Wants' seem to work in this way, utilizing what could be termed a 'High Modernist' conception of mythic structure. Both poems borrow the narrative structure of the previous myth (the Immram Mael Duin, or the Trickster cycle), and map a new narrative on to it. However, the fragmented poetic narrative continually resists interpretation in terms of the older mythic narrative, as the mythic source is relegated in importance to the level of other 'found' material, and alternative modern narratives (such as the history of Howard Hughes in 'Immram', and the events taking place in Gertrude Stein's Paris in 'The More a Man Has'). Just as Muldoon's sly references to mythic sources for the poem's meaning parody the search for narrative coherence in a mythic correlative, so the fragmented structure of the poems themselves,

[51] The relationship between oatmeal and bran (dear to health-conscious consumers) lends a rather different significance to the lines. It gives a more unsavoury, Swiftian connotation to the kind of 'letting go' and 'moaning' witnessed in the first stanza.

with their arbitrary connections between different types of narrative suggest that the myth no more holds the key to the poem than any other of its sources. But myth also works paradigmatically suggesting mythic significance through a fragment. So 'Bran' uses a tiny slice of a myth to denote the whole—the name works as a synecdoche of myth. Here what is important about the myth is not its structure but its theme, the function of which is to play off and enrich the poetic sense.

For Barthes the interest in myth is occasioned by a fear of history: 'the very end of myths is to immobilise the world'.[52] And this trans-historical nature of myth suggests that it is not well suited to writing about contemporary events. Myth and fairy-tale are in Bakhtin's sense 'monologic' genres—they project a 'universal' story, a stable signified which remains untouched by layers of historically changing signifiers (a myth is a myth however you represent it).[53] As such, as I discussed in relation to the use of myth in Heaney's *North*, myth can be used to 'legitimate' a new narrative by presenting it in terms of the older, established, and unchanging mythic significance. It is in the context of this practice that Muldoon's attempt to fragment and 'privatize' mythic references (so that the personal significance of the 'oatmeal' labrador vies with the mythic significance of Bran the voyager as a determinant of meaning) becomes significant. Once emptied and reconstituted the myth works less as a means to 'legitimate', to find an authoritative father, and become a son, than as a parody of precisely this practice.[54] The reconstitution of the narrative using mythic fragments undoes stability, as the significance becomes enslaved to a new meaning.

It is as though the mythic references in the poems alternate between the strength of their ability to pull the poetic narrative into the separate, isolated, and eternal world of myth, and their

[52] Roland Barthes, *Mythologies*, trans. Annette Lavers (London: Granada, 1973), 155.

[53] On the 'epic distance' of the national myth see Mikhail Bakhtin, 'Epic and Novel', in *The Dialogic Imagination*, ed. Michael Holquist (Austin, Tex. University of Texas Press, 1981), 3–40.

[54] One could read the paternal quest of Mael Duin/Muldoon in 'Immram' as among other things a quest for a precursor, a poetic father to give legitimization to the new version of the myth, whether that precursor be the original myth, or Tennyson's or MacNeice's version. But the new poetic narrative does as much to destroy as to nourish any potential father figures. And significantly the father is never found—he is always one move farther west.

weakness in being dragged into the world of the present by the contemporary, personal, and historically contingent narrative. Thus the privatization of mythic meaning stands opposed to the legitimization of a communal narrative through myth. However, it would be mistaken to assume that Muldoon is pitting the truth of personal experience against the mystifications of myth. It is not that personal experience is opposed to public or communal concerns. For just as the use of mythic paradigms is undercut, at the same time the enclosed personal world of the small boy is ironized by being set against the experiences in the world of the grown man. Thus while the narrator might wish to imply the radical disjuncture between authentic experience in the rural community (the small farm), and the narrator's failed attempts at communication in the modern, urban world of casual sexual encounters, the poem insists that the first is created as a fantasy through the 'experience' of the second. The contentment afforded by the small community and the simple pleasures of rural life exist only in tension with the supposed lack of communication in the complex modern society. Moreover, one might argue that the narrator is fooling himself if he thinks he can gauge the quality of the women's sexual experience—like the narrator's own personal experiences this is in a sense irreducibly private, unknowable, and therefore arbitrary. The narrator fantasizes their pleasure as much as his own childhood contentment. The notion of 'authentic' experience is radically undercut in the poem, and with it the possibility of using such authenticity as a guarantee of representativeness. The poem simultaneously undermines any attempt to authenticate its claims through myth or through the truths of personal experience, suggesting instead that private and public arenas, personal and communal modes of discourse, are fundamentally imbricated with one another from the start.

Throughout my readings of Muldoon, McGuckian, and Paulin in Part II of this book, I will emphasize the characteristic disruption of mythic paradigms, and reconfiguration of the boundaries between public and private spheres in the work. Naturally, there are different ways of affecting this reconfiguration, and the three poets I have chosen to discuss each exemplify alternative strategies. As a preliminary to the more detailed discussions below, I will briefly sketch their differences here, and indicate some of the difficulties with each method.

Most importantly for my argument, the barrier between public and private worlds is drawn differently by the poets, and their modes of disruption accordingly differ. While McGuckian characteristically reads public and political events through the changes occurring in her own body, thereby offering a new perspective on both, for Muldoon and Paulin it is the world of language and communication itself which constitutes the public sphere, and entails a difficult negotiation on the part of the public and published poet. The poets' conceptions of the division between public and private differ also in their *content*. For Muldoon and Paulin the private world constitutes specific personal events and histories, while for McGuckian (and this is in part a circumstance she shares with Irish women generally) it constitutes the whole area of sexuality, which is in a sense already part of the public world although not accepted as so (in other words, sexuality is publicly 'owned', for example by the Catholic Church in Ireland—as in the contested constitutional prohibitions on divorce and abortion—or more generally in acceptable definitions of the division between feminine and masculine, in a way that actual personal histories cannot be). But whereas the poetry undermines attempts to read them as spokespeople or representatives, the success of their strategies depends to a large extent on what constitutes an acceptable reading of their work—it is defined by a necessarily limited field of reception.

Muldoon's collection *Quoof* introduces in its title-poem the notion of a private or familial world which needs to be translated if a wider audience is to be addressed: a 'quoof' is a hot water bottle in the private language of his family. But this exploration of personal or closed modes of communication, the privacy of a hermetic language, is not merely 'ostrich-like' behaviour, a shutting-out of the outside world, since it works to disrupt normative codes of literary discourse and to change accepted definitions of the public sphere by including or reading through aspects of the personal life. The link between public and private worlds and between private poetic worlds (the world of the lyric) and political statement becomes a conscious *theme* in Muldoon's work, as narcissistic self-enclosed narratives (in language and experience) are used as metaphors for the political situation in Northern Ireland as well as for the self-enclosed nature of the individual. Muldoon uses the fact of language's inability to communicate intensely private experience directly to express the lack of communication between people and sections of the community in Northern Ireland. So in a certain sense he is using privacy as a metaphor for the political situation. However, this is a double-edged strategy: this privatization of mythic discourse amounts to a translation of a public discourse into personal terms, and as such it differs widely from Heaney's attempt to use myth as a way of opening up to communal concerns. By contrast, as I have discussed, Muldoon's technique involves taking the myth out of the official public sphere (though this does not exhaust all public space in a colonized culture). But several methodological and theoretical problems follow from this strategy. First, of course, there is the difficulty of using a private hermetic discourse to discuss public events, which leads to an almost circular method of interpretation: it is only possible to understand how the poems are in fact dealing with public issues by following up the private hermetic self-reflexive references. Secondly, it is not clear simply from Muldoon's wish not to engage in a straightforwardly public and political narrative, that he rejects the theorization of the relationship between a self-consciously aware literature and a mystificatory myth discussed earlier.[55]

Rather than an ironic comment on the lack of connection between public and private worlds, McGuckian's use of the contours of her body, her experience of sex and childbirth, and her exploration of women's lack of control of public life as metaphors for the political situation suggests instead the impossibility of approaching the public world except through the prism of private or individual experience. Even her attempt to uncover the history of Irish women is carried out through an exploration of her own experience as a woman. It is her experience of women's lack of authoritative roles which suggests a lack in the traditional concepts of passive or virago women in history. But there is a danger that she will merely reinforce traditional conceptions of women's concerns as essentially private. In order to change notions of the public sphere and allow women's lives to gain a place she must find some way of bringing the private life into conflict with official public norms. Here she comes across

[55] In order to answer this question it will be necessary to examine his construction of the political world in relation to myth; see my discussion of 'Becbretha' in Ch. 3.

the problem of the limitations of reception, and the traditional reading of women's texts as private and autobiographical. If her work is read as simply another example of a woman writing about personal concerns, how is it possible for this private discourse to have impact on the social world. It is not as simple as choosing to publicize a private language.[56] On a more metaphorical level there is a danger that her poems will offer little more than a private vision of public events (as I will discuss in relation to 'Dovecote'). As the private narrative is used as a metaphor for the political, it becomes generalized, opened up in its significance. But does the political narrative thereby become particularized, losing its political character?

An antithetical danger courts Tom Paulin's work, such that despite the poetry's careful interweaving of personal and political levels, and the consequent destabilization of each, Paulin's professed commitment to political poetry ('almost invariably . . . a political poem is a public poem') obscures his work's reconfiguration of the public realm. Indeed Paulin's theoretical arguments for political poetry betray a very traditional notion not only of poetry, which is defined primarily in terms of its content, but also of politics. As Peter Middleton points out, according to Paulin's theory, 'Contemporary poetry must appear to speak as if there is a direct continuity with the pieties, orders and ideas of the class-structured English world before the first world war, and link that in turn with preceding centuries, as if poetry were as much a matter of ancestry and inheritance as landed property.'[57] Yet it is precisely such a homogeneous understanding of culture and tradition that his poetry undermines. Paulin has a slightly asymmetrical relationship to the debate I have outlined: since his poetry is primarily concerned with delineating the nature of the Protestant community in Northern Ireland the relationship between mythic irrationalism and politics may seem to have little bearing on his work. Nevertheless, despite its ostensible commitment to the civic and rational values of the Enlightenment tradition in Ireland, his poetry continually reveals the mythic and tribal nature of con-

[56] See Clair Wills, 'Upsetting the Public: Carnival, Hysteria, and Women's Texts', in David Shepherd and Ken Hirschkop (eds.), *Bakhtin and Cultural Theory* (Manchester: Manchester University Press, 1989), 130–51.

[57] Middleton argues that experimental poetry is better suited to the political conditions obtaining in the contemporary public sphere. Peter Middleton, 'Language Poetry and Linguistic Activism', *Social Text*, 25/26 (1990), 249.

temporary forms of politics, including British neo-imperial politics. While in his critical prose Paulin often seems to accede to the division between the rational and atavistic which is by now a convention in discussions of Irish identity, his poetry questions the value of such oppositions. Paulin has associated his vision of a secular Irish republic both with the New Ireland Forum and with the 'fifth province' of the imagination heralded by the editors of the *Crane Bag*. Moreover, in his introduction to the *Faber Book of Political Verse*, he singles out Heaney and Muldoon as writers whose work is able to represent in the aesthetic realm alternative possibilities to the current political and social conflict between communities in Northern Ireland: 'To oppose the historic legitimacy of that state [Northern Ireland] and at the same time refuse the simplicities of traditional nationalism is to initiate certain imaginative positives and offer a gracious and civil trust'.[58] In this formulation the value of art again inheres in its capacity for an aesthetic resolution of politics rather than in its active engagement with the political realm. However, the linguistic strategies of Paulin's poetry insist not on their own role in bringing together the state and the family, the 'civil' and the 'primitive', but instead on the *prior* interpenetration of these forces in contemporary culture.

Throughout this chapter I have emphasized the ways in which the established paradigms of the relationship between poetry and politics in Northern Ireland fail to recognize the formal difference of the younger writers, and to comprehend its real significance. Clearly the fragmentation of mythic narratives, the parody of established forms, and their claims to significance and legitimacy cannot be separated from international movements in poetry. Similarly the emphasis on local or particular narratives, such as the narrative of maternal sexuality, is incomprehensible outside of the cultural aura of postmodernism, and the transformations in our understanding of the nature of the political (I am thinking, for example, of the influence of the women's movement in establishing the public relevance of the private sphere of the home, or of post-colonial political movements in establishing the relativity of European ideas of culture and progress). Such social and

[58] Tom Paulin (ed.), *The Faber Book of Political Verse* (London: Faber and Faber, 1986) 43. See also id., *Ireland and the English Crisis* (Newcastle Upon Tyne: Bloodaxe Books, 1984), 17.

cultural movements clearly have bearing on the formal nature, the style, and the thematic concerns of the poetry, but at the same time the poetry is instrumental in formulating our understanding of the divisions between public and private spheres in contemporary society. In refusing the claim to authenticity, either through myth or through personal experience, the poetry forces a reassessment of the status of the lyric, and of the notion of privacy on which it depends.

2

Women Poets
The Privatization of Myth

'POETRY is now opposed—to what?', ask the editors of a recent collection of essays on contemporary poetry and modern theory.[1] Whereas in the past, they suggest, the 'other' to poetry has been ordinary or natural language, as often as not the poetic now turns to the language of emotion, confession, plain speech, and lived experience as a bulwark against an increasingly global bureaucratese. Or, alternatively, it opposes itself to rational communication in its entirety, couching itself in terms as far removed from plain speech as possible. Both forms of opposition concur in their resistance to the mechanistic, bureaucratic, media-polluted language and thought of the contemporary world. These two seemingly alternative strategies of subversion, or opposition, are played out in contemporary women's poetry in nuanced ways, yet certain lines of demarcation can be drawn. On the one hand there is, in overt opposition to the perceived exclusion of women's concerns, and women's narratives in much contemporary poetry, a strategy of representation—of giving voice. One of the arguments I want to make here is that the belief in the efficacy of such representation depends on a fundamental faith in representative politics, or more broadly the public realm of democratic politics. Moreover, the link between political and aesthetic representation hinges on the representativeness of the poetic narrative—the fact that what is being represented is not merely of significance to one individual, but forms a link between a personal and a public or national narrative. My use of the term 'representativeness' to apply to poetry here then denotes the process whereby a poem constitutes a political demand, as it stands in for the demands of a marginalized community, in this case women. Hence representativeness does not necessarily entail

[1] Anthony Easthope and John O. Thompson (eds.), *Contemporary Poetry Meets Modern Theory* (Hemel Hempstead: Harvester Wheatsheaf, 1991).

a form of concurrence with existing modes of discourse, so much as a process of legitimization through shared modes of address. On the other hand there is a poetic strategy which, in its enigmatic refusal of clarity and interpretation, throws into question the notion of both representation and representativeness, and with it the dominant definition of the public realm.

This division suggests the two routes that post-Movement poetry has taken in its rejection of public language and public policy: a poetry of the marginalized voice, and a poetry which resists, or refuses to engage in, the process of communication (violently truncated by the State and other systems of social organization), refuses to use the voice—in order to throw that process into question. In the simplest terms the choice for the poet seems to be between a reinflection of the notion of the lyric voice so that it can stand not simply for a personal but for a communal experience, and a rejection of the expressive voice as complicit with the status quo—and here I am thinking of theorizations of the politics of postmodern poetry and of experimental writing practices associated with LANGUAGE poetry. Yet this opposition, which is perhaps relatively clear-cut in America and Britain, becomes skewed in the context of the particular political demands of anomalous situations such as Ireland, and of the asymmetrical relationship of women poets to this debate. Moreover, such anomalies may require us to rethink our assumptions about the politics of poetic form as a whole. What I want to suggest is that current discussion of the politics of form in contemporary poetry is caught in a false binarism, between, on the one hand, 'traditional' lyric, which while it may carry a political content belies its message through its slavery to conventional forms, and, on the other, 'experimental' or avant-garde poetry, which in its conscious problematization of language itself forgoes political content in favour of linguistic counter-conventions, a rejection of the authoritative lyric voice, a destabilization of meaning. In this book I have chosen to discuss mainstream contemporary poets (poets published by established publishing houses), but I argue that they are none the less working with forms which question the function of representation and representativeness. However, it is only possible to see this if you admit of a blurring of this distinction between expressive and experimental poetry. In contrast, the experimental poet and critic

Wendy Mulford has claimed that McGuckian writes in the 'traditional mode' where 'language is not seen as problematic', and she opposes this to poetry which 'resigns the authority of the individual poetic voice'. Experimental poetry (such as language poetry) lacks a unified lyric voice:

> In its place, we, the readers, follow the text in all its provisionality, its multiple meaning, its erasures, silences, chora. Into the darkness, along the glass sliver edge between consequentiality and inconsequentiality, assuming a poetics of play and gesture.[2]

The politics in all this arises from the consequent disruption of authoritative forms and conventions of public language (and therefore, so the larger argument goes, public policy). My disagreement with this rests not in the designation of McGuckian as an 'expressive voice' poet, but with the assumption that because she believes in the efficacy of the individual lyric voice, her poetry does not question the boundaries between private lyric and public world. My counter-claim would be that whatever McGuckian intends by her use of the expressive voice, her work brings us no nearer to an understanding of her personal experience of femininity and motherhood—what it does instead is what is so often claimed for experimental poetry—it problematizes the communicative function of poetic language, and thereby questions the grounds for reaching consensus, and the boundaries of the public sphere itself.[3] I examine McGuckian's work in some detail in Chapter 5; here my purpose is to situate her poetic strategy in the context of contemporary women's writing in Ireland, with particular reference to the manner in which debates over the figure of the motherland have determined the concerns of Irish women poets.

Much recent poetry by women has been marked by a rejection of the conservative politics associated with the stereotypical images of Ireland as a passive and suffering maiden or militant mother figure, and a drive to represent the real history and experiences of Irish women in their stead. I will argue that this strategy fails when it is conceived primarily as making public

[2] Wendy Mulford, '"Curved, Odd . . . Irregular": A Vision of Contemporary Poetry by Women', *Women: A Cultural Review*, 1:3 (1990), 261–74.

[3] For a discussion of this issue in relation to the politics of radical or experimental poetry, see Peter Middleton, 'Language Poetry and Linguistic Activism', *Social Text*, 25/26 (1990), 242–53.

(including publishing) the previously ‘private’ experiences of women unaccounted for in male-dominated civic or national historiography. There is a danger not only that such an approach will tend to reconfirm the view that women's concerns are focused on the home and the family, but also that the radical dislocation of the private sphere in modern society will remain unacknowledged. Far from being contained within the confines of the home, women (the female body, sexuality, and reproduction) are at the centre of public policy and legislation.[4] Indeed, as the figure of the motherland should alert us, in certain ways the body of the Irish woman (and her analogue in conservative nationalist discourse, the home) is the very ground—both figural and material—of the national enterprise. Yet this public function destabilizes not only the ideal of the home, but that of the nation too, as the abstract national image is continually in danger of falling back into its particular (sexual and bodily) narrative. So Belinda Loftus has argued that the authority which images of Mother Ireland retain derives not from their stereotypical nature but from their transgressive potential:

> These figures are fascinating and fearful not only because of the roles they play, or their political and religious symbolism, but because they combine the public and the private. They are not clear and clean-cut, but dangerous, dirty *boundary* figures.[5]

As I will maintain, representations of the female body in Ireland are not the arena of the private or the personal, but precisely the place of interpenetration of public political discourse, and notions of private ownership and personal identity, a fact which has important consequences for a reading of contemporary women's poetry.

Women Writers and the Poetic Tradition

Possession, dispossession, and repossession, in the context of literature by contemporary Irish women, are not only powerful reminders of Ireland's colonial and post-colonial history, but also

[4] Working-class women, and women in agricultural economies, have always been present within the public arena as members of the work-force, though of course this has not given them the power of self-determination.

[5] Belinda Loftus, *Mirrors: William III and Mother Ireland* (Dundrum: Picture Press, 1990), 86.

image a way of approaching women poets' relation to tradition. When the nation is represented as one version of femininity, the motherland, when the dispossession of the Irish is figured in terms of exile from the mother's body, the mother's tongue, what access to legitimizing roles, what means of 'possessing' a history or a tradition do Irish women have? The desire to legitimize oneself (all too often confounded with the process of legalizing one's position), to submit to an authority (that of the father) in order to accede to it, presupposes acceptance of the supremacy of tradition. The process of legitimization asks us to fit ourselves in to a family narrative in which goods, and the authority to own them, pass from father to son. But the daughter's inheritance requires not simply a diversion of familial chattels; it necessitates a disruption (an evolution) of tradition. In the literary system it performs a mutation of genre. This chapter focuses on the generic disruption effected in work by contemporary Irish women poets (specifically Eavan Boland and Medbh McGuckian) and examines poetry which questions current definitions of cultural and national identity in Ireland, in particular the repeated association of the use of myth and the writer's attempt to link himself with, to repossess, a history and a community.[6]

It is now a commonplace that the inherited tradition constitutes a difficulty for women poets. As Margaret Homans points out in *Women Writers and Poetic Identity*, where the major literary tradition normatively identifies the figure of the poet as masculine, and the voice as masculine property, women writers 'cannot see their minds as androgynous, or as sexless, but must take part in a self-definition by contraries'.[7] For Homans there are two main difficulties facing the woman poet: her association with nature, and her exclusion from the traditional identification of the

[6] I cannot hope to do justice to the diversity of women's poetry in Ireland here. Indeed it is through the differences between and among the poets discussed here and other writers such as Eiléan Ní Chuilleanáin, Nuala Ní Dhomhnaill, and Rita Ann Higgins that notions of what constitutes the traditional Irish community are called into question. Two useful anthologies of Irish women's writing are A. A. Kelly (ed.), *Pillars of the House: An Anthology of Verse by Irish Women from 1690 to the Present* (Dublin: Wolfhound, 1987), and Ruth Hooley (ed.), *The Female Line: Northern Irish Women Writers* (Belfast: Northern Irish Women's Rights Movement, 1985).

[7] Margaret Homans, *Women Writers and Poetic Identity* (Princeton, NJ: Princeton University Press, 1980), 11.

speaking subject as male. Within the Irish tradition, however, the woman writer must also inevitably come to terms with the Catholic representations of the female as virgin handmaiden or equally desexualized mother, and with the nationalist trope of Ireland as the motherland. In an important sense this trope derives from the colonial moment in Ireland, whose legacy thus poses certain problems for the Irish woman writer. For as Irish feminists have pointed out, the feminization of Ireland and the Irish as a whole in colonial discourse has shaped post-colonial attempts to redefine Irish identity and the traditionally nationalist post-colonial 'renaming' of Ireland serves only to reconfirm the mythology of woman.

In a recent essay entitled 'The Floozie in the Jacuzzi,' Irish feminist Ailbhe Smyth ponders the particular problematics of culture and identity for Irish women, and specifically the difficulty of finding a place from which to rename themselves. Where femininity stands as symbol of the nation, how can woman 'consume' the symbol without 'erasing' herself?[8] She points out that, long denied the power to name, naming in post-colonial Irish culture has achieved an overdetermined status. Smyth draws a parallel between the colonization of Ireland and the patriarchal definition of woman but maintains that women experience dispossession differently—because doubly colonized they do not have access to the naming process by which definitions of Irish identity are promulgated. Delineations of the lost motherland take place through the metaphor of woman and 'we are lured into a belief in the *significance* of the representation. But the message carried is paradoxically (?) one of our in/non-significance. Woman-as-image and woman-as-spectator participate in the reproduction of our own *meaninglessness* in culture.'[9] Moreover, already 'inhabited' by meanings, what strategies are open to women whereby they may define their own meanings without thereby feeding into the existing mythology? Smyth approaches the issue in terms of the possible strategic defence positions available to women; she advocates a type of 'écriture feminine', an oblique discourse from women's marginalized position which will disrupt spurious notions of Irish unity of culture and identity. And indeed, this analysis of the role or mask the

[8] Ailbhe Smyth, 'The Floozie in the Jacuzzi', *Irish Review*, 6 (1989), 7–24.
[9] Ibid. 9.

woman writer should adopt as a shield against the public female stereotype does correspond to the writers' own understanding of their projects.

The feminist critique of the motherland myth has been of paramount importance in combating the conservative Catholic and nationalist use of the female body to project an oppressive vision of the nation's identity, centring on the idealization of an undefiled (non-sexualized) female 'home'. However, it also courts the danger of assuming that all figurations of the nation as female are equally retrograde, the self-evident signs of nationalism's patriarchal structure. Moreover, this critique of the sign finds it hard to account for the affective dimension of the motherland image or allegory, the psychic investment which must be present in order for the figure to function successfully as a vehicle for collective identification. This makes it difficult to appreciate the productive or progressive elements in appropriations of the motherland image, even those of the women writers themselves. Therefore, while I shall emphasize the negative aspects of the image of the motherland for Irish women in this chapter, I also hope to show that certain 'improper' uses of the allegory (focusing on the body and sexuality) serve an important political and aesthetic function in destabilizing the very grounds of the conservative nationalist appeal.

For contemporary women poets continually return to the identification of woman and land, reinflecting it in various ways. All the poets under discussion are concerned with the possibilities of using woman as a metaphor without merely reducing her to a figure for something else. Moreover, despite their many differences both political and aesthetic, these poets have tried to find ways in which they can work to some extent within the Gaelic or native Irish tradition, rather than simply rejecting it outright, since to reject it would involve accepting some sort of place within an English tradition—more particularly the English tradition of the well-made Movement lyric, with its aesthetic of 'privacy'. Particularly for McGuckian, as for the Irish language poet Nuala Ní Dhomhnaill, this process has involved an attempt to invest an older figure of femininity with a positive meaning for women.[10] Proinsias MacCana argues that what occurs as colo-

[10] See Nuala Ní Dhomhnaill, *Selected Poems*, trans. Michael Hartnett (Dublin: Raven Arts Press, 1986).

nization progresses is a desexualization, through the twin pressures of Catholicism and Celticism, of the more positive and powerful Gaelic figure of the land of Ireland as sovereignty goddess.[11] Since in eighteenth- and nineteenth-century Irish literature in English the available roles for women seem to be polarized into virgin daughter on the one hand, or equally chaste mother on the other, the poets have attempted to reach further back into the Gaelic tradition, and to retrieve from the mythic and early Irish past an image of woman as sexually and socially active, desiring, and powerful.

And yet a number of theoretical problems are posed by this reading of contemporary work in terms of a reconfiguration of tradition. To interpret the rewriting of the myth of the motherland by poets such as Boland and McGuckian in terms of an attempt to negotiate a place in a retroactively created Irish literary tradition, obscures the radical redefinition of the role of poet in Ireland which their work necessitates. The acknowledged desire on the part of these poets to legitimize their work by deferring to the authority of their literary heritage (a practice Jurij Tynyanov terms 'traditionalism') obscures their poetry's disruption of the very basis of the tradition itself.[12]

As I will argue, the poets are engaged in a tropological 'privatization' of the myths of Mother Ireland, but, once this strategy is defined as an attempt to undermine the existing stereotype of Irish femininity by the 'truths' of women's personal experience (in other words, poetry of the expressive voice), it becomes all too easy to fault them for simply creating new stereotypes. For example, along with the turn to archaic sexualized femininity marked in Ní Dhomhnaill and McGuckian's work, come new problems of stereotyping which bear on the ability of the woman to take an active role in the history of the nation. There is a danger, more or less present in all these writers, that they will simply replace a passive female figure waiting for her sons to fight for her, with a sexually, but not politically, active earth mother, again dependent on her sons for a link with actual history. For the

[11] See Proinsias MacCana, 'Women in Irish Mythology', *Crane Bag*, 4:1 (1980), 7–11; and Elizabeth Cullingford, 'Thinking of Her as Ireland', paper presented at Yeats Annual Summer School, Sligo (Aug. 1988), 7–13.

[12] See Jurij Tynyanov, 'On Literary Evolution', in Ladislav Matejka and Krystyna Pomorska (eds.), *Readings in Russian Poetics* (Ann Arbor, Mich.: Michigan Slavic Publications, 1978), 77.

figure of the sovereignty goddess is one which confers power and kingship on the men who sleep with her, rather than retains it for herself. Furthermore, a more general difficulty with an analysis which concentrates on the personalization of early Irish female myth and folklore is that the use of such personae may merely serve to reinforce a concept of the eternal feminine. The body of the myth thus acts as a 'container' for the body of the woman. If definitions of femininity and nationhood are to be questioned such symbols require interrogation rather than reconfirmation, but recent interpretations of the poets' work have tended to stress their continuity with, rather than their difference from, tradition. So, for example, in an examination of modern Irish poetry's re-use of folkloric themes Gearoid Denvir notes how Ní Dhomhnaill's recourse to ancient Irish female 'archetypes' such as the goddesses Mor-Rion, Badb, and Macha enables her to express the 'most genuine voice of the female experience', and he comes close to a dangerous equation between the two.[13] The theoretical distortion involved in such interpretations lies in their acceptance of the myth as origin, compromising any alternative message the contemporary utterance may carry by denying that historical and individual articulations of myths have bearing not only on their meaning, but also on their function in contemporary writing. Thus I will argue that the privatization of the myths of Mother Ireland must be understood not as a personalization or subjectification of mythic concerns (with the connotations of truth and the authenticity of personal experience which go along with this), but as strategies of concealment and secrecy, which foreground the historical contingency of everyday life, its arbitrary nature.

[13] Gearoid Denvir, 'Continuing the Link: An Aspect of Contemporary Irish Poetry', *Irish Review*, 3 (1988), 40–54. In the same way Bríona Nic Dhiarmada claims that Ní Dhomhnaill's use of mythic personae enables her 'to explore what she considers to be the very essence of being female, especially the dark side of female nature'. As a counterbalance Anne O'Connor points out that such folkloric themes are not 'natural' or archetypal, but have ideological and propaganda value for contemporary definitions of femininity. See Nic Dhiarmada, 'Tradition and the Female Voice in Contemporary Gaelic Poetry', in Ailbhe Smyth (ed.), *Women's Studies International Forum: Feminism in Ireland*, 2:4 (1988), 391–2, and Anne O'Connor, 'Images of the Evil Woman in Irish Folklore: A Preliminary Survey', ibid. 281–5.

Mother Irelands

As I have outlined, recent discussion of the relationship between myth, or tradition in Ireland, and the future has tried to suggest ways in which the past can be raided in order to create a Utopian vision of Ireland which differs from both traditional and modernist conceptions. Women poets, however, are characteristically ignored in studies of the rereading of tradition, despite an awareness, notably in Cairns and Richards's work, that questions of national identity are intimately bound up with questions of sexuality.[14]

In its most conservative manifestations the mythic paradigm of Ireland as a woman fosters an exclusive rather than a cosmopolitan sense of community, one in which women do not have equal subjectivity and citizenship. As critics such as Elizabeth Cullingford and Richard Kearney have argued, the progressive idealization of Irish womanhood can be traced in the literature from the seventeenth century, and it is connected, among other things, to the fact of English colonialism in Ireland.[15] As Cullingford points out, historically, the allegorical identification of Ireland with a woman, variously personified as the Shan Van Vocht (the poor old woman), Kathleen Ní Houlihan, or Mother Eire, 'has served two distinct ideological purposes: as applied by Irish men it has helped to imprison Irish women in a straitjacket of purity and passivity; and as applied by well-meaning English cultural imperialists it has imprisoned the whole Irish race in a debilitating stereotype, or in a fruitless inversion of that stereotype'.[16] The motherland trope in all its guises then is like a pin which connects sexual stereotyping with political and cultural domination of the Irish—thus the ways in which the poets are radical in terms of sexual and gender politics bear on issues of imperialism, and definitions of national identity.

As a consequence, merely to assume the role and function of

[14] See David Cairns and Shaun Richards, *Writing Ireland: Colonialism, Nationalism and Culture* (Manchester: Manchester University Press, 1988).

[15] See Cullingford, 'Thinking of Her as Ireland', and Richard Kearney, 'Myth and Motherland', *Ireland's Field Day*, ed. Field Day Theatre Company (London: Hutchinson, 1985), 61–80. See also David Lloyd, '"Pap for the Dispossessed": Seamus Heaney and the Poetics of Identity', *Boundary 2* (Winter/Spring 1985), 322–3.

[16] Cullingford, 'Thinking of Her as Ireland', 1.

poet depends on a certain stance in relation to this trope of the motherland. For the representation of the Irish land as a woman stolen, raped, possessed by the alien invader is not merely one mythic narrative among many, but, in a literary context, it is *the* myth, its permutations so various and ubiquitous it can be hard to recognize them for what they are. The trope functions not only as the means by which the poet can lament the loss of the land, but also, through his linguistic embodiment of it, the means by which he may repossess it. The structure through which the poet obtains this mandate is complex, but its critical ingredient is an already poeticized (mythic) political discourse of the nation which enables the poet to act as spokesperson for his community—public voice of his mute and beleaguered rural 'tribe'. The nationalist poet's role is to bear witness, thus enabling 'a restoration of the culture to itself', a restoration which, like all restorations, opposes itself to modernity, losing itself in a nostalgic celebration of a pure, organic, and monocultural society. It would of course be inaccurate to claim an uncritical celebration of the virtues of the organic society in contemporary Irish poetry—the vacillation between tradition and modernity in Heaney's poem 'Hercules and Antaeus' is a case in point. None the less the very fact that the poem has achieved the status of a kind of text for our time, the fact that it is read as summing up the Irish dilemma, goes some way to prove the strength of the rural, organicist nostalgia.

Thus the motherland trope poses a very specific problem for the Irish woman writer. For the writer who rejects the association of woman and land thereby questions the relationship between poet and community, and the type of community it posits—one which excludes women. In her essay 'The Woman Poet in a National Tradition', Eavan Boland points out that the question of her relationship to the English tradition is complicated by a femaleness which sets her apart from 'the sense of community which came early and easily to male contemporaries'.[17] Put crudely the problem is that not all members of the community can relate to the received public and universal myth successfully.

[17] Eavan Boland, 'The Woman Poet in a National Tradition', *Studies*, 76 (Summer, 1987), 152. See also ead., 'The Woman Poet: Her Dilemma', *American Poetry Review*, 16:1 (Jan./Feb. 1987), 17–20.

I wanted to relocate myself within the Irish poetic tradition. A woman poet is rarely regarded as an automatic part of a national poetic tradition. There has been a growing tendency, in the past few years, for academics and critics to discuss woman's poetry as a sub-culture within a larger tradition, thereby depriving both of a possible enrichment. I felt it vital that women poets such as myself should establish a discourse with the idea of a nation, should bring to it a sense of the emblematic relationship between the feminine experience and the national past.

The truths of womanhood and the defeats of a nation. An impossible intersection? At first sight perhaps. Yet the more I thought of it, the more it seemed to me that if I could find the poetic truth of the first then, by virtue of that alone, I would repossess the second. If so, then Irishness and womanhood, those tormenting fragments of my youth, would at last become metaphors for one another.[18]

To gain a place in the construction of an idea of a nation Boland turns to experiential testimony. The linkage of femininity and the idea of the nation is accepted, and her objections turn on the simplifications which both have undergone in male writing. Her alternative is summed up in a poem like 'Mise Eire'.

'Mise Eire' ('I am Ireland') was the normal response of the beautiful and radiant maidens of the eighteenth- and nineteenth-century Aisling ('Vision') poems on interrogation concerning their identity. After a series of questions had been put to them by the male poet, such as 'Are you Venus, or Aphrodite, or Helen fair? Are you Aurora, or the goddess Flora?', the maiden would reply, 'I am Ireland and I am sick because I have no true and manly husband' (since the men in Ireland had been cowed into submission by the force of English imperialism). Boland replaces the generalized, idealized Aisling figure whose function is to remind her menfolk that they must fight the English for her (or await Jacobite forces) if they are to repossess their homeland, with the imagined history of a single emigrant woman. Her deprivation and prostitution in England or America, Boland implies, stand as an historical corrective to mythic representations of the nation:

No. I won't go back.
My roots are brutal:

[18] Boland, 'Woman Poet in a National Tradition', 156–7.

I am the woman—
a sloven's mix
of silk at the wrists,
a sort of dove-strut
in the precincts of the garrison—

who practises
the quick frictions,
the rictus of delight
and gets cambric for it,
rice-coloured silks.

I am the woman
in the gansy-coat
on board the 'Mary Belle',
in the huddling cold,

holding her half-dead baby to her
as the wind shifts East
and North over the dirty
water of the wharf . . .[19]

Rather than draw a metaphorical parallel between one woman's personal history, her loss of national heritage, and the breach in the presumed continuity of Irish history caused by English colonial rule, the poem insists on the radical disjuncture between the histories of the emigrant woman and her nation. It is impossible to use the woman as a symbol for the fate of the land because she has left it; unlike the deserted maidens of the traditional Aisling she is not there at home to be repossessed.[20] Hence, for Boland, the 'real story' of Irish women will combat the falsification and abstraction of the motherland myth. Her argument could be summed up as a version of 'No taxation without representation'; Boland, in effect, is a suffragette. She seeks not to challenge the basis of the poet's authority, but to widen the political constituency, adding women to the electoral rolls.

[19] Eavan Boland, 'Mise Eire', *The Journey and Other Poems* (Manchester: Carcanet, 1987), 10.

[20] In any case the woman's heritage would not have been the possession of land, a privilege reserved solely for sons. Emigration, undertaken at a greater rate by women than men, though often a result of Ireland's disadvantaged economic relationship with Britain, was contributed to by the traditional system of land inheritance and marriage. See Jenny Beale, *Women in Ireland: Voices of Change* (Basingstoke: Macmillan, 1986), 33–40. For a brilliant overall study of Irish emigration see Kerby A. Miller, *Emigrants and Exiles: Ireland and the Irish Exodus to North America* (Oxford: Oxford University Press, 1985).

But of course poetry cannot simply add the private or personal experience of women to its dominant structures, and Boland herself does not so much represent female experience as trope it.

This desire to celebrate personal truths arises out of a confusion regarding the status of privacy and the domestic in relation to the public national image of femininity. For the domestic image has a legal as well as a poetic expression. In post-colonial Ireland it stands alongside the legal construction by the Irish Free State of a sphere of private domesticity, and De Valera's insistence on a constitutional definition of a woman's place as in the home (or, as he might have put it, the comely maiden's place in the cosy homestead).[21] Paradoxically, it is *because* of the construction of such a sphere that the concept of 'mothering' can continue to stand as ideological confirmation of the representation of the Irish nation as a traditional rural community. To investigate the personal dimension of the motherland myth is thus a contradiction in terms, not merely because a myth cannot be undone by reality, but because that personal experience is already public. Privacy, defined as the domestic, is not the residence of the unique and individual, the non-communicable. It is a social institution with genres, codes, and a semantics. Moreover 'Mise Eire' knows this. For all that we seem to be offered a woman's private thoughts on her personal situation, what the poem in fact stresses is that her sexuality is publicly owned (through prostitution), her personal story *is* a public narrative. So even though one might want to reject the symbolization of the dispossession of the nation through a woman's rape, any attempt to be possessive in one's turn, even self-possessed, is doomed to failure. In this sense the slogan 'the personal is political' carries not the liberal message that the lot of individual women should be added into the account, but the message that (in the context of Irish motherhood) the personal as individual is a chimera.

What is actually at stake in these arguments is not a modification of tradition to fit changing social circumstances, as Boland suggests, but, following Tynyanov, a mutation of the lit-

[21] For example, women's traditional familial role was institutionalized in the Republic by a marriage bar which forced women in certain jobs to give them up on marriage. See Evelyn Mahon, 'Women's Rights and Catholicism in Ireland', *New Left Review*, 166 (1987), 56. For a general study of the ideology of femininity of the Irish Republic see Beale, *Women in Ireland*.

erary system in which the semantics of domesticity takes on a particular literary function. A trope of privacy appears in place of the motherland trope, the function of which is to allow women to accede to the role of poet.

Of course, if woman as national monument is all too public a figure, women's traditional confinement in the private sphere of the home is mirrored by a tendency to read women's writing in terms of its personal significance, for what it has to say about love, marriage, and the condition of being female, rather than for its insights into the world of work and politics.[22] The difficulty of analysing privacy as a code for the domestic is compounded by the traditional habit of reading women's texts through an autobiographical grid. Nevertheless, despite the dangers of a reading which would merely serve to reconfirm notions of women's concerns as primarily personal, it is important to be aware of the ways in which a seemingly personal or confessional poet (such as McGuckian) is radical precisely in her attempts to talk about public and political events through the medium of private symbolism. The recontextualization or reaccentation of myths of womanhood can be read as a personalization or privatization of the myths of Mother Ireland, but it is for its consequences for the relationship between poet and community, rather than for its 'truthfulness', that we can read in this gesture of privatization, that beacon of Thatcherite values, the mark of political responsibility.

Medbh McGuckian is generally read as a poet obsessively concerned with femininity, with her personal life, even with the dimensions of her house, to the exclusion of wider, more public concerns. She characteristically reads public and political events through the changes occurring in the contours of her body, and her experience of sex and childbirth. This is perhaps precisely because as a woman writer she lies outside the tradition of poetry

[22] In the Gaelic poetic tradition this traditional division is encapsulated in the generic separation of the (male) role of professional poet from feminine modes of love and grieving poetry. Bríona Nic Dhiarmada points out that: 'The professional poet or "file" with his socially integrated status generally spoke through conventions and on behalf of the tribe rather than personally.' See Nic Dhiarmada, *Women's Studies International Forum*, 389. Nic Dhiarmada notes that a fusion of 'traditional' and 'personal' modes has a precedent in the Danta Gra of the late 17th cent. See also Eiléan Ní Chuilleanáin, 'Women as Writers: Danta Gra to Maria Edgeworth', in ead. (ed.), *Irish Women: Image and Achievement* (Dublin: Arlen House, 1985), 111–26.

as public statement—she does not have access to the language of poetic 'responsibility'. Indeed her only public discourse is one about women, but it is inevitably read in terms of its private significance (i.e. as confessional, rather than as an intervention in Ireland's public or civic discourses about sexuality and nationhood).

However, it is odd that she should be read as a confessional poet, as in fact it is impossible to glean much about her life from the typically enigmatic, veiled style the poems employ. In her explorations of sexuality the body is never approached directly, but through a system of symbolic correspondences (flowers and rain, planetary configurations, houses and geographical locations). For example, in 'Rowing' the representation of the feminine and masculine principles in the acts of love and anger (playing on the homonym in 'rowing') is characteristically obscure, requiring of the reader not only considerable patience in unravelling the metaphorical correspondences, but also a keen ear for literary echoes (in this case the echoes are of Heaney's 'Hercules and Antaeus' and Yeats's 'Byzantium'):

> There are two kinds of light, one perfect
> Inside, pear-coloured, shedding that cool
> Classical remorse over the angered field,
> The other gifted with an artlessness too
> Painful to live with, like a spur
> Eloping from the room below, its nurtured
> Discipline of dark tobacco golds.

McGuckian seems to be looking for a way to speak about women's experience which avoids being investigated—a riddling discourse which will be public and at the same time distinctively different, disruptive of the normative codes of literary discourse. She uses a repeated image of language as a veil which may be lifted only for the ideal reader who will not react by simplifying the complex nature of the life which is being offered up for inspection.[23] Openness connotes betrayal; she wants to tell a personal narrative, the story of giving birth, or of a marriage, but she is wary of 'opening herself up' to be probed by a public readership. So she says, in discussing the difficulties of writing about a private life: 'I feel that you're going public—by writing the poem

[23] See also the discussion of 'Venus and the Rain' in Ch. 5.

you're becoming a whore. You're selling your soul which is worse than any prostitution—in a sense you're vilifying your mind. I do feel that must be undertaken with the greatest possible fastidiousness.'[24] Such explanations of her project naturally encourage readings of her work as concerned with individual female experience. A different reading would argue that the poems provide not veiled representations but allegories of privacy; the difficult style connotes or signals private meaning, through a play on the ambiguity of the term privacy. (Although, again what this equivalency suggests is the individuality of the private sphere. Codes of domesticity mesh with codes of impenetrability to imply that rather than a social institution, a shared or typical life, domesticity is experienced personally, femininity is unique.)

Nevertheless, many readers would aver that to argue for the public reference of McGuckian's work requires considerable special pleading. For example, a poem entitled 'Sky-Writing', in *Marconi's Cottage*, which represents a woman's difference from herself during pregnancy, implies that her outlook upon the world is narrowed not merely to the personal but to a very corporeal 'inwardness'. The 'home' of the woman's body becomes distorted and alien, as a new 'room', the womb, grows within it:

> What can I do against this room
> I was obliged to let grow and grow
> In the new space all through the winter?
> October dawns seeking the distance
> Of their unfolding are startled
> By a vessel so restricted holding them.
>
> I forfeit the world outside
> For the sake of my own inwardness . . .

McGuckian's abiding concern is with the question of a woman's shape (full in pregnancy, or pinched in at the waist like 'being emptied | From bottle to bottle'), her function as a container, and her fragmentation not only into different body parts, but into different selves. The fragmentation of the woman's body in the poem mirrors the disruption of the fabric of the poem itself; the body within the body is not only a double, but a foreign body which disrupts any sense of self, and the possibility of saying 'I'.

[24] Medbh McGuckian, personal interview (20 Nov. 1986).

Should we read the consequent fragmentation in language (and ownership of the 'expressive' self) as a purposive statement about the inadequacy of the traditional lyric voice, or is this merely a retreat into the exploration of a divided psyche? One might bear in mind here Habermas's theory of the transformations of the public sphere, and in particular his argument that, with the demise of the 'authentic' public sphere of rational-critical debate, culture has lost its civilizing mission—the function of literature in the modern world is to create the illusion of bourgeois privacy, rather than to communicate the values born out of the private or intimate sphere.[25] For Habermas the intimate sphere is defined as the complex of personal relationships within the family. He argues that this arena of the personal secedes from the private sphere proper as that becomes deprivatized, through the intrusion of bureaucratic and educational institutions into the socialization process of the bourgeois family. The family increasingly functions as a consumptive rather than a productive group, losing its power as an agent of personal internalization, and leading to the construction of the contemporary sphere of 'pseudo-privacy'. Read in the light of Habermas's theory, it might seem as though, rather than any productive engagement with the social world, all McGuckian's poetry can offer the reader is the fantasy that a realm of meaningful individual and familial experience still exists—untouched by the invasion of technological media into the home, and the separation of politics from everyday life. Moreover the veiling of personal experience, behind a cloak of obscurity and semantic indeterminacy, merely intensifies the suggestion that significant truths lie within. Secrecy becomes both a form of protection and of seduction.

Moreover, such 'secrecy' seems to bear out Habermas's strictures on the relation between autobiography and individualism; he points out that the subjectivity of the privatized individual was related from the start to publicity. The opposite of intimacy, whose vehicle was the written word, was indiscretion, and not

[25] See Jürgen Habermas, *The Structural Transformation of the Public Sphere* (Cambridge, Mass.: MIT Press, 1989), 171. While I find this part of his theory productive, Habermas's work on the public sphere has often been criticized for its inadequacy in relation to women. I think also that his theory cannot account for the strangely skewed emergence of anything like a bourgeois public sphere in a colonial or neo-colonial context, nor for the non-individualistic nature of Irish Catholic socialization, which derives in part from the ideology of the family.

publicity as such.[26] You could argue then that McGuckian's style bears the mark of a hopeless desire to communicate through the personalized address (the letter, the diary) in an era of the market and the mass media. Faced with the problem of how to avoid becoming a prostitute or public woman, if you want your book to sell, the answer is perhaps to learn something from the courtesan—be discreet.

Despite its continuing resonance, there are I think several difficulties with this theory of the relation between private and public spheres in contemporary society, both with regard to the role of women, as has often been remarked, and in terms of its relevance to colonial and post-colonial situations. My aim here is to sketch, albeit tentatively, some of the ways in which these two issues are articulated together in Ireland. Part of Habermas's critique of the decline of a meaningful intimacy centres on the dismantling of paternal authority, which leads to a type of refeudalization of culture, as individual family members are socialized by society. What he is complaining about is a kind of emasculation of the family unit, as domesticity is severed from public life, and handed over to the (limited) control of women.[27]

There are two principal difficulties with this theory. Many critics of Habermas have questioned the idea that a public sphere of rational-critical debate ever existed, and that it carried the progressive political potential which he maintains. But it can certainly be argued that, if it did function as Habermas suggests, it did so only within a narrowly defined bourgeois entrepreneurial class—and it is this fact that should alert us to the difficulties of applying to Irish society orthodox theories of the Enlightenment division between public and private spheres. For while there was undoubtedly an emergent bourgeoisie in eighteenth-century Ireland, under the Union with Britain it was stripped of the power to create and regulate its own public sphere. One could argue that far in advance of the damage caused by mass culture and consumerism, the loss of paternal authority in Ireland can be

[26] Ibid. 48–9.

[27] See e.g. Jessica Benjamin's discussion of the early Frankfurt School's theory of the family in 'Authority and the Family Revisited: Or A World Without Fathers?', *New German Critique*, 13 (1978), 35–58. However, in his later work Habermas is more willing to acknowledge the progressive potential of the modern family.

linked to historical events such as the dissolution of Grattan's Parliament, the Act of Union, and the management of Irish affairs by the Castle administration. Within liberal political theory the private sphere is defined as that which is by right protected from state interference, but in Ireland, to some extent, that private sphere became associated with the nation-as-family in opposition to the alienated and bullish British state. This process was clearly determined to some extent by the role of Catholicism (and religious discourse on the Virgin Mary) in creating a 'public' sphere outside of British jurisdiction. And indeed this family complex throws further light on the representation within nationalist discourse of the Irish nation as a (forlorn and abandoned) mother, suggesting that, for all its stereotypical qualities, the figure of Mother Ireland is the sign of an incomplete separation between public and private spheres.

The theory of the feminization of Irish society through the nineteenth and twentieth centuries has been forwarded in many guises, from racial arguments about the essentially feminine nature of the Celts, to sociological analysis of the structure of the Irish Catholic family in which authority is invested in the mother through her alliance with the priest.[28] It is not the place here to enter into a detailed assessment of the validity of these theories, though I should make it clear that it is certainly not the case that the symbolic power given to women, for example in the representations of Mother Ireland and the authority invested in the figure of the Virgin Mary, has resulted in any greater role for women within society. Quite the reverse, the requirements of purity within the family and the nation have forced women into the most restricted modes of behaviour in order to conform to the Catholic and nationalist ideology of femininity. Nevertheless, it must be acknowledged that the divisions between private (feminine) authority and the public and political sphere are drawn differently in Ireland, if primarily at the level of representations. However, since poetry works at the level of representations, it may be that work which turns 'inward' on to and into the female body is not disengaging from public and political discourse. As McGuckian states in 'On her Second Birthday' there is a corre-

[28] See e.g. Tom Inglis, *Moral Monopoly: The Catholic Church in Modern Irish Society* (Dublin: Gill and Macmillan, 1987).

spondence between the material nature of the world, and the material of our own bodies:

> It seems as though
> To explain the shape of the world
> We must fall apart,
> Throw ourselves upon the world,
> Slip away from ourselves
> Through the world's inner road,
> Whose atoms make us weary.

At the risk of repetition it is important to emphasize here that McGuckian's poetry is engaged in a reconstruction of the division between public and private spheres not because of its personal content (its 'expressive' potential) but because of its emphasis on sexuality and the body. The complex rhetorical strategies of her work recognize, and force the reader to recognize, the interpenetration of these spheres on the social level. As I have discussed, this process is partly related to the status of the figuration of motherhood and maternity in Ireland, where the mother figure stands to some extent as the 'affective' dimension of rational political processes set against imperial power (though she is also co-opted by the discourses of the nation-state). But in addition to this historical condition (peculiar to a post-colonial society such as Ireland), modern developments in the construction of social life also suggest a need to reassess the separation between public and private spheres of activity.

The second difficulty with Habermas's theory can illuminate this issue, and indeed suggests that its relevance extends far wider than Irish society. Habermas seems unwilling to acknowledge the progressive aspects of the 'emasculation' of the bourgeois male. However, as Seyla Benhabib has argued, the patriarchal authority of the father within the family conflicts with the requirements of justice in the private sphere. So while it may be true that, as the power and autonomy of the bourgeois male declines, social and bureaucratic processes invade the intimate arena of family life, at the same time the family is inscribed within an external social sphere. Domesticity, sexuality, and reproduction are reinscribed on to social life, albeit a different kind of public life, leading to an incomplete separation between public and private spheres. Therefore it may be mistaken to read intimacy of concerns as inevitably part of a withdrawal from the public and political arena, despite McGuckian's suggestions to the contrary. As I argue in more detail in Chapter 5, the worlds inside and outside the body continually interpenetrate, and require readjustments from one another.

I have argued that McGuckian cannot be read as an 'expressive' poet giving voice to her experience of the intimate sphere, not only because the formal strategies of her poetry fragment the lyric voice, but also because feminine and familial 'privacy' in Ireland is orientated towards a public and political domain. The arena of privacy must be interpreted not simply as the realm of women's personal experience of family and home, but as the body itself (the most intimate of spheres). To a certain degree McGuckian's investigation of her own maternal sexuality can be interpreted as 'authoring' her own interior, in defiance of the elision of the woman's body in traditional representations of femininity. And here we may find an alternative link between literary and political representation. For McGuckian, neither the body, nor its metaphorical equivalent, the home, is 'private'; therefore, despite her ostensible lack of interest in history or the lives of Irish women in the past, she views her work as giving voice to other women in a similar mute condition. For in fact she shares with Boland the belief that one of the functions of her writing is to speak for the community of women, so that the personal recording of her everyday life becomes analogous to a type of history writing:

> I'm trying to make the dead women of Ireland, who I am the living memory of, I'm trying to give them articulation, if anything. In that sense I'm trying to make their lives not a total waste, that they didn't live in vain, that they have no record at all.[29]

However, McGuckian's metaphorical approach is strikingly different from Eavan Boland's. Boland wants to use women's experience as an example of what has been erased from Irish history and literature. But for McGuckian it is not the content of women's histories and experiences which suggests a lack in the national ideal, for in a sense McGuckian's obscure and enigmatic private worlds are *contentless* (she thus eschews liberal 'representative' politics). Instead she presents women's experience as

[29] Personal interview (20 Nov. 1986).

unknowable and therefore *useless*. Her project is the very opposite of Boland's; by figuring sex and childbirth in language which serves to veil rather than represent she emphasizes the integral relation between sexuality and the public sphere, the ways in which the female body is already inscribed in public life.[30] The politics of the body is thus not a metaphor, or a substitute, for genuine national self-determination, but is bound up with it—and this is more apparent in conditions (such as those that hold in a post-colonial culture) where the boundary between the public and the private is not so clearly drawn. In the following section I will explore these ideas through a reading of McGuckian's most direct reworking of the association between woman and land, 'The Soil Map'.

Privatization and Historical Responsibility

If one problem with the repeated metaphor of woman-as-topography, the motherland, is the effacement of the materiality of the woman's body, the reduction of her sexuality to her status as the passive object of desire (what McGuckian calls 'all those poems about Ireland laid out as a passive woman on a bed and mounted'),[31] a more general difficulty is the elision of history which the use of such mythic metaphors demands. Heaney's poem 'Act of Union' describes sex with his wife as the rape of Ireland by the male English soldier: 'And I am still imperially | Male, leaving you with the pain, | The rending process in the colony, The battering ram, the boom burst | from within. The act sprouted an obstinate fifth column | Whose stance is growing unilateral'.[32] The Act of Union becomes a struggle between primitive, landed, situated femininity and rational, social, organized masculinity which creates the inhabitants of the bastard province Northern Ireland.[33] In questioning the symbolism of

[30] This strategy of resistance has similarities with Luce Irigaray's advocacy of a 'riddling' enigmatic discourse for women as a way of undoing their objectification, although there are obviously important differences between Irigaray's radical feminist deconstruction of representation and McGuckian's stated wish to educate a male audience in the complexities of femininity.

[31] Personal interview (10 Jan. 1986).

[32] Seamus Heaney, 'Act of Union', in *North* (London: Faber and Faber, 1975), 49–50.

[33] Witness Heaney's description of the roots of the Troubles: 'To some extent the enmity can be viewed as a struggle between the cults and devotees of a god

such poems of dispossession, and linguistic repossession, I do not want to deny the traumatic effects of the plantation and the mass dispossession of Catholics in Gaelic Ulster and the rest of Ireland. Rather my concern is with what is historically elided in the attempt to describe such events through the metaphor of the motherland. The desecration of the motherland signals a fall into history, into the discontinuities of modernity. The feminine becomes the sign of secure national identity, the body of the woman is both the site where a breach in national continuity and tradition has been effected (the result of the rape) but also the place where that breach may be healed, through a return 'home' from linguistic exile.

McGuckian's trope harbours a different politics; the mother is an extremely unstable guarantee of identity, and patriarchal continuity. Her poetry repeatedly stresses women's dispossession and their displaced relation to the land, and therefore also the language—for there is a sexual as well as a racial element to dispossession. Continually and arbitrarily displaced, moved from one home, one piece of land, to another, what kind of secure motherland can woman represent? Though the land may be represented as a woman, the woman herself has no rights over the land, which is passed, along with her sexuality, from father to husband. But while authority and possession for women is always by chance 'slips', always second-hand, through motherhood the woman's relationship to the nation is supposed to be anything but secondary.[34] Women play a crucial role in the furtherance of the nation through their reproductive labour. As Gayatri Spivak points out in her essay on the short story 'Breast-giver', the term 'proletarian', defined as one who serves the State with no prop-

and a goddess. There is an indigenous territorial numen, a tutelar of the whole island, call her Mother Ireland, Kathleen ni Houlihan, the poor old woman, the Shan Van Vocht, whatever; and her sovereignty has been temporarily usurped or infringed by a new male cult whose founding fathers were Cromwell, William of Orange, Edward Carson, and whose godhead is incarnate in a Rex or Caesar resident in a palace in London. What we have is the tail end of a struggle in a province between territorial piety and imperial power', *Preoccupations: Selected Prose, 1968–78* (London: Faber and Faber, 1979), 57. On this opposition between a mythic motherland and a historical masculinity see David Trotter, *The Making of the Reader: Language and Subjectivity in Modern American, English and Irish Poetry* (Basingstoke: Macmillan, 1984), 188.

[34] See McGuckian's poem 'Slips', in *The Flower Master* (Oxford: Oxford University Press, 1982).

erty but only with his offspring, carries an effaced mark of sexuality.[35] And specifically in the context of a national struggle mothering belongs to the sphere of politics and ideology, as rearing children becomes an investment in the future of the nation.

If the child in 'Act of Union' is symbolic of a bastard fifth column, the source of the trouble, in McGuckian's poem 'The Heiress', the male child is a way to regain land. In 'The Heiress', McGuckian allies the position of women to that of Gaelic Ulster—defeated by the plantation, dispossessed after the Flight of the Earls, they must retreat to higher, more barren ground. From her vantage point the woman addresses a man who reveals his 'good husbandry' in relation to her 'pinched grain'.[36] McGuckian has said that the genesis of the poem lies in the story of Mary, Queen of Scots—denied her heritage in her own life, Mary's son became King James of England (during whose reign the major plantation of Ulster was carried out):

> But I am lighter of a son, through my slashed
> Sleeves the inner sleeves of purple keep remembering
> The moment exactly, remembering the birth
> Of an heiress means the gobbling of land.

Whereas her birth has led to the loss of land, the birth of a son through the 'slashed sleeves' of her Tudor dress and the torn body of the woman in childbirth, will regain the land (although Ulster will thereby be gobbled). So the heiress of the title is precisely the one who has been usurped; only through her children will she inherit. The final stanza implies that in order to regain her rightful position, the marginalized woman must place herself at the very limits of society—neither the hill nor the fields but the shore.

> I tell you dead leaves do not necessarily
> Fall; it is not coldness, but the tree itself
> That bids them go, preventing their destruction.

[35] Gayatri Chakravorty Spivak, 'A Literary Representation of the Subaltern: A Woman's Text from the Third World', in *In Other Worlds* (London: Methuen, 1987), 252, 255.

[36] See Cairns and Richards, *Writing Ireland*, 28, and Seamus Deane, 'Civilians and Barbarians', *Ireland's Field Day*, ed. Field Day Theatre Company (London: Hutchinson, 1985), on the colonizers' use of metaphors of husbandry during and after the plantation, in arguing for the necessity to combat Irish wildness by planting and cultivating English civility.

> So I walk along the beach, unruly, I drop
> Among my shrubbery of seaweed my black acorn buttons.

Here the sand is associated with fertility; the speaker finds a place where she can plant the seed of her authority on the beach—which is without order and authority in itself, 'unruly'.[37] The implication is that if the writer/woman is underrated, her poems/children may have citizenship, lend weight to her statement. Similarly, if Irish Catholics have been banished to barren ground, it is not by identification with the land that they will gain power. The intermediate realm between traditions, between land and sea, may be productive. In this way Ireland could be mother of a new history. But the problem with the poem is that by placing woman on the margin between history and flux, land and sea, the mother is reduced to a passage for history to pass through in the shape of her (male) child. Secondly, the poem does not offer an alternative to the use, or co-option, of the figure of the woman as a metaphor for the state of the nation. McGuckian seems to be simply reinflecting the identification of woman and land.

McGuckian's poem 'The Soil Map' may offer an alternative to the use of the figure of the woman as a metaphor for the nation. I read the poem as a parody of a 'place-name' or Dinnseanchas poem. Dinnseanchas was a major poetic genre in the Gaelic tradition, a celebration of rootedness, of knowing one's place through the etymological understanding of the roots of the place-name and the history that goes with it. In the typical scenario the poet's loving resurrection and exploration of the Irish or dialect name for the locality undoes the alien rape of the ruined maid, who can thus return to be possessed by her rightful kin. McGuckian's poem is addressed to a house (biographically the large Victorian house where McGuckian lives in Belfast, in an area built for wealthy Anglo-Irish Protestants though now inhabited almost entirely by Catholic families). The soil map is of course the map of Ireland on which the house stands, but the house is also a woman: 'I am not a woman's man, but I can tell, | By the swinging of your two-leaf door, | You are never without

[37] See Heaney's poem 'Shore Woman', which takes as its epigraph the Gaelic proverb—'Man to the hills, woman to the shore', in *Wintering Out* (London: Faber and Faber, 1972), 66.

one man in the shadow | Of another.' The woman in Irish myth who was 'never without one man in the shadow of another' was Queen Medhbh. Territorial goddess as well as legendary queen, she conferred kingship on all those who slept with her. (She is self-possessed rather than possessive). In contrast to the purity and chastity inscribed in the Aisling tradition, the essence of the myth is sexual, and Medhbh is not a mother but a seductress. This woman/house has lifted her skirts to all comers, Irish and English, Protestant and Catholic. It is therefore not necessary to lay siege to the house, the woman does not need to take possession with the 'hardness' of a male, because the Anglo-Irish big house tradition has already failed: 'Anyone with patience can divine how your plaster work has lost key | The rendering about to come away'. So the house is open, but to ignore the tradition of previous inhabitants is foolhardy because the present includes the layer of Anglo-Irish history as it does the earlier pre-colonial era. Where Heaney's or Montague's place-name poems imply that it is possible to disinter from the land a piece of history that has remained untouched by subsequent events, as though the past could simply visit the present, McGuckian uses the metaphor of the mud on which Belfast is built, rather than bog. While the seepage and mud flats are the reason for the house not being well preserved, the wet soil has also caused all the historical traditions to become mixed up. The motherland is extremely unreliable:

> I appeal to the god who fashions edges
> Whether such turning points exist
> As these saltings we believe we move
> Away from, as if by simply shaking
> A cloak we could disbud ourselves,
> Dry out and cease to live there?

The saltings and movements of water have changed the lie of the land. The act of possession may give the illusion of a break with previous history, but the poem implies that the inhabitants of the North are rooted in a contradictory position and it is useless to ignore any strand of it.

So far woman and house again serve as allegorical semes for the motherland; in opposition to the 'rape' theory of colonization the poem brings to the fore the copulative as well as the reproductive body, stressing the woman's active sexual desire. In fact McGuckian's self-proclaimed 'modesty' of style veils a celebration of sexual openness which itself stands as analogue for the opening up of community. To combat the Catholic/nationalist ideal of chaste, passive femininity, McGuckian foregrounds the unfaithfulness of both woman and nation, thereby undercutting notions of racial purity. One might argue that, again, this identification fails to expand the thematics of the woman's political body. The sexualization of the nationalist trope of the motherland is not going to help transfer the woman from her status as ground of the nationalist teleology to active participant in the nation's history. However, by emphasizing the unregulated nature of her sexuality, McGuckian foregrounds the impropriety of the figure. The woman/house stands both inside and outside the domain of the national at the same time; the figure reveals the ways in which national representations depend on sexuality, and at the same time undermines rationalist notions of the public sphere which would deny its imbrication with the private arena of the body, domesticity, and affectivity. In addition, as the public sphere is privatized, the concerns of the private, domestic sphere are revealed to be public ones, ensuring that the constructions of both home and nation are destabilized. Moreover, it is possible to focus on the figure of the woman as gendered subject in the poem, rather than as a metaphor for the nation. The place-names on this map, which shows the contours of historical change, are English women's Christian names—the only names women tend to keep. Carrying women's identification with the landscape to its logical conclusion, the Anglo-Irish houses were built for women with English names, and taking possession of the house should mean taking on its female name:

> I have found the places on the soil map,
> Proving it possible once more to call
> Houses by their names, Annsgift or Mavisbank,
> Mount Juliet or Bettysgrove.

But the names are a joke since women, exchanged along with the land, do not have the right to name it. It is because of her economic dispossession rather than her sexual excess that woman is an unstable guarantee of the nationalist teleology. The land is not something she has lost along the way, something that has been usurped from her, but something she never owned.

Much of the force of the poem resides in what I have termed the characteristic personalization of public narratives engaged in by these poets. They aim to disable one aspect of myth's power—its claim to universality—introducing discontinuity into their version of the myths by privatizing them, by taking them out of the public realm in which they are everybody's story and everybody knows their significance. But the poems in fact show that the woman's body is already public—thereby simultaneously calling into question public narratives of nationhood and community, and the private (familial) narratives of traditional femininity on which they depend. At the same time, both Boland and McGuckian imply that one of the functions of their work is to speak for the community of Irish women, though they differ radically in the strategies they adopt for such articulation. And yet this organicist position, which assumes a continuity between the writer and her people, is denied by those very writing strategies which force a change in the relation between poet and community, and thus a structural alteration in the generic tradition.

Conclusion

My discussion of the function of privacy in McGuckian's work began with a consideration of the politics of poetic form, and it is important to emphasize the fundamental connection between McGuckian's formal strategies and her representation of an intimate domain. For the nature of the relation between the private domestic sphere and the public allegory of the nation is cut across by the question of private and public languages, which are filtered through the body. Rather than an attempt to change public or national forms of representation by 'including' feminine narratives, McGuckian's work suggests instead the impossibility of separating domestic and national histories to begin with. The drive towards the increased representation of women's narratives is in danger of ignoring the politics inherent in the use of the traditional lyric form, focusing instead on the content of the feminine experience (both personal and communal) which must be introduced into the literary institution. The obscurity and indeterminacy of McGuckian's poetry, far from opening up experience in this way, parodies the very idea of a private or intimate domain; instead of intimacy we are confronted with secrecy, a refusal to offer the narrative up for inspection, and at the same time we are stalked by the nagging suspicion—as a historical narrative is glimpsed in fragmented form through the articulation of intimate body parts—that these are not private narratives anyway, but political allegories.

Why has the significance of this use of poetic form been misunderstood? I think this issue can only be properly grasped when placed in the context of current debates about postmodern poetic form in Britain. For, as I discussed in Chapter 1, semantic indeterminacy, enigmatic statement, and secret symbolism have been heralded as the defining characteristics of contemporary poetry by critics such as Blake Morrison, Andrew Motion, John Kerrigan, and Alan Robinson. All suggest that the 'obliqueness' and 'relativism' of current poetic forms have their roots in the changed nature of society, which has destroyed all faith in the Enlightenment values of truth and progress. However, by interpreting the significance of poetic form as the *result* of changing social formations, liberal critics such as Morrison and Motion concur with Habermas's pessimistic view about the loss of culture's civilizing role, since the public dimension of poetry is seen as collapsing inaccessibly into private narratives. Yet, as I have suggested, this poetry, even at its most obscure and enigmatic, is not simply seceding from the public realm of a degenerate consumerist culture into an area of pseudo-privacy. The refusal of communication, the resistance to interpretation, the parody of privacy through secrecy is directed outwards. At a more fundamental level, what I am arguing for is a more nuanced and contextual understanding of the function of particular literary forms. For the fragmentation of historical narrative, and the parody of public or official forms of discourse have a very specific function in colonial and post-colonial cultures; they are not necessarily, or not only, the signs of a global postmodernism. Moreover, given the particular, politicized functions of parody and fragmentation in women's discourse, one might argue that McGuckian's case is somewhat overdetermined. To return to Wendy Mulford's guarded dismissal of McGuckian as a non-experimental, and therefore less radical, poet—I would argue to the contrary that it is only because of the elements of representation in her work that McGuckian can hope to engage fruitfully with the particular construction of public and political discourse in Ireland. I hope I have indicated that what is at stake in her work is not the investigation and protection of interior space, it is not even the *addition* of that interior or private story to the public narrative. Instead this kind of aesthetic representation has an interventionist function. While engaging with the construction of political discourse in Ireland, it is saying to an iniquitous system of political representation, to, if you like, an unrepresentative bureaucracy—the normal processes of political negotiation have failed, and I will take no part in them.

3

Language Politics, Narrative, Political Violence

A STRANGE neologism has crept quietly into the discourse of politicians and media spokespeople who tackle Northern Ireland: the British mainland. It is a term which crystallizes within itself the dangers and difficulties of discussing neo-colonialism in Ireland, when the occupation of part of the island has, as far as large sections of the community are concerned, nothing 'neo' about it. Introduced as a way of avoiding some of the logical contradictions inherent in discussing the relationship between Northern Ireland and Britain, the word carries a weight of ideological contradictions of its own. For 'the British mainland' is meaningless as a political term: mainland marks a geography and in a sense defines itself against political entities such as the United Kingdom or Great Britain (which does not include Northern Ireland anyway) since it expressly omits parts of these. So for the Unionist it stands as an implicit rebuke: he or she can never be truly joined to Britain, and yet what use is that treasured Britishness if it can suffer divisions in this way? The word makes of Northern Ireland a region even as it sutures England, Wales, and Scotland into a single entity (though excluding their islands). Meanwhile for the nationalist it carries a similar smart: not only does the word imply a relationship to the wrong political and geographic entity but ironically it also dissolves the border between Northern and Southern Ireland (to use safely geographical terms). For mainlands have neighbouring islands, not parts of islands (is it the whole island of Ireland which is deemed to snuggle in the seas of the British mainland?). And here it is perhaps worth noting that Gibraltar's mainland is of course Spain, not Britain (or rather England–Scotland–Wales).

The logical contradictions of 'the British mainland' are just one example of the difficulties inherent in using language to mirror or represent national allegiances, and an illustration of the fact that such allegiances are fissured even for the British. (Indeed regionalist developments in the media, and particularly in broadcasting (where the term arose), reveal the fragmented nature not only of 'British' national identity, but of its 'official' language. It would obviously be mistaken to imply that the language of the media mirrors a conservative ideology handed down from above, as it may have done thirty years ago. Nevertheless, to deny the real influence governments still have over the media representation of events would be equally shortsighted.) Paradoxically the phrase acts as a reminder that the issue of Ireland's national status is not simply a question of the relation of one nation-state to another; the opposition is between a nation which is not a state, and a geographical entity, which is neither. Moreover, the problem of Northern Ireland's national or regional status takes on a new dimension in the context of the political movement towards a transnational Europe. The question of how national struggles operate within the framework of the European nation-state, both as their goal and as their foe, must be reframed in the light of the ideal of a Common European Home. But on a more material level, the complexities accruing to the regional status of Northern Ireland have by no means newly arrived, and it is the history of attempts to regionalize the area which is played out in contemporary debates around the politics of language. The fact that Northern Ireland is not only economically dependent on Britain but also occupied by the British military obviously has important consequences for any discussion of neo-colonialism in Ireland, as does the fact that there too Irishness and Englishness are cut across by varieties of Britishness. (The 'British presence' is altogether too English for some Unionists).

But the history of colonialism in the island as a whole throws up yet more contradictions, which stem primarily from the fact that Ireland is not one of Europe's 'others'. Is the Irish nationalist movement, the Easter Rising, and its aftermath to be classed among the varieties of nineteenth-century Western nationalisms, or as a non-Western post-colonial movement for liberation, like the one it influenced in India? This difficulty of placing Ireland is compounded by the absence of the visual marker of skin-colour difference which was used to legitimize domination in other colonized societies. Of course the English had and still have various methods for delineating the difference between themselves and the barbarian race of the Irish, even if some of those Irish choose to call themselves British. Despite some pseudo-Darwinian attempts to match Irish with black physiognomy, in general, stereotypes of the 'wild Irish' have tended to concentrate on their habits and life-style (poverty, laziness, dirt, and drunkenness), and, most importantly for my argument, on their *language.*[1] Whether it is a patronizing approval of lyrical Celticism, or horrified revulsion from the degenerate Irish accent, Irish men and women are marked by their voices, their (mis)use of the English language. So much is this the case that recently an interviewer for the BBC Radio programme *Today* asked a Conservative politician quite seriously whether his exhortations to the public to be vigilant in the fight against terrorism meant treating those with Irish accents with suspicion. Of course the equivalence between Irish person and terrorist has a long history too, and, as Seamus Deane points out, it is the logical consequence of characterizing the Irish as a whole as 'barbarian', and outside the law.[2]

In the following pages I will approach the barbaric pollution of the English language by the Irish from the other side, discussing issues of post-colonial identity in Ireland by examining theoretical arguments about the language question in Northern Ireland, and its relation to nationality. (Given the different political, social, and literary parameters of the Irish language in the South I do not attempt to deal with it here.) I will differentiate several ways of viewing both the historical fate of Irish as a living language, and the contemporary situation in which most people in Ireland speak one of several dialects of English. My analysis foregrounds a basic distinction between those who argue for an intrinsic connection between language (either Irish or Irish-English) and Irish identity, and those who find in Irish dialects not the expression of 'Irishness' but a mark of difference from 'Englishness'. (Again, identifications with 'Britishness' may be forced uncomfortably to straddle this divide.) While one may look for the signs of this struggle in straightforwardly political arguments about language, such as those associated with Sinn Féin and Ulster separatists, it is in contemporary Northern Irish writing, and particularly

[1] See Liz Curtis, *The Roots of Anti-Irish Racism* (Information on Ireland).

[2] Seamus Deane, 'Civilians and Barbarians', in *Ireland's Field Day* (London: Hutchinson, 1985), 33–42.

poetry, that the relationship between narrative form and the national role of language is set into relief.

As my analysis of the version of Irish history presupposed by the genre of Dinnseanchas poetry will show, all these theories of language and nationality harbour theories of historical narrative. The question of the type of narrative a nation, group, or tribe tells itself has always been of immense importance in Ireland where dates, heavy with the weight of overinvested identities, war with each other: 1690, 1798, 1912, 1916. But in the shadow of another date, 1992, and stalked by post-national and trans-national ideals such as the common European home, how will national (English, Irish, British) narratives evolve? Will the importance of Ireland's relationship with 'the mainland' recede? Nationalist Irish politicians and commentators both North and South see in a new Europe the possibility both of some kind of resolution to the Northern Irish problem, and of a revival of the economic fortunes of the Republic. And, on a theoretical plane, writers such as Richard Kearney have argued that the fragmentation of narrative characteristic of postmodernism is in some sense symptomatic of the fragmentation of conservative, nationalist, and by implication also Unionist, historical, and political narratives.[3] Kearney celebrates postmodern style in Irish writers as almost a prefigurement of post-nationalist possibilities for Ireland within the framework of a new, federalized Europe. His analogy between postmodernism and post-nationalism depends on interpreting events such as 1992 and the fragmentation of the Eastern Bloc as a dissolution of overarching imperialist or nationalist narratives, whether British, Irish, or Soviet, in favour of regions and regional histories. In contrast, one of the present British Government's fears is that the opening up of national borders will enable Irish 'men of violence' to bring their version of historical narrative all the more frequently into savage conflict with others. In this sense, as I will explore, perhaps postmodernity's celebrated fragmentation, its ability to freely mix past, present, and future may find itself host to the pre-modern nostalgia of terrorism's narrative of crisis.

[3] See Richard Kearney (ed.), *Across the Frontiers: Ireland in the 1990s* (Dublin: Wolfhound Press, 1990), 7–28.

Language as Resistance

Any discussion of the politics of language use in Ireland today must initially take account of the conflictual history of the English language in Ireland, and the complex historical relationship between the various languages and dialects in use in the present. In the major part of the island Irish steadily declined in use during the English colonization in the period from the sixteenth to the mid-nineteenth centuries, at which time Irish remained a first language, as it does today, only in areas in the far west of the country (now called the Gaeltacht, with native speakers estimated as 2 per cent of the population). The decline in Irish shouldn't be interpreted simply as the result of actively repressive domination by the English; as David Lloyd points out in *Nationalism and Minor Literature*, Ireland's geographical closeness to Britain resulted in its 'undergoing the transition to hegemonic colonialism far earlier than any other colony'.[4] In addition to a growth in the demand for literacy, the rapid decline in Irish in the nineteenth century was due in large part to the forces of bureaucratic centralization, exemplified by the national schools and the ordance survey, which were introduced in Ireland far earlier than in England.[5] Moreover, as Tom Paulin points out,

> English was the language of power, commerce and acceptance, and the Irish people largely accepted Daniel O'Connell's view that Gaelic monolingualism was an obstacle to freedom. Particularly after the famine, parents encouraged their children to learn English as this would help them make new lives in America.[6]

Thus the more complete picture is of the English language proceeding by means of 'prestige and active consent', rather than domination by coercion and passive consent, in line with Antonio

[4] David Lloyd, *Nationalism and Minor Literature* (Berkeley, Calif: University of California Press, 1988), 3.

[5] See John Andrews, *A Paper Landscape: The Ordnance Survey in Nineteenth-Century Ireland* (Oxford: Oxford University Press, 1975), and Brian Friel's dramatization of the effects of the mapping on the Irish language, and particularly on place-names, *Translations* (London: Faber and Faber, 1981). Both the national school system and the ordnance survey can also be interpreted in terms of repressive domination, of course, since they were introduced as part of an educational experiment in Ireland.

[6] Tom Paulin, 'A New Look at the Language Question', in *Ireland's Field Day*, 10.

Gramsci's theorization of hegemony.[7] But Irish was not completely suppressed or rejected; in the period since its most rapid decline Irish has been championed by the Young Ireland movement and the Gaelic League among others, and as a result of the struggle for independence it was reinstated as the national language of the Irish Republic, although used by a small minority. The programme of the Young Irelanders, and of figures such as Patrick Pearse (who called for an Ireland 'not free merely, but Gaelic as well') has been continued by, among others, Sinn Féin's cultural department which calls for the reintroduction of Irish as a crucial step in the attempt to heal the breach with the past caused by the domination of Ireland by imperial English culture, and to create a future unaffected by global multinational capitalism.

Albeit from a very different perspective, Seamus Heaney sums up this feeling of loss and separation caused by the disappearance of the language, in a discussion of Stephen's 'tundish' from *A Portrait of the Artist as a Young Man*:

> Stephen feels excluded from the English tradition, which he senses as organic and other than his own. His own tradition is linguistically fractured. History, which has woven the fabric of English life and landscape and language into a seamless garment, has rent the fabric of Irish life, has effected a breach between its past and its present, and an alienation between the speaker and his speech . . . Whether we wish to locate the breaking point of Gaelic civilisation at the battle of Kinsale and the Flight of the Earls in the early seventeenth century or whether we hold out hopefully until the Jacobite dream fades after the flight of the Wild Geese, there is no doubt that the social, cultural, linguistic life of the country is radically altered, and the alteration is felt by the majority of Irish people as a kind of loss, an exile from an original whole and good place or state.[8]

Through Stephen, Heaney's remarks deny the heterogeneity of the use of English by the British, for there is of course no organic

[7] For a concise account of Gramsci's theory of hegemony see Perry Anderson, 'The Antinomies of Antonio Gramsci', *New Left Review*, 100 (Nov. 1976–Jan. 1977), 5–79. For the relation of hegemony to language politics see Antonio Gramsci, *Selections from Cultural Writings*, ed. David Forgacs and Geoffrey Nowell-Smith, trans. William Boelhower (London: Lawrence and Wishart, 1985), 164–95.

[8] Seamus Heaney, 'The Interesting Case of John Alphonsus Mulrennan', *Planet*, 41 (1978), 35.

connection between the varietes of British English throughout these islands and an English literary tradition. And indeed there is a strain of English literary conservatism which laments this diversification of speech forms as the sign of a similar infraction on the smooth progress of an English literary tradition. Heaney's description of the fate of the history of the language as a breach in continuity, a division between before and after, Irish and English, obscures the more complex historical situation, nowhere more so than in the North of Ireland. For example, Scottish settlers, fleeing from religious persecution under Elizabeth, introduced Scots Gaelic and culture into the north of the country, particularly counties Antrim and Down, even before the seventeenth-century Ulster plantation (when land freed by the flight of native Catholic chiefs was granted by James I to be planted by English and Scots settlers).[9] As John Braidwood observes, there are now three main dialect types in Ulster: east and northern Ulster Scots (Lallans), a central Ulster dialect mainly of English origin, and in the border and survival areas a more Anglo-Irish type (which he terms mid-Ulster English to distinguish it from the Hiberno-English of the South of Ireland).[10] So the major dialect divisions correlate in a general way with the plantation pattern. However, this pattern has been complicated still further by the presence of significant numbers of people born in England, with varieties of English accent and dialect, living in the North of Ireland. In addition there are a growing number of primary schools in Northern Ireland which teach Irish as a first language, and small numbers of Irish Republicans who attempt to use only Irish for their everyday purposes. Most obviously for Republican prisoners, communicating in Irish is a very concrete way of using language as a form of resistance.

Within this region characterized by extreme diversification of languages and dialects, arguments abound about the possibility that language may act as a sign or expression of national or tribal identity. Albeit in very different ways, the attempt to use language, whether Irish, Ulster Scots, or Irish English, as a counter-hegemonic force, resistant to British cultural imperialism, informs

[9] See Marianne Elliott, *Partners in Revolution: The United Irishmen and France* (New Haven, Conn: Yale University Press, 1982), 19–20.

[10] John Braidwood, *The Ulster Dialect Lexicon* (Belfast: Queen's University Press, 1969), 7.

the various projects of the Field Day Company, Sinn Féin's cultural department, and figures such as Ian Adamson who argue for a separatist Ulster. As will become clear, arguments regarding the efficacy of a specific language both to foster and represent such resistance tend to depend on the nature of the political history which is embedded in the linguistic one, the link which may be drawn between the history of a language or dialect's emergence or decline, and its ability to mark or express Irish or Ulster identity. Putting aside specific cases in favour of particular languages, I want first to address the broader theoretical questions concerning the possibility of a cultural form such as a language to be 'resistant'. Such a question naturally touches on the role of poetry, and cultural production more generally, in the formation of a national culture.[11]

In the complex situation detailed above, the question for the writer opposed to British or English cultural hegemony is which language or dialect to choose as an instrument of counter-hegemony. This is a general problem confronted by ex-colonial nations, both those which resist and those which keep and adapt the colonial language. In 'Minority Discourse and the African Collective', Josaphat B. Kubayanda points out the contradictory history revealed in the use of the colonial language:

> Language itself contains the world, and minority discourse borrows the language from the dominant world, which in its purely negative form negates or diminishes the minority subject. What, then, does the minority literature do with such a dominant tongue? Shakespeare's Caliban is admittedly the supreme example in the Western literature of the minority subject crushed by the language of the majority. But Caliban saves himself through a counter-discourse which 'deterritorializes' the borrowed English tongue with curses.[12]

As Kubayanda points out, in using the dominant language as a weapon against the dominant culture, the writer chooses not to be pitted against the canon and hegemonic centres, but to

[11] See David Cairns and Shaun Richards, *Writing Ireland: Colonialism, Nationalism and Culture* (Manchester: Manchester University Press, 1988), for a discussion of this topic in relation to 19th- and 20th-cent. literature.

[12] Josaphat B. Kubayanda, 'Minority Discourse and the African Collective', *Cultural Critique*, 6 (1987), 116. See also Gilles Deleuze and Felix Guattari, *Kafka: Toward a Minority Literature*, trans. Dana Polan (Minneapolis: University of Minnesota Press, 1986).

recontextualize and reframe the dominant language by undermining its 'purity of grammar', its pretensions to transcendence and universalism. For the dominant language can only claim universalism by a denial of otherness. Kubayanda's reframing is analogous to Homi Bhabha's theory of colonial mimicry, which 'introduces a hole in colonial authority' by creating a hybrid form of discourse as the colonized or minority people ask questions of authoritative discourse in the dominant language. Hybridity 'causes the dominant discourse to split along the axis of its power to be representative, authoritative'.[13] The language becomes 'polluted' not only by its transformation into a pidgin, creole, or dialect in the mouths of the colonized people, but also simply by its articulation by the 'barbarian' or 'other'.[14]

In Bhabha's formulation 'voice' is understood as a mark of difference, rather than as an expression of identity—it works as a sign of outer recognition of the 'native' rather than as an inner mirror of his being (in other words it has no intrinsic connection

[13] Homi Bhabha, 'Signs Taken for Wonders: Questions of Ambivalence and Authority under a Tree outside Delhi, May 1817', in Francis Barker *et al.* (eds.), *Europe and its Others*, ii (Colchester: Essex Conference Papers, 1985), 89–106. On Bhabha's concept of colonial mimicry see 'Of Mimicry and Men: The Ambivalence of Colonial Discourse', *October*, 28 (1984), 125–33. The 'deterritorialization' of a language, which takes place through its repetition in the mouth of the 'other', also has obvious affinities with Luce Irigaray's theory of subversive mimesis.

[14] For both Bhabha and Kubayanda the crucial sign of otherness is skin colour, a difference which naturally does not apply to the relationship between the Irish and their English colonizers, despite attempts to figure Irish physiognomy as akin to that of the apes, as for example in this statement of 1860 by Charles Kingsley: 'I am haunted by the human chimpanzees I saw along that hundred miles of horrible country. I don't believe they are our fault. I believe that there are not only many more of them than of old but that they are happier, better and more comfortably fed and lodged under our rule than they ever were. But to see white chimpanzees is dreadful; if they were black, one would not feel it so much, but their skins, except where tanned by exposure are as white as ours', quoted in Richard Kearney (ed.), *The Irish Mind* (Dublin: Wolfhound Press, 1985), 7. See also L. P. Curtis, Jun., *Anglo-Saxons and Celts: A Study of Anti-Irish Prejudice in Victorian England* (Bridgeport, Conn.: Conference on British Studies of University of Bridgeport, 1968), and Deane, 'Civilians and Barbarians'. However, the fear of 'cultural pollution' of the English by the Irish was none the less strong, and importantly for my argument it concentrated on the barbarism of the Irish accent. See Cairns and Richards, *Writing Ireland*, 6. In contrast, 1930s Gaelic League propaganda advocated the preservation of the Irish language and the Gaelic way of life to combat the danger of Ireland becoming 'a hybrid people'; see D. George Boyce, *Nationalism in Ireland* (Baltimore: Johns Hopkins, University Press, 1982), 353–4, on this desire for cultural homogeneity as a means of resisting the history of the English presence.

with 'native culture'). What is at stake is a positioning of the dominant discourse, a perception of its relativity through an awareness of difference. This opposition between viewing language as an expression of national identity, or alternatively as a mark of difference and therefore possible point of resistance to the hegemonic language, may be fruitfully mapped on to the language question in Ireland. My contention is that in contrast to those who argue for an intrinsic connection between the Irish (or Ulster Scots) language and Irish (or Ulster Scots) identity, writers such as Seamus Heaney, Tom Paulin, Paul Muldoon, and Medbh McGuckian exploit the possibilities of language, whether English or Irish-English, to be recontextualized by its Northern Irish usage, at the same time uncovering the variety of discourses and the diversity of speech forms within Official English itself. In addition to the use of dialect which Paulin advocates (and which will be discussed in detail in the following section), such a recontextualization is achieved by the parodic use of the official (political, religious, media) language typical of Muldoon and McGuckian. Parody can also be unconscious of course (and this is precisely because standard British English is not as univocal as it pretends); as Paulin points out in 'A New Look at the Language Question', the Unionist who retains a marked Irish accent, while arguing for the complete cultural integration of Britain and Northern Ireland, 'is either an unconscious contradiction or a subversive ironist'.[15]

But with the introduction of the possibility of unconscious parody the problem of intention arises. Is the dominant discourse reframed only if this is the writer's or speaker's intention? Moreover, does the parodic recontextualization need to be recognized in order for it to exist? As Heaney points out, the long history of the English language in Ireland brings about a situation in which 'English is by now not so much an imperial humiliation as a native weapon'.[16] But how is it to be utilized as a weapon? The choice of writing in the dominant language, published in the neo-colonial metropolis, gives writers access to a wide public, but how is it possible to avoid absorption into the dominant canon, thereby forfeiting the possibility of reframing it? Paulin has asserted that 'the Irish writer who publishes in Britain has a

[15] Paulin, 'Language Question', 5.
[16] Heaney, 'John Alphonsus Mulnennan', 40.

neo-colonial identity', identifying the 'central question' for such a writer as 'whom am I writing for?'[17] Yet Irish and English readers may respond very differently to some of the obscurities in Irish writing, since what to one may be a hidden reference to the other may be a local allusion. In the same way the fact that critics have largely ignored the linguistic irony present in much Northern Irish poetry may have as much to do with their own critical assumptions and 'responsibility' as anything else. As Edward Said asserts in *The World, The Text, The Critic*, 'critics create not only the values by which art is judged and understood, but they embody in writing those processes and actual conditions in the present by means of which art and writing bear significance'.[18] In approaching Irish poetry critically there is a need to be alert to the ways in which the use of dialect and Irish words may introduce cracks in the representations of standard English. So place-names such as Broagh, Anahorish, and Eglish, or words and sounds such as 'glipes', 'sheugh', and 'ack' may be read not only for their local colour but in terms of their political function and effect. Only in this way, by the cultivation of reading strategies alert to the distinction between the use of voice as a mark of difference or alternatively as a mark of identity, can the presence of a politically oppositional voice in contemporary Northern Irish poetry be recognized for what it is.

National Language

The history of a language is often a story of possession and dispossession, territorial struggle and the establishment or imposition of a culture.[19]

One of the mainstays of national identity in its modern form has been the ideal of a unifying common language. Moreover it is clear that forms and representations of discourse play a crucial role in the operation of both national and imperial hegemony. As Cairns and Richards argue in *Writing Ireland*, the political domi-

[17] However, on a new-found authority in recent Irish language writing, see Dermot Bolger, Introduction, in id, (ed.), *The Bright Wave/An Tonn Gheal: Poetry in Irish Now* (Dublin: Raven Arts Press, 1986), 12–22.

[18] Edward Said, *The World, the Text, and the Critic* (originally published 1983; London: Faber and Faber, 1984), 53.

[19] Paulin, 'Language Question', 1.

nation of the Irish has been intimately connected with a cultural imperialism, exemplified by writings such as those of Ferguson and Arnold, and consisting not only of the imposition of the English language as the norm, but also of English literature.[20] But if language is the site and sign of imperial domination, it is also, and because of this, crucial in the formation of a national counter-hegemony. It functions as a paradigm for the operations of social change and the achievement of hegemony. David Forgacs points out that Gramsci's concept of hegemony was derived at least in part from the work of the 'spatial linguists' at Turin, who argued that linguistic change was brought about by the effect of the prestigious speech community's language in its contact with the languages of non-dominant neighbouring groups.[21] Thus Gramsci asserts the need for groups opposing existing hegemonies to formulate a linguistic programme which can unify disparate sections of the community. His own historical situation, in an Italy where communication between provinces and regions was difficult, if not impossible, due to the marked language differences, required a unitary standard language as a prerequisite to political mobilization. (His argument is not that it is the language which unifies, but rather that it serves as a vehicle for the processes of unification already active across a number of institutions.) And yet there is of course no necessary correlation between a unitary language and a language which unifies; for example, a language which can unify the various sections of the community in the island of Ireland must necessarily be one which can accommodate difference. In other words, for a language to be politically forceful it is not necessary for it to be 'monoglossic', in Bakhtin's terms, to ignore or reduce differences.[22] The question for Tom Paulin and the Field Day Company of which he is a part is how to bring together the various different languages and dialects in use in Ireland in order to create a 'standard' Irish English which would have the authority

[20] See Cairns and Richards, *Writing Ireland*, 25–31, 43–9. See also Lloyd, *Nationalism* 6–13, 49–77.

[21] Forgacs, Introduction to 'Language, Linguistics and Folklore', in Gramsci, *Cultural Writings*, 164–7.

[22] See Mikhail Bakhtin, 'From the Prehistory of Novelistic Discourse', in *The Dialogic Imagination* (Austin, Tex.: University of Texas Press, 1981), 41–83.

to counter standard English, without at the same time denying cultural difference within Ireland.[23]

In 'A New Look at the Language Question' Paulin stresses the political nature of a nation's choice of language, and asserts implicitly the necessity of a language programme for any group which aspires to cultural hegemony. Language is important in two interconnected ways—firstly as a means of creating a contemporaneous community through a shared field of language, and secondly as a link with a particular, national history. But as I have argued, in Ireland the weight of history which seems to inhere in the language is geographically fractured, as the language has performed different historical functions in different areas, and among different classes.[24] The difficulty then for anyone attempting to introduce questions of language into the contemporary political arena, is how to be faithful to the conflictual and heterogeneous history signified in and by the language, while acknowledging the politics inherent in the relation between the 'dominant' and the 'minority' nation. In other words, in analysing the politics of language in a particular region, it is not sufficient to emphasize only the polyglossic nature of the linguistic situation *within* the region (in Northern Ireland this would involve taking account of Irish, Irish English, Ulster Scots) if this analysis excludes consideration of the more binary or oppositional relation of the region to the colonial centre.

Tom Paulin's essay could be read as an example of the contemporary politics of dialect; it brings together the issues of history and contemporary community in arguing for a federal concept of language and dialect in Ireland. Through, among other things, the institution of a dictionary of Irish English, such a concept would be able to take account of differences within the community, thereby preserving historical differences, while affirming a functional or positional similarity between dialects, in

[23] However, though received pronunciation and standard English usage do gain a particular force and the illusion of universality through educational and media promotion, actual English usage is of course characterized by a diversity of speech forms. (And indeed it is the case that within the media and the political world regional accent is now as common as BBC English.) An alternative language programme might emphasize the fact that, like Paulin's Irish English, standard English could accommodate differences in lexicon and accent, in which case Irish English would be a part of it.

[24] And there may also of course be a gender difference in relation to the national language. As I discussed in Ch. 2, women occupy a displaced position in relation to the concept of the standard language as a vehicle for national identity.

that they occupy the same position (non- or substandard) in relation to standard British English.[25] Paulin is scrupulous in his examination of the relations between languages and between standard and non-standard versions within languages, as political relations. He points out that the process of ascertaining the English language has been intimately connected with the English Parliament: 'Fundamentally the language question is a question about nationhood and government, and some lexicographers perceive an occult connection between the English language and the English constitution.'[26] In addition, opposition not simply to the Irish language, but to the Irish accent (together with other regional accents), can be read as a political stance in favour of a unified culture, symbolized in the standard English accent embracing England and Ireland. Paulin's dialectal counter-hegemony would be achieved by the elevation and organization of two aspects of the language—accent, or regional pronunciation, and lexicon, or regional vocabulary. (One could argue that recently the concept of 'standard English' has successfully been dethroned in terms of the former, but has given hardly any space at all to the latter.) His project seems to comprise the creation of a new concept of standard Irish English which, since it would be an *organized* linguistic entity, would have the power to resist standard British English, much in the same way as Noah Webster planned for his Dictionary of American English.

But it is important to be aware of how Paulin's project also differs from other republican linguistic programmes such as the American one. As Paulin points out, for Webster local accent within America hindered a sense of national identity, and he argues instead that 'uniformity of speech' will help to form national attachments.[27] Thus Webster's projected American

[25] Paulin's insistence on the relative 'equality' between dialects is open to question, however, for, coming from the other side of the colonial, cultural, and religious divide, Hiberno-English necessarily makes for a very different form of hybridity than its Ulster counterparts.

[26] Paulin, 'Language Question', 7. However, Paulin's argument here seems to depend on a problematic homogenization of parliament with nationhood. See also Tom Nairn, *The Enchanted Glass* (London: Radius Press, 1988), 351–2.

[27] But see Charles Swann, 'Noah Webster: The Language of Politics/The Politics of Language', *Essays in Poetics*, 13.2 (Sept. 1988), 41–82, on the complex relation between Webster's language programme and his political position. See also John Barrell, *English Literature in History, 1730–80: An Equal Wide Survey* (London: Hutchinson, 1983).

language is a version of the 'platonic standard' which Paulin opposes, but without the universal claims attached to British English. Webster's decision to ignore race and gender differences in the interests of national unity firmly defines his projected language as a 'monoglossia' in Bakhtin's sense, ie. a language which accounts social difference a threat and banishes it. But Paulin's conception of Irish English does not seem to be monoglossic in the same way;[28] rather than an attempt to raise Irish English to the level of an abstract standard, Paulin seems intent on revealing the false basis of any standard which is violently abstracted from the particular social situation from which it arises, whether that be the British House of Commons or the more socially disparate situation in Ireland. His dictionary would elevate local accent and dialect words to the status of the national language, rather than ironing them out in the interests of unity. His federal concept of Irish English would, he claims:

> redeem many words from that too-exclusive, too-local usage which amounts to a kind of introverted neglect. Many words which now appear simply gnarled, or which 'make strange' or seem opaque to most readers, would be released into the shaped flow of a new public language. Thus in Ireland there would exist three fully-fledged languages—Irish, Ulster Scots and Irish English. Irish and Ulster Scots would be preserved and nourished, while Irish English would be a form of modern English which draws on Irish, the Yola and Fingallian dialects, Ulster Scots, Elizabethan English, Hiberno-English, British-English, and American English. A confident concept of Irish English would substantially increase the vocabulary and this would improve the written language. A language that lives lithely on the tongue ought to be capable of becoming the flexible, written instrument of a complete cultural idea.[29]

From the standpoint of colonial or minority discourse theory such a project would constitute a reversal of values by which Irish English has been designated marginal, since Irish accents

[28] Here I would take issue with Tony Crowley's otherwise excellent discussion of language politics in Northern Ireland. See 'Bakhtin and the History of the Language', in Ken Hirschkop and David Shepherd (eds.), *Bakhtin and Cultural Theory* (Manchester: Manchester University Press, 1989), 88.

[29] However, although Paulin isolates three languages in use in Ireland he elevates only one of them, Irish English, to the level of a standard and relegates the others to the role of 'nourishment'. The danger is thus that the Irish-English language would become a standard in the sense of 'level of excellence' rather than a vehicle for the promised equality.

and dialect vocabulary are, in the absence of any defining visual features, the most obvious marks of difference, and thus the sign of the substandard. Moreover, it is only by the organization of Irish English that the recontextualization or reframing of British English discussed earlier can be recognized for what it is. However, there is a tendency for Paulin's definition of Irish English to slide into a concept of the expression of the Irish or the Irish way of life through his stress on a particular content for the language. This is problematic since once a language is accepted as expressive or representative of a people, it may easily be frozen into a trans-historical standard which ceases to be moulded by, and to respond to, the changes in the nation: particular words and phrases can be read as signs of authentic Irishness. While for both Paulin and Gramsci the political qualities of language are related to its material formations, its place and function in the institution, rather than in the lexicon, there is no institutional basis for Irish English at present and in its absence Paulin is reduced to using a lexicon (the projected Dictionary of Irish English) to fight a number of British institutions.[30] Thus, while it is obviously important to ground the new standard Irish English in its social base, the danger is that certain words will become 'representative' of a class or a people and therefore necessary to the principle of national unification (in the way that Ian Adamson, for example, uses the evidence of Scots Gaelic to prove Ulster the most 'Irish' territory in the island of Ireland).[31] As I will argue in the following section, a similar theoretical difficulty, in which a language, because it is viewed as representative or expressive of a region or a tribe, is invested with political force and the power to resist imperial hegemony, recurs in many contemporary 'place-name' poems; here dialect words and names tend to become symbolic of a people and a whole history of their dispossession and are therefore entrusted with the task of repossessing the land.[32] At issue here is the relation of

[30] His position, he admits, is founded on an idea of identity which as yet has 'no formal or institutional existence'; see 'Language Question', 11.

[31] Ian Adamson, 'The Language of Ulster', in id., *The Identity of Ulster: The Land, the Language and the People* (Belfast: Adamson, 1982), 73–81.

[32] Whereas for Gramsci the aim of linguistic intervention should not be a specific unified language, designated in advance, (with the consequent danger that the standard would be merely symbolic or aesthetic) but one whose final shape will depend on the action of the people: 'One will obtain a *unified language*, if it is

Irish English to the variety of other non-standard dialects and accents of English. Will the unification of Irish English create a language which can dialogize and challenge standard British English? Irish English, if it is to be truly oppositional, has to express not only the nation, but also the position of the nation in relation to England, not only a region, but the position of the non-standard in relation to the centre.

It is therefore politically significant that Paulin argues not for the reintroduction of Gaelic, Scots, or Irish, as intimately connected to Gaelic culture and inherently oppositional to British cultural hegemony, but for the elevation of dialects of English. Here he differs both from politically separatist accounts of language in the North of Ireland, such as that of Ian Adamson who argues for the preservation of Ulster Scots (Lallans), along with Irish, within an independent Ulster, and from Sinn Féin and Republican arguments for Irish as the link with two thousand years of Gaelic continuity. So, for Padraig O Maolchraibhe in *The Role of the Language in Ireland's Cultural Revival*, a pamphlet published by Sinn Féin, the present position of the Irish language represents not just a breach with Gaelic culture but also with Gaelic values, which he asserts are implacably opposed to British materialism, and which moreover are inherent in the language: 'Our traditional Gaelic culture held values of human dignity, of cooperation, of socialism which are directly opposed to the materialism, consumerism, individualism, competitiveness which predominate in the Anglo-American culture of today.'[33] As I have

a necessity, and the organised intervention will speed up the already existing process. What this language will be, one cannot foresee or establish: in any case, if the intervention is "rational", it will be organically tied to tradition, and this is of no small importance in the economy of culture' (Gramsci, *Cultural Writings*, 183).

[33] Padraig O Maolchraibhe, *The Role of the Language in Ireland's Cultural Revival* (Belfast: Sinn Féin, 1984), 4. This purist strand in Sinn Féin's thinking is in tension with arguments for the acceptance of the heterogeneity of cultural forms in modern Ireland. For example, Gerry Adams, though at times he seems to endorse O Maolchraibhe's restorationist view, emphasizes the fact that arguments for the revival of Gaelic language and culture need not necessarily entail notions of the preservation or restoration of the past: 'We do not seek to recover the past but to discover it so that we can recover the best of our traditional values and mould them to the present. Our national culture should reflect the combination of the different influences within the nation: urban and rural, Gaeltacht and Galltacht, northern and southern, orange and green. The revival of the Irish language as a badge of identity, as a component part of our culture and as the filter through which it is expressed, is a central part of that reconquest'. This valoriza-

argued, at issue in these differing linguistic projects is a tension or a contradiction between a view of language as expressive of national, regional, or racial identity (i.e. inherently bound up with certain values), or alternatively as a political tool in the creation of a community resistant to an imperial cultural hegemony. (These differing views in turn correspond to Homi Bhabha's distinction between a concept of 'voice' as a mark of authentic identity, or alternatively as a mark of social and political difference.)

National Narratives

The issues I have discussed have been concerned primarily with the political inflections which are given to the history of the language in Northern Ireland. Arguments for and against languages arise because of the political history which is thought to be buried in the linguistic one, and it would of course be short-sighted in the extreme to argue that the destruction of the Irish language should, or could, be greeted by Irish people with equanimity. I wish to turn now, however, to the ways in which contemporary English-language poets write of the loss of the language. I have suggested that the distinction between 'identity' and 'difference' which I have been delineating is integrally connected to alternative versions of historical narrative, and it is in contemporary poetry that the link between narrative form and the national role of language is revealed most clearly. A writer's choice of language, or the inflection he or she gives to a language, is not merely a question of which of the available tools to utilize, but of his or her relation to tradition. Moreover, as I shall argue, it is crucially bound up with views about the construction of the community.[34]

tion of Irish for its function as a 'badge of identity' in a culturally fragmented modern nation ('young people with Doctor Martin boots, knee-high denims and punk hairstyles peppering their talk with Irish phrases') has much in common with Bhabha's formulation of voice as a mark of difference. See Gerry Adams, *The Politics of Irish Freedom* (Dingle: Brandon Books, 1986), 139, 145.

[34] The alternative versions of tradition can be fruitfully mapped on to Mikhail Bakhtin's distinction between 'epic' and 'novelistic' discourse; see Bakhtin, 'Discourse and the Novel', in *Imagination.* For an analysis of contemporary Irish poetry which makes detailed reference to Bakhtin's theory, and to the work of Benedict Anderson on the construction of national communities, see the earlier version of this essay, 'Language Politics, Narrative, Political Violence', *Oxford Literary Review*, 13 (1991), 20–60.

I have suggested that the celebration of a particular language as expressive of the true identity of a people or a region has affinities with a mythic or trans-historical notion of tradition, and I instanced in this regard claims for the intrinsic connection of the Irish language with the old Gaelic culture, and its consequent ability to heal the divisions caused by British cultural imperialism. The danger here is that Irish words will be taken for non-arbitrary signs, with an inherent connection to a value or a way of life. I will relate this tendency to find in particular words the sign and symbol of a culture to the Dinnseanchas or 'place-name' tradition in Irish poetry in which names are investigated, either through pronunciation or etymology, for their connection with the history of the land. As I discussed in Chapter 2, through their use of the trope of the motherland, such poems tend to present a mythic version of history which mirrors the propensity in some approaches to the language question to analyse the disappearance of the Irish language in terms of a breach in continuity and an exile from a true linguistic home. However, my claim that the dominant opposition in discourse on these matters falls between femininity, nature, and continuity on the one hand, and masculinity, culture, and discontinuity on the other, should not be interpreted as applying to all formulations of the language question. Indeed, I maintain throughout this book that several Northern Irish writers distance themselves from the dominant paradigm by figuring the feminine and the home as fragmented and discontinuous, a source of impropriety (both in the sense of indiscretion and non-possession) which affects Irish cultural tradition as a whole.

Dinnseanchas was a major poetic genre in the Gaelic tradition, a celebration of rootedness, of knowing one's place through the etymological understanding of the roots of the place-name, and the history that goes with it.[35] And most of the contemporary male poets in the national tradition have gone through a 'place-name' period. Paul Muldoon's first book was called *Knowing My Place* and poems such as 'Macha' and 'Seanchas' fall squarely within this tradition, as do many of the poems in John Montague's *The Rough Field*, and Heaney's *Wintering Out*. Even Tom Paulin's 'Mount Stewart' could be read as an ironic version

[35] See Ciaran Carson, '*Sweeney Astray*: Escaping From Limbo', in Tony Curtis (ed.), *The Art of Seamus Heaney* (Bridgend: Poetry Wales, 1985), 141–8.

of Dinnseanchas: the place was named, imperially and royally, after a Jacobean planter, Sir William Stewart, but the local people replaced the name by calling it what it actually is, i.e. five miles from the nearest villages: 'That some military man | should have planted his own surname | on a few sloping fields, | then had it rubbed out by the local demotic'.[36] However, women occupy a difficult position in relation to this tradition of laying claim to the land through its name. On the one hand the woman symbolizes the matter, the land which is to be named, the object to which the language is supposed to be knit as a guarantee of identity. But on the other, as I discussed in my reading of 'The Soil Map', the fact that women have owned neither land nor name introduces a rupture into the presumed symbiotic relationship between language and the mother, the motherland. Thus women and their relation to language further undermine the attempt to invest the language with the power of a monoglossic standard because of their unequal claim to the authority the use of such a standard would bring.

The crucial requirement of the place-name poem is that it should tell a history, whether of dispossession or of repossession.[37] And this history is crystallized in the name itself. Though Irish names have been corrupted, both through natural means and through Anglicization during the Ordnance Survey in the nineteenth century, original meanings may be discovered through etymology. In fact, for P. W. Joyce, writing *The Origin and History of Irish Place Names* in 1889, etymology was almost unnecessary since he regarded the Irish language as virtually incorruptible. He ascertained meanings by, among other things, going to the place and matching the topography with the name, but also by asking local people to pronounce the name, so that its meaning would become clear despite orthographical corruption. For him the face of the country was a book where,

not only are historical events and the names of innumerable persons recorded, but the whole social life of our ancestors—their customs, their

[36] Tom Paulin, *Fivemiletown* (London: Faber and Faber, 1987). The new name, Fivemiletown, is a 'motivated' name. Like the Irish place-names, it is motivated by its geographical connection with the place, and by analogy with other Irish names.

[37] See A. J. Gwynn (ed.), *The Metrical Dindschenchas* (Dublin: Royal Irish Academy, 1903–35).

superstitions, their battles, their amusements, their religious fervour and their crimes—are depicted in vivid and everlasting colours. The characters are often obscure, and the page defaced by time, but enough remains to repay with a rich reward the toil of the investigator.[38]

Despite some rather wild suggestions for the meanings of names which have since been revised, Joyce's methods were fruitful in the main. But this was partly because he did not rely purely on etymology to ascertain meanings. For, as I will argue below, etymological investigation often works to deny history—and this refusal of actual history becomes clearer when it is connected to the concept of the motherland. In *Preoccupations*, Heaney describes the roots of the Troubles in terms of a battle between history and myth:

To some extent the enmity can be viewed as a struggle between the cults and devotees of a god and a goddess. There is an indigenous territorial numen, a tutelar of the whole island, call her Mother Ireland, Kathleen ni Houlihan, the poor old woman, the Shan van Vocht, whatever; and her sovereignty has been temporarily usurped or infringed by a new male cult whose founding fathers were Cromwell, William of Orange, Edward Carson, and whose godhead is incarnate in a Rex or Caesar resident in a palace in London. What we have is the tail end of a struggle in a province between territorial piety and imperial power.[39]

The struggle here is between a mythic motherland and a historical masculinity. As David Trotter has argued, the conflict within the realm of culture is referred to a supposedly self-evident and immutable distinction in the realm of gender.[40] Heaney issues a refusal of history as he draws up usurping historical characters, Cromwell and William of Orange, against a mythological deity above and beyond history, as if to suggest that history itself, in the shape of male imperialism, were the intruder. So, as in 'Act of Union' where the land is opposed to the arbitrary kingdom, there is a distinction between the authority of creation which, god given, is invested in the land, and the law of society set up by human and political means. In linguistic terms Heaney sets the self-confirming mother tongue against the patri-

[38] P. W. Joyce, *The Origin and History of Irish Place Names*, 3 vols. (Dublin: McGlashan and Gill, 1889), i. 86.

[39] Heaney, *Preoccupations: Selected Prose, 1968–78* (Faber and Faber, 1979), 57.

[40] See David Trotter, *The Making of the Reader: Language and Subjectivity in Modern American, English and Irish Poetry* (Basingstoke: Macmillan, 1984), 188.

archal symbolic order. It is not simply that there are two languages, Irish and English, but that there are two species of language; one natural, rooted in the soil, connected to the living power of speech, the other arbitrary, male, alien. The entry of the arbitrary into language, like the entry of the imperial male into Ireland, thus taints the very life of the language, and with it the 'spirit' of the nation. The Irish nation impresses its past in words, language becomes the repository of the nation's genius, the site of the nation's heritage, as the 'truth' of the oppressed culture inheres in its territory, or the language which embodies it. In taking issue with this tendency I do not wish to argue that language is not the site of history, but rather that that history is not singular and indivisible—it is not the ground of a unified identity. Heaney is being only partly ironic when he complains about his inclusion in the *Penguin Anthology of British Poetry:* 'Names were not for negotiation | Right names were the first foundation | For telling truth'. Some names, he implies, come closer to the truth of an identity than others.

Heaney's interest in the connection between land and language in *Wintering Out* divides into two areas—that of pronunciation and that of etymology. In 'Fodder' and 'Anahorish' he employs phonetic terminology to investigate the regional distinctiveness of accent; he establishes a distinctive regional identity, and at the same time reveals the difference which such identity implies. And in 'The Other Side' that difference is not merely geographical but religious, as the Puritan neighbour dismisses with 'the tongue of a chosen people'. Language segregates, isolates the nation in its nationhood; however, in 'Broagh' Heaney shows how language use also works to bring different strands of the community together. Because of their inability to pronounce the place-name English outsiders are set against the Northern Irish, both Protestant and Catholic, whose shared accent draws them together: 'That last gh strangers found difficult to manage'.[41]

[41] This last phrase, and the assumptions of exclusivity attendant on it, are ironized by Muldoon in 'The More A Man Has The More A Man Wants'. Gallogly, the shifty character of uncertain racial identity, has been shot: 'Gallogly, lies down in the sheugh | to munch | through a Beauty of | Bath. He repeats himself, *Bath,* | under his garlic-breath. | *Sheugh,* he says, *Sheugh.* | He is finding that first 'sh' | increasingly difficult to manage.' Gallogly's identity is displaced through the etymology of his name which links him to gallowglass (a mercenary soldier, probably Scottish, who was employed by feudal Irish landlords to keep

Apart from pronunciation, one of the central themes of *Wintering Out* is the etymology of place-names; but unlike the poems which emphasize shared speech, Heaney's historical/etymological investigations tend to deny the possibilities for a national language to work in an inclusive manner, because of the nature of the history which the language is deemed to represent. Language and soil are both rich in historical evidence, poems have 'the aura and authenticity of archaeological finds'.[42] In his review of *Field Work*, Terry Eagleton argues that Heaney 'textualises' nature, allows it to be read, at the same time recognizing that language is in some sense material.[43] This 'materiality' is seen as linked to a view of history inhering in the land, which Eagleton casts as a defining feature of much Northern Irish poetry. He finds a radical, anti-imperialist commitment in the theme of 'disinterring' history and tradition which runs through Heaney's 'Bog' poems, Montague's *The Dead Kingdom*, and some of Longley's and Mahon's work. For Eagleton, radical or revolutionary thought, in the manner of Walter Benjamin, reverses what he terms the ruling-class 'denial of history' by rewriting the present in terms of a past that refuses to die:

> Much recent Irish writing has been 'political' less in its explicit declarations and allegiances than in this ceaseless nurturing of historical traces, this disinterring of concealed geological strata stacked beneath a surface which mistakes itself for all there is.[44]

Eagleton is undoubtedly correct in terming this archaeological unearthing a positive project. However, as in Benjamin's theory,

order). The word derives from Gaelic '*gall*' (foreigner) and '*oglach*' (youth, warrior), but Muldoon's etymology links it through '*Golightly*' and 'Ingoldsby' to 'English' (*Quoof* (London: Faber and Faber, 1983), 58). A further irony is perhaps gained by the knowledge that *sheugh* is one of the few dialect words to have been 'elevated' in the manner Paulin suggests. Braidwood points out that the word probably derives from Irish *sioc*, but it is recorded everywhere in use in Scotland. Moreover, because of the confusion over the meanings of 'ditch' and 'dyke' in Ireland, '*sheugh*' has been introduced into the publications of the Northern Irish Ministry of Agriculture, as the only word which means unambiguously that border of a field you would fall into rather than climb over. Here is a dialect word then which has worked in an inclusive rather than an exclusive way.

[42] Heaney, *Preoccupations*, 41.

[43] Terry Eagleton, 'Recent Poetry', rev. of Seamus Heaney, *Field Work*, in *Stand*, 23:1 (1980), 77.

[44] Terry Eagleton, 'New Poetry', rev. of John Montague, *The Dead Kingdom*, in *Stand*, 26:2 (1985), 67.

the historical find needs to be placed in a significant relation to contemporary events, rather than merely offered as an explanation for them. The danger is that Heaney's finds will comprise merely the remnants of history, not its living force. So in the place-name poems in *Wintering Out* he disinters an epic past from layers of bog which have preserved moments of time pure and intact. In 'Toome' the 'blastings' of mouthing the word parallel blastings into the subsoil:

> prospecting what new
> in a hundred centuries'
>
> loam, flints, musket balls,
> fragmented ware,
> torcs and fish-bones
> till I am sleeved in
>
> alluvial mud that shelves
> suddenly under
> bogwater and tributaries,
> and elvers tail my hair.[45]

The word 'Toome' derives from the Irish *tuaim* (Latin *tumulus*), and of course it is not without connections to the English 'tomb'; it is inside this grave mound that Heaney finds his buried history. The history is one of imperialist advance, new objects are the relics of war.[46] So the word is valuable because it is a symbol of dispossession, but the poem does not place that symbol in a significant relation to the present. The problem with the poem is that both word and find become museum pieces, mere curiosities to be visited and contemplated in isolation.[47] In contrast, Muldoon's place-name poem, 'The Right Arm', investigates the meaning of the name 'Eglish', uncovering a contradictory

[45] Seamus Heaney, *Wintering Out* (London: Faber and Faber, 1972), 26.

[46] It was in Toome that the United Irishman Roddy McCorley was hanged, suggesting that a very particular narrative of rebellion is being uncovered here.

[47] The value of John Clare's language, as Paulin shows, lies in its connection with specific social practices denied by political centralization and normalization—linguistic and economic. When the dialect word becomes abstracted from these practices it ceases to act in an oppositional way, deconstructing the monolithic standard language, and works merely as a symbol of identity (it performs the function Bakhtin analyses as the function of national myth). Rather than a means of bringing together a community, it acts as a sign of a community. See Tom Paulin, 'Clare in Babylon', rev. of Mark Storey (ed.), *The Letters of John Clare*, in *Times Literary Supplement* (20 June 1986), 675–6.

history which lives on the surface of the word (it lives in the present). His arm is sleeved not in mud but in glass, and glass which reveals not the 'Irishness' of the word but its relation to French and Latin:

I would give my right arm to have known then
how Eglish was itself wedged between
ecclesia and *église.*

The Eglish sky was its own stained-glass vault
and my right arm was sleeved in glass
that has yet to shatter.

The turn to history, and more specifically etymology, as a means of understanding or explaining contemporary political events is ironized by Muldoon in his poem 'Becbretha', which means 'the bee judgements'. The poem is in part a parody of the 'place-name' poem, but more particularly this parody is used to criticize notions of racial exclusivity, and the magical nature of political manœuvres. Muldoon has mentioned his impatience at the invitation of writers to the signing of the Anglo-Irish Agreement at Hillsborough in 1985, believing that writers have no special warrant to talk about politics. Here the speaker of the poem, described by Muldoon as 'somebody like me' is invited to an imaginary Garden Party at Hillsborough under a former Secretary of State, Merlyn Rees. His name, and the disembodied presence of Marvell in a misquotation from his poem 'To his Coy Mistress' ('rolled all its thingamy into one ball'), suggests that we are going to witness wonders, a magician's tricks. The party is disturbed suddenly by the warning aggression of a swarm of bees, whose racial identity become a focal point of the poem. In the confusion, the speaker finds himself next to Merlyn Rees:

I'm not sure what possessed me
to suggest he ask Enoch Powell
over from Loughbrickland.
I suppose that when I think of bees
I think of a row of hives
running up the side of an orchard
in Loughbrickland,
and then I think of Enoch Powell.

It is by a process of random association that the speaker arrives at the Unionist, alien to Ireland, Enoch Powell. Left in control of the floor he continues his process of association, and this time the various strands are drawn together by their common relation to the etymology of the name 'Loughbrickland'. This Unionist home is given an origin, by the speaker, in Irish language and history:

> I described the 'brick' in Loughbrickland
> as 'a stumbling block'
> and referred to Bricriu Poison-Tongue
> of Bricriu's feast.
> Then I touched on another local king,
> Congal the One-eyed.
> who was blinded by a bee sting.
> This led me neatly to the Becbretha,
> the Brehon judgements
> on every conceivable form
> of bee dispute,
> bee-trespass and bee-compensation.

As Muldoon has pointed out in interview, the 'brick' is a stumbling-block in more ways than one, since there is a debate over whether 'Bricriu' is a Viking or an Irish name. The difficulty of assessing racial identity is stressed by the fact that the rules laid down for sorting out disputes over ownership are foreign—Brehon, like the British presence in Ireland. (Though the Brehon laws are frequently called upon as proof of Ireland's integral Celticism.) One of the results of the Anglo-Irish Agreement was a Unionist and Protestant fear that their identity would be swamped by the Southern Catholics, if Dublin was given a say in the government of the North of Ireland. In contrast here the speaker is distressed at the loss of his audience to a figure who claims his subject (the bees) as British 'subjects'. A man in a hat and veil,

> (whom I still take to have been Enoch Powell)
> had brushed the swarm into a box
> and covered it with the Union Jack.
> Try as I might to win them back
> with the fact that 90 per cent of British bees
> were wiped out by disease
> between 1909 and 1917
> I'd lost them . . .

The speaker's attempt to force the associations of words into a unitary, mythical notion of nationality fails beside the magician's tricks carried out by the man who may have been Enoch Powell, and the virtuoso Merlyn, who knows how to manipulate the crowd. Muldoon describes the speech in this way:

> It's completely true in the sense that everything he says is true, but it's irrelevant. Or at least the order he's put things in. Well, no, you see he's got quite a good argument going and then there's a diversion; it's not an educated diversion but people happen to be distracted from what he's saying just as he's getting to the point. It's hard to imagine what his point would be mind you—it's something fairly facile I would say. At the end he's scrabbling around for bits of data to substantiate what his argument might be—it's an old style ridiculous Northern Ireland speech of which a couple are made every day. Yes, it's a speech about racial purity . . . it's about notions of purity.[48]

But the very method the speaker chooses to prove his argument about racial purity—the pure etymology and single meaning of words—betrays him. The origin of the word is not pure and univocal but is a struggle over meanings. In 'Language as History History as Language', Derek Attridge points out the anti-historical nature of the etymological argument, which replaces the social and historical determination of meaning (operating on the arbitrary sign), with a transcendent 'true' meaning.[49]

While the speaker attempts to use a historical argument (though it is spurious history), Merlyn's magic tricks play with surface appearances not depth of meaning—he dresses up his actions, such as using a secret door, with the flourish consonant with marvels. Nevertheless, while both types of rhetoric are in some sense 'false', both have real social effects. The magic tricks have the force of government behind them, and so they work (Merlyn wins the contest). In the same way, though it may be logically mistaken to assimilate the current meanings of words to their etymological derivation, within Northern Irish society the two are inseparable (in this sense the glass has yet to shatter). It is important to emphasize here that the narrative form itself denies the 'epic' purity deemed essential for the conservative national

[48] Paul Muldoon, personal interview (June 1988).

[49] See Derek Attridge, 'Language as History/History as Language: Saussure and the Romance of Etymology', in *Peculiar Language: Literature as Difference from the Renaissance to James Joyce* (London: Methuen, 1988), 90–118.

narrative, as word associations and the speaker's subjective impressions offer what is almost a caricature of Bakhtin's 'novelistic' form. Yet at the same time Muldoon's poem calls up echoes of the meandering story-telling technique of the traditional *seanchai*, suggesting that while he distances himself from one Gaelic tradition through parody, he relies for its effect on another.[50] The poem itself seems to acknowledge the impossibility of standing outside the parameters of the traditional community, which retains its hold through historical and literary tradition, while at the same time asserting the need to go beyond it.

Terrorism and Narrative

My argument so far has been concerned with the way that a language viewed as expressive of a people may also be judged as representative of that nation's history, symbolic of a construction of the nation's past which in turn draws its strength from a mythical rather than a historical narrative. In the Irish Republic this mythic rewriting of the past can be traced in the consolidation of a rural, Gaelic, Catholic ideology of Irish nationalism by the Free State. As Carol Coulter points out, Free State nationalist ideology not only sought to deny the diverse radical strains in Irish republicanism, but also the reality of Ireland's experience of colonization itself:

> A new past and a new character were created for Mother Ireland, de Valera's metaphorical bride, by Fianna Fail. If Ireland was a woman, she was also Irish speaking, catholic and (paradoxically) a virgin. If she had once been kidnapped and raped, no offspring ensued and thus no provision needed to be made for them and it could all be put behind her and a new, pure life built. History was rewritten to present successive nationalist movements as expressions of an uninterrupted fight for the catholic faith. Nationality was presented as identical with religion, thus removing any necessity to look closely at the real social, political and cultural content of colonial domination.[51]

[50] Ciaran Carson's work, particularly the long poems in *The Irish for No* and *Belfast Confetti*, plays brilliantly with this device of the story-teller. Unfortunately I do not have the space to discuss his work here, though I would emphasize the fact that his reworking of the Gaelic tradition again suggests the need for a more nuanced interpretation of the term 'postmodernism'.

[51] Carol Coulter, *Ireland: Between the First and the Third Worlds* (Dublin: Attic Press, 1990), 12.

If conservative constitutional nationalism interprets the course of Irish history as the adulteration of a pure essence by an alien intruder, so too republicanism, as it is interpreted by certain strands within Sinn Féin and the IRA, tends towards a mythic or epic construction of the national narrative, parallel to the conception of history I have delineated in Sinn Féin's linguistic and cultural politics.[52] In this final section I want to look more closely at the kinds of historical narrative presupposed by some strands of nationalism and post-nationalism in Ireland, and in particular to examine the theory of narrative suggested by acts of political violence.

The image of political prisoners in Northern Ireland (not all of them Republicans) communicating in Irish, even battling to learn it when dying on hunger strike, is one graphic reminder of the way language is invested with the power of resistance because of the history it is deemed to represent. It is here too that attachment to what I have termed epic or mythic narrative histories slides into tragedy. I have argued that mythic constructions of Irish history are built upon a fundamental anti-modernism—a resistance to the impurities born with the fall into historical narrative. But as Franco Moretti points out, when we turn our attention to the revolutionary politics which take their justification from such history, the generic conflict is no longer one between epic and novelistic discourse, but between the novel and tragedy.[53] Moretti's analysis of the structure of modern tragedy takes its cue from Lukács's description in *Soul and Form* of the moment of crisis, the reversal of everyday life which will usher in the truth, in which time is 'deprived of temporality'. It is in this denial of the growth of awareness as an evolutionary process (the fundamental premise of the novel), in the interdependence of truth and crisis in tragedy, that Moretti finds similarities with the rhetoric of revolutionary politics: 'This worldview finds its centre not just in politics, but in a tragic version of political struggle. In

[52] It should be noted, however, that there is nothing intrinsic to the arguments of militant nationalism which binds it to restorationist myths. Indeed one could argue against revisionist and post-nationalist claims that militant nationalism sets itself against pluralism, diversity, and heterogeneity, that the very indeterminacy of violence runs counter to the notion that it sets up a narrative of unity. Revolutions properly conceived are about narratives of crisis and discontinuity.

[53] See Franco Moretti, 'The Moment of Truth', in *Signs Taken for Wonders*, 2nd edn. (London: Verso, 1988), 249–61.

the notion of conflict as something which must inevitably lead to a crisis, and of crisis as the moment of truth'.[54] His fundamental argument with theorists such as Georges Sorel, and revolutionary activists such as Italian left-wing terrorists, lies in their refusal to acknowledge the everyday quality of life, the way it proceeds by means of half-truths and, importantly, through dialogue. The willed purity of these tragic forms has affinities with the valorization of an epic past, hermetically sealed against the contamination of the present, which informs certain types of linguistic nationalism in Ireland. Yet, as I will argue, there may be important distinctions to be drawn here between the violence heralded by a nationalist revolutionary struggle (whose enabling myth, as in the case of the IRA, concerns a return to the truth of a pre-colonial past) and the reversal of order celebrated by groups such as the Red Brigades and the Red Army Faction (the Baader–Meinhof group). Notwithstanding these distinctions, the question remains; can terrorism, in all its various forms, be said to harbour a theory of narrative and temporality?[55] In other words, is it possible to analyse the theoretical correlates of terrorist violence by examining its means, rather than its aims or projected ends, as theorists of postmodernism such as Jean Baudrillard, Paul Virilio, and Umberto Eco suggest? Moreover, if the terrorist 'crisis narrative' shares with forms of linguistic nationalism a resistance to impurity and accretion, how is it that it seems to thrive in an era of postmodernism?

It is frequently argued that the narratives set in play by acts of political violence within Europe constitute a denial of historical process, through their attack on nations which derive their legitimacy from the post-Enlightenment ideals of representation, dialogue, and consensus; in this sense the terrorist attack is deemed to be postmodernist in its will to destroy the 'grand' narratives of the nineteenth century. But there is an apparent contradiction between the postmodernity of the Irish struggle and its seeming

[54] Ibid. 253.

[55] I use the term 'terrorism' as a substitute for political violence advisedly, since part of my discussion will focus on the ways that the designation 'terrorist' serves to depoliticize violent nationalist struggle. However, 'political violence' is too broad a definition for the specific type of violence I am discussing. Moreover, I wish to retain a distinction between guerrilla warfare and the activities of the 'terrorist' cell, and since most of the critics and theorists I discuss use the term, I have kept it for the sake of simplicity.

atavisms. Nationalist and post-colonial political violence seems to present us with a difficulty, since not only does it take place in the name of the nation, child of the nineteenth century, but it also claims political representativeness. Moreover, like groups such as Islamic Jihad, who claim hostage-taking as a traditional and legitimate form of political engagement, militant Irish Republicans can situate their activity within an (albeit discontinuous) tradition of guerrilla warfare, political violence, and hunger strikes in Ireland. In other words, Republicanism can draw on a long national narrative of violence for its legitimization. On the other hand, as Baudrillard and Virilio argue, the necessarily arbitrary nature of a terrorist bombing campaign—its dependence on anonymity, rupture, the sudden disappearances of people and buildings—all speak against the possibility of narrative at all, setting in place in its stead a kind of violent, postmodern '*bricolage*'. But observations made to this effect are rarely innocent. For it is this kind of concentration on terrorism's means, this analysis of the structure of the terrorist act, which is most often used to show its lack of political representativeness. For example, Paul Virilio makes a familiar distinction between popular protest, or the face-to-face nature of guerrilla warfare, and the technologization of both 'pure war' on the one hand and terrorism on the other.[56] According to this argument the arbitrariness and anonymity of the terrorist attack becomes in effect the embodiment of alienation, in a culture where the 'social' has receded in the face of multinational, capitalist, and defence systems. Virilio argues that there is a reciprocal relationship between the systematized postmodern state and acts of terrorism, but in discussion with Sylvere Lotringer one important distinction becomes clear:

> the State absorbs techniques of the nomad war-machine, the secret of the warrior who takes advantage of the surprise-effect to win. The urban guerilla also uses camouflage, but his actions must be as spectacular as possible in hopes of rousing the masses and shaking the State's power. The only true terrorism is state terrorism, as it isn't answerable to anybody.[57]

[56] Paul Virilio and Sylvere Lotringer, *Pure War* (New York: Semiotext(e), 1983).

[57] Sylvere Lotringer, ibid. 89; See also Umberto Eco, 'Striking at the Heart of the State', in *Travels in Hyperreality* (London: Pan, 1987), 113–18.

'Pure' terrorism arises when representativeness is no longer an issue, when 'it isn't answerable to anybody'. (And, we might add, true terrorism can only exist where there are no perceivable agents, or the agents cannot be tried, as is the case when they are employed by the State.) But this is a dangerously circular argument; on the one hand it is claimed that national revolutions (signalled by guerrilla warfare and popular defence) can no longer take place because of the technologization of the multinational global machine, which atomizes protest.[58] And on the other, that very atomization is taken as proof that the terrorist's aims lack any link with a broader social movement, and that they are, at basis, non-political. It is this understanding of terrorism as the end of representation which I wish to question.

Any discussion of contemporary nationalist trends in Ireland must necessarily situate them within the broader context of European national fragmentation and consolidation, a process which has historical if not necessarily theoretical correlates in postmodernism. Recent discussion of the peculiarly Irish postmodern condition, notably in Richard Kearney's work, has tended to emphasize a theory of postmodernism which sees it as a means of transcending divisions between nostalgic traditionalism and modern cosmopolitanism. Kearney positivizes the usually critical definitions of postmodernism as pastiche, and, somewhat optimistically, celebrates the new narrative possibilities opened up by a cultural postmodernism as the best of all worlds.[59] An unstated but critical ingredient of his argument is the importance of postmodernism's ability to harness the artistic products of modernism's nostalgia and to rework them. Translated on to the nationalist/post-nationalist axis, the claim is that only in a post- rather than an anti-nationalist framework will the genuine nostalgia of people in Ireland for a past unadulterated by foreign influences be included and thereby appeased. In the editorial to a recent collection of essays analysing Irish society in 1990 and beyond, he turns to the possibilities afforded by the new formation of Europe in 1992 as a similarly positive means of

[58] It was only relatively recently (in 1978) that the IRA changed its organizational structure from that of a guerrilla army, with brigades, battalions, and regiments, to the less easily infiltrated formation of the terrorist cell.

[59] See Richard Kearney, *Transitions: Narratives in Modern Irish Culture* (Dublin: Wolfhound Press, 1988).

transcending both inward-looking nationalism and a cosmopolitanism which rejects the national past:

> We need to move beyond the established, and ultimately failed, model of the Nation State towards a society without frontiers. But 'without frontiers' should not mean—in the European or Anglo-Irish contexts—'without differences' . . . On the contrary, the more we transcend national boundaries the greater the need for decentralized regional government. What we are talking about then is not the liquidation of nations but their supercession (*aufhebung*) into a post-nationalist network of communities where national identities may live on where they belong—in languages, sports, arts, customs, memories and myths—while simultaneously fostering the expression of minority and regional cultures within each nation.[60]

It should come as no surprise of course that Tory neo-imperialist nationalism does not see itself reflected in this postnationalist vision—an opposition which is crystallized in resistance to European integration. But the question I should like to pose here is, to what extent are fears that the opening up of national frontiers will become an enabling event for revolutionary national narratives related to an actual correlation between forms of anti-modern myth and the structure of a Common European Home? Could the postmodern attack on overarching historical narratives, embodied in the European context in the relaxation of border controls, lend space to the crisis narrative of forms of revolutionary violence?

Such enquiry may seem at the same time both brutal and academic. On one very practical level there is an obvious link between the opening-up of Western European frontiers, and terrorist movements (though this is balanced by increased co-operation between anti-terrorist organizations, including those of the constitutionally nationalist Irish Republic). And it is here, as recent events show, that the dangerously parasitic relation between tourism and terrorism becomes lethal. In one scenario three IRA operatives can walk into Gibraltar as tourists, and in another three unarmed tourists are shot dead by the security forces. Mistaken identity touches the genuine tourist too, as it did for the two Australian tourists shot as members of the British Army in Holland. Like the spy, it is in the terrorist's anonymity

[60] Kearney, *Across the Frontiers*, 17.

that the danger lies (a surface anonymity which, again and again, is judged as betrayed by an Irish accent). But, unlike spying, anonymity and the arbitrariness of violent attack can become generalized into danger for all.[61] (At least, this is the case outside Northern Ireland, where the structure of anonymity cuts both ways. But the arbitrariness of attack and of suspicion is alien to Northern Ireland, where court procedures are predicated on the assumption that everyone knows who is guilty. As I will argue below, it is the very lack of anonymity, or the fact that anonymity is preserved by the group not the individual, in Northern Ireland which forces a reassessment of the structure of representation underlying political violence.)

Anonymity is indeed central to any link between the structure of Western postmodern society and national political violence, and this, as I will argue, in more than purely practical terms. Beyond these practical considerations, my enquiry concerns the possibility of a hidden convergence between the anti-modernism of certain forms of terrorism—even for nationalist ends—and a postmodernism which has as one of its political correlates the rejection of the logic of enlightenment rationality dominant in the European nation-state. At one very basic level, of course, it is impossible to separate the crisis of modernist narrative from the consequences of European colonization, which includes the necessary violence of anti-imperial struggles.[62] But recently there have been attempts by several critics to draw a more precise link between revolutionary violence and the breakup of the nation-state. For example, Julia Kristeva's psychoanalytic interpretation of terrorist violence locates it as a 'symbolic denominator' within

[61] From the opposite end of the spectrum, Hannah Arendt points to the way that anonymity becomes generalized horror when a state becomes dependent on terror for its continuing existence: 'Terror is not the same as violence; it is rather the form of government that comes into being when violence, having destroyed all power, does not abdicate but, on the contrary, remains in full control. It has often been noted that the effectiveness of terror depends almost entirely on the degree of social atomization, the disappearance of every kind of organised opposition, which must be achieved before the full force of terror can be let loose. This atomization—an outrageously pale, academic word for the horror it implies—is maintained and intensified through the ubiquity of the informer, who can be literally omnipresent because he no longer is merely a professional agent in the pay of the police but potentially every person one comes into contact with' ('Reflections on Violence', *Journal of International Affairs*, 23:1 (1969), 21).

[62] See Edward Said, 'Representing the Colonized', *Critical Inquiry*, 15:2 (1989).

the transnational construct, Europe. Noting the large numbers of women in European terrorist organizations, Kristeva suggests that their motivation springs from a denial of the socio-symbolic contract (the 'linear' time of national history) in the name of a mythic purity: 'Each time the mobilization takes place in the name of a nation, of an oppressed group, of a human essence imagined as good and sound: in the name, then, of a kind of fantasy of archaic fulfillment which an arbitrary, abstract, and thus even bad and ultimately discriminatory order has come to disrupt.'[63] Kristeva's distinction echoes that between mythic and historical narrative which I have discussed in terms of language politics; however (despite the fact that her essay was written in 1979, before the start of the Palestinian Uprising), her argument is flawed by her refusal to make distinctions between the anti-colonial national struggle in Palestine, and the revolutionary violence of post-1968 Western Europe. (And even within Europe a distinction needs to be drawn between anti-capitalist groups, which are not nationalist, and those movements which are continuing the history of nineteenth-century nationalism.)

A similar blindness to the difference between the liberation struggle and the terrorist act confounds Jean Baudrillard's attempt to find theoretical common ground between the 'masses' of postmodern society and the structure of the terrorist attack.[64] Baudrillard's argument centres not on the narrative behind revolutionary violence, but on the violent act itself, and, through its focus on terrorism as 'means', it returns us to the question of anonymity and arbitrariness. Baudrillard accepts the Sorelian definition of political violence as the substitution of crisis for historical narrative, and maintains that, precisely because of its non-representational character, terrorism lies not only outside constitutional politics, but is symptomatic of the 'end of the social'. He draws an analogy between the 'inertia' of the masses which confounds all social and political schemes (and in particular puts paid to any idea of popular revolutionary *movement*) and the structure of terrorism:

[63] Julia Kristeva, 'Women's Time', in Nannerl O. Keohane, Michelle Z. Rosaldo, and Barbara C. Gelpi (eds.), *Feminist Theory: A Critique of Ideology* (Brighton: Harvester, 1982), 47.

[64] See Jean Baudrillard, *In the Shadow of the Silent Majorities* (New York: Semiotext(e), 1983), 48–58.

Nothing is more 'cut off from the masses' than terrorism. Power may well try to set the one against the other, but nothing is more strange, more familiar either, than their convergence in denying the social and in refusing meaning. For terrorism claims to really aim at capital (global imperialism, etc.) but it mistakes its enemy, and in doing so aims at its true enemy, which is the social.[65]

Here a comparatively well-rehearsed argument about the structure of political violence, which sees it as arising out of the breakdown of social mobilization, is transposed on to a disquisition on the asocial structure of postmodern society, in which Baudrillard's own nostalgia for a socially organic community is barely masked.[66] In his description of revolutionary violence as a denial of the whole system of democratic representation, Baudrillard seems to mean groups such as the Red Brigades and Baader–Meinhof; however, he goes on to discuss Palestinian hostage-taking as the perfect example of the arbitrariness of terrorism's targets, and it is here that the notion of 'representativeness' comes into question. For is it not in the Palestinian terrorist's truly representative function, in the fact that he or she is not without popular support, that the real danger lies for the enemies of the Palestinian nation? Indeed, even violent operations which are not undertaken for nationalist or anti-colonialist ends, must rely on a certain degree of support. Baudrillard's theory cannot countenance the notion of sympathizers, upon whose existence the success of an operation must to some extent depend.

Baudrillard argues that the very structure of the terrorist act denies itself historical continuity—it is absolutely without legitimacy, and this lack of validity is due to the terrorists themselves. In comparison Edward Said emphasizes the need for the narrative and history which the terrorist act aims to put into play to be balanced against the way that narrative, and the power of explanation, is denied to certain terrorist groups (though not to all). For Said, terrorism's quality of 'arbitrariness' is in part the result of the deliberate stripping away, on the part of the terrorist's enemies, of the roots and causes of the violence:

The very indiscriminateness of terrorism, actual and described, its tautological and circular character, is anti-narrative. Sequence, the logic of

[65] Ibid. 50.

[66] See e.g. Sidney Tarrow's excellent analysis of Italian political violence in *Democracy and Disorder* (Oxford: Oxford University Press, 1989), 298–306.

cause and effect as between oppressors and victims, opposing pressures—all these vanish inside an enveloping cloud called 'terrorism'. Israeli commentators have remarked that the systematic use by Begin, Sharon, Eytan and Arens of the rubric 'terrorist' to describe Palestinians made it possible for them to use phrases like 'terrorist nests', 'cancerous growth' and 'two-legged beasts' in order to bomb refugee camps. An Israeli paratrooper said that 'every Palestinian is automatically a suspected terrorist and by our definition it is actually true'.[67]

The underlying irony which Said fails to bring out here is that even as the designation 'terrorist' separates Palestinian fighters from the history which gave birth to them, the extension of that term to Palestinians in general reinstates the fighter in a position of national representativeness. When all Palestinians are terrorists it can hardly be denied that theirs is a national struggle. If this is the case in the Occupied Territories, where Palestinians are denied political representation, it is only emphasized in Northern Ireland in the dual attack by Sinn Féin and the IRA of the bullet and the ballot box. The Catholic community's willingness to vote for imprisoned members of the Republican movement is in itself an indication of their representativeness, albeit a fluctuating one. Indeed in Northern Ireland, on both the Unionist and Republican sides, violence is allied to a system of political representation, though with varying degrees of popular support. But more important perhaps than democratic representation (since Sinn Féin MPs do not take up the representation of their constituents in Westminster) is the symbolically representative function of militant Republicanism's actions.[68] (Although the two are not separate, since the more symbolically resonant the event, such as the Hunger Strikes of 1981, the higher the political party's popular poll.) The importance of the IRA's symbolic representativeness was recently revealed in a strongly anti-nationalist article by Conor Cruise O'Brien. In discussing the actions of the IRA he found himself unable to dismiss them as a few 'men of violence' since, as he admitted, they do represent a huge body of nationalist public opinion in both the North and South of the

[67] Edward Said, 'Permission to Narrate', *London Review of Books* (16–29 Feb. 1984), 14.

[68] For a discussion of Yeats's relation to the post-Treaty division between democratic and symbolic representativeness, see David Lloyd, 'The Poetics of Politics: Yeats and the Founding of the State', *Qui Parle*, 3:2 (1989).

country, emphasized above all by the Republic's constitutional dedication to national reunification.[69] The point is that in the context of Irish militant nationalism, political violence and the rejection of British constitutional politics does not at the same time constitute a rejection of representation. The IRA member's very anonymity, given its ultimate representation by the masked gunmen who fire salutes at IRA funerals, is absorbed into an image of the nation's aspirations. This discussion of the isolation of atomistic forms of terrorism from the community it purports to represent, interestingly raises similar problems to the social construction of the atomistic 'privatized' sphere of lyric poetry discussed in the previous chapter. My contention is that within the specific context of Irish political and literary tradition, such allegedly 'isolated' spaces can be socially imbricated and 'representative' of the history and political demands of the community.

The point of my disagreement with Baudrillard thus lies in the occlusion in his theory of the political aspects of political violence, the national narrative which such violence may carry.[70] In opposition I have argued that political violence in Ireland is implicated in a structure of representation, albeit a symbolic one. However, I am aware of the danger here of falling into the trap which confounds much revisionist Irish historiography. One might characterize this as the inverse of Baudrillard's argument, which concentrates on an analysis of the structure of the terrorist *act* in order to argue for its lack of political representativeness. In contrast, some revisionist historians focus on the mythic and symbolic *rhetoric* of Republicanism (for example by stressing the aspects of blood sacrifice in the Easter Rising, and the sacrificial

[69] Conor Cruise O'Brien, 'A Tale of Two Nations', *New York Review of Books* (19 July 1990), 33–6. I am grateful to Luke Gibbons for bringing this to my attention.

[70] For an interesting reversal of Baudrillard's nostalgia, see the debates on the relationship between Autonomia and the Red Brigades in Italy in the 1970s. At the same time as Baudrillard and Virilio are lamenting the end of politics as the demise of a possibility of social agency, theorists such as Deleuze and Guattari, *and for the very same reason*—the belief that the structure of political representation has been superseded—are proclaiming the advent of a new politics of 'concrete struggle' and 'molecular revolution'. For them the end of representation means the return of politics in a new, radical, and more efficient guise. Most interestingly, rather than view terrorism as the result of a breakdown of social mobilization, they entertain the possibility of a move *from* terrorism *to* guerrilla warfare. See Sylvere Lotringer and Christian Marazzi (eds.), *Autonomia: Post-Political Politics*, 3:3 (New York: Semiotext(e), 1980),

elements in more recent Republican activity, such as the Hunger Strikes) in order, similarly, to argue for the non-political character of Republican activity.[71] Now, while I want to offer a critique of this process of symbolic representation at the points where it seems to underwrite a purist or exclusive version of Irish history, or where it is used as a rationale for a rejection of the political arena, I do not argue that the symbolic aspects of representation necessarily set themselves against more obviously political or democratic modes of representation. For not only is it impossible to draw a sharp distinction between national myths and progressive Enlightenment politics (and in this sense all politics has a symbolic dimension), but also an emphasis solely on the mythic dimensions of the arguments of militant nationalism, its stress on the restoration of a putative Gaelic continuity, obscures the radically disruptive and discontinuous aspects of the physical force tradition (which is uneasily linked to conservative nationalism's valorization of the Gaelic past), as well as the clearly political nature of Sinn Féin's position.

Conclusion

It is by now clear from recent events that the simultaneous fragmentation and consolidation of new European alliances has given force not only to a politics of the region, as champions of post-nationalism desire, but that it has also been the motor force behind a resurgence of nationalist feeling. Moreover, this resurgent nationalism is a defining feature not only of the politics of contemporary Eastern Europe, but also, and infamously, of that of the most well-established nation-states, such as Britain. In which case, despite its qualities of arbitrariness and anonymity, its disregard for borders, the structure of terrorism's strange alliance with the trans-national European ideal may have less to do with a shared postmodernity, than with a return to the values of the European nation-state, a desire for the nation which relies as much on structures of symbolic representation as on democratic representativeness.

[71] The force of the revisionist argument became very evident in the embarrassment shown by the Irish political establishment on the 75th anniversary of the Rising. For a critical appraisal of arguments about revisionism see Tom Dunne, 'New Histories: Beyond "Revisionism"' *Irish Review*, 12 (1992), 1–12.

My discussion of postmodernist interpretations of the structure of revolutionary violence has found fault with their characteristic elision of the political context of the violence. In relation to Ireland I have maintained that violence has to be understood both as part of a mythic or symbolic narrative, and as fundamentally imbricated within the political structures of the nation-state. It is perhaps this very hybrid character which encourages the postmodern analysis, since to merge nostalgia and the hypermodern is taken as one of the defining features of a global postmodernism. In the same way, I would argue, much contemporary Northern Irish poetry refuses easy categorization, rejecting at the same time the securities of mythic narrative, and the temptation to dispense with the language of community and nation as a whole. But the presence of such parody and pastiche in the poetry (and this is particularly true of Muldoon) is insufficiently explained by the description 'postmodern' since, as I have discussed in relation to the legacy of Enlightenment in Ireland, it cannot do justice to the specific history of cultural forms and their literary variants.

Part II

4

Tom Paulin: Enlightening the Tribe

MY discussion of the limits of both Enlightenment and Romantic perspectives on Northern Irish literature and politics would be incomplete without a close examination of the work of Tom Paulin, the contemporary poet who most consistently espouses a political vision derived from the classical and secular republican ideals of the eighteenth century. Among the most frequently voiced of his opinions are his commitment to a cosmopolitan and universalist ideal, and his related impatience with the conservative romantic strain in English politics and literature. For Paul Muldoon, in 'Madoc—A Mystery', the failed United Irishmen rebellion of 1798 offers primarily a point from which to explore the complex interrelationship of cosmopolitan and nationalist ideals, imperial myth-making, and colonization in the history of Western revolutions, art, and philosophy. In comparison, Paulin's imaginative use of the politics of 1798 in *Liberty Tree*, is at once a means of exploring the contours of a political ideal which is still deemed valid, and a measure of the political complexities of the present.

Unlike either Muldoon or McGuckian, Paulin publicly professes a political standpoint on the situation in Northern Ireland—signalled not only in his discussion of Ireland in *Ireland and the English Crisis* and *Minotaur*, but also by his membership of the Field Day Company (of which he is one of the directors) and his support for the cultural ideal of a 'fifth province' (discussed in Chapter 1). Indeed Paulin has gone so far as to relate (albeit tentatively) his ideal eclectic concept of Irish identity and political community, 'which has as yet no formal or institutional existence', to the report of the New Ireland Forum.[1] In *Ireland and the English Crisis* Paulin explains his principled commitment to a resolution of Ireland's 'national question' as in part the result

[1] Tom Paulin, *Ireland and the English Crisis* (Newcastle Upon Tyne: Bloodaxe Books, 1984), 18.

of a growing disillusionment with a provincialism 'hostile to the idea of institutions, formality, opera, educated southern accents, the necessary insincerities of good manners'. This introduces a recurring idea in Paulin's work, that particular beliefs and customs (for example, in religion) need to be overcome within a formal and institutional frame—a sign of his continued commitment to the rationalist ideals of the Enlightenment, and of his faith in the value of modernity: 'In my view it is impossible to achieve a wide and cosmopolitan outlook without beginning—like a diver kicking off from a springboard—from the idea of a secular republic.'[2] Yet alongside this dedication to a form of universalism, Paulin emphasizes the importance of historical and linguistic particularity and diversity. I have considered the tensions in this view in my discussion of his project for a dictionary of Irish English, where there is to some extent a conflict between the wish to preserve the particular timbre and the vitality of a community's language, and the felt need to give it formal and institutional existence. Just as he asserts the value of the experiences of a marginalized community, so it is important to emphasize that Paulin is not arguing for a modern secular ideal which would dismiss the past in a kind of collective historical amnesia. On the contrary, as I will argue, his work engages in a sustained examination of history's hold over the present, determined by an awareness that, for modern political structures to have force and authority, they must be capable of a flexible appropriation of tradition.

Paulin's poetry deals with a central concern in contemporary political and literary theory—the limits of the values of the Enlightenment. He is dedicated to a post-colonial and post-imperial outlook (evidenced by his persistent drive to 'deconstruct' the notion of Englishness), while maintaining the critical insights of the Enlightenment, in particular its commitment to a rational democratic politics. To a certain extent his exploration of the limits of the secular ideal is forced on him by its obvious failure to take hold in Ireland (and indeed in England), a failure which is evidenced not only in the injustices of the political system, but also in the biases of literary criticism. His valorization of the civic domain of public political life, over the claims of custom

[2] Tom Paulin, *Ireland and the English Crisis.*

and tradition, is clearly related to his search for an aesthetic form which is opened up to the public and political arena—as he has claimed, 'almost invariably . . . a political poem is a public poem'. Yet Paulin's poetry necessarily confronts the problem of what now constitutes public space in contemporary Britain and Ireland. On a broader level the issue touches on the possibility of literature's public address in a complex modern society, where the ideal of a rational civic domain is no longer viable. This development can be interpreted negatively as the destruction of the public space of politics by 'social life' which transforms individuals into consumers rather than producers of culture. However, as Seyla Benhabib points out, the ideal of civic virtue and the *res publica* are classical forms dependent on a closed system of political participation (the exclusion of slaves and women for example). Both clash with the demands for universal political emancipation which were the mark of the French and American Revolutions (despite the fact that these legitimized themselves through reference to classical symbolism).[3] Given his commitment to the inclusion of marginalized sections of the community within a transformed political structure, the progressive alteration of the division between public and private spheres is something that Paulin's poetry cannot hope to ignore, despite its ostensible commitment to a civic ideal. In the following pages I will examine ways in which the changing construction of a sphere of privacy (for example, in sexuality and religion) determines Paulin's aesthetic concerns.

Such matters clearly relate to the issue of postmodern style which I discussed in Chapter 1. The increasing hermeticism of Paulin's work seems to cut directly across any commitment to poetry's public address, and to conflict with his interest in dialect and the vernacular. On the other hand, one could argue that (as with Muldoon) the stylistic complexity of the work is a formal

[3] As Benhabib argues, 'With the entry of every new group into the public space of politics after the French and American revolutions, the scope of the public gets extended. The emancipation of workers made property relations into a public-political issue; the emancipation of women has meant that the family and the so-called private sphere become political issues; the attainment of rights by non-white and non-Christian peoples has put cultural questions of collective self- and other-representations on the "public" agenda . . . The struggle over what gets included in the public agenda is itself a struggle for justice and freedom' (Seyla Benhabib, *Situating the Self: Gender, Community and Postmodernism in Contemporary Ethics* (Cambridge: Polity, 1992), 94).

recognition in poetry of the complexities of, and dissonances within, the political communities in Britain and Ireland. But the general description of Paulin's style as 'postmodern' does not acknowledge the political dimension of his attempt to formulate a poetics in opposition to the post-Romantic aesthetics of privacy, which Paulin sees as linked to a conservative politics. Rather than reflecting in its formal innovations the impossibility of literature's public address in a complex modern society, Paulin's work is directed towards the construction of a new public poetry which would be adequate to new social developments.

Sex and Civility

It must be possible to speak plainly for a new civility.[4]

The first lines of Paul Muldoon's poem 'History' ('When and where did we first have sex? | Do you remember?') emphasize above all the arbitrary and even insignificant character of a history dependent on memory and choice for its construction. History, Muldoon suggest, is created out of what we decide to remember. The poem distils a common trope in Muldoon's work, in which often vague or enigmatically constructed narratives of personal sexual experience represent the poet's relationship to historical and political events, as well as the inconclusive and non-productive narrative of history itself.[5] As in McGuckian's work, the metaphorical relationship between sexual and political history is tangential and oblique, foregrounding the separation between public and private histories, or at least emphasizing the complex nature of their relationship. A similar process can be noted in Tom Paulin's most recent collection *Fivemiletown* where poems repeatedly draw analogies emphasizing the parallelism between personal and institutional histories, only then to undercut the stability of each. But we must be wary of any too simple correlation between the practices of these poets; the meaning of history and tradition carries a very different weight for Muldoon and McGuckian than for Paulin who takes as his subject-matter contemporary Protestant identity and the politics of Unionism. Moreover, the 'privatization' engaged in

4 Paulin, *Ireland and the English Crisis*, 22.
5 See e.g. the discussion of 'Bran' in Ch. 1, and of 'Quoof' in Ch. 6.

by Paulin and Muldoon as male poets will naturally differ greatly from the process I have analysed in women's poetry, because of a gendered and asymmetrical relationship to civic life. As I have discussed, while it may appear to confirm their concerns as primarily personal and autobiographical, for women to write about sexuality at all necessitates a disruption of the boundaries between public and private discourses. But where the primary concerns in a reading of Boland and McGuckian's tropes of sexuality was with the relationship between the individual experience of feminine sexuality, and the national myths built upon the feminine symbol, it is the link between violence and sexuality which is most striking in Paulin's and Muldoon's work. Critics have tended to interpret many of the poems in *Fivemiletown* and *Quoof* as distasteful confessions, or as simple metaphors for the violence in Northern Ireland, but to do so is to ignore the ways in which the poets use these narratives to explore the complex relationship between personal and national histories. The temptation is to interpret these strategies as part of a generalized postmodern scepticism about the value of overarching teleological narratives. Such a reading does have the merit of acknowledging that the importance of the poetic form lies in what it reveals about the changing relationship of the poet to his poetic or national community, and the narratives which sustain them, but can any more specific analogies be drawn between the narrative construction of these stories and their political content?

In Muldoon and McGuckian's work the political often seems almost synonymous with nationalist myth-making, an association which renders any attempt to construct an alternative vision of politics problematic for both poets. Paulin's work by contrast deals far more directly with the issues of constitutional representation and democracy in Northern Ireland and Britain—in other words with institutional politics and its confrontations with 'tribal' affiliations. None the less his more recent poetry mirrors the strategies I have discussed in its choice of sexual narratives as a means of representing the institutional realm. The violent, often sordid nature of the sexual encounters in *Quoof* is reflected in Tom Paulin's most recent collection *Fivemiletown*. 'Waftage', 'Breez Marine', and 'Really Naff' represent attempts at sexual communication in the absence of love, and betray what some reviewers found to be a distasteful anal obsession. (One possible interpretation of this is as a counterpart to the 'oral childhood' of 'Mythologies', which like many of the poems in the volume arises out of a reflection on childhood or adolescent experience, or perhaps it is a wry acknowledgement of the symbolic importance of faeces in Northern Ireland where, through the prison dirty protests, quite literally 'we've had x years of blood and shit'?) On one level the poems seem to be concerned with the ways in which we relate our personal histories to ourselves, how we reflect on our experiences. Even the tender and moving 'Mount Stewart' entertains the possibility of an alternative, both sordid and insignificant, retrospective narrative:

Now, in the dream of our own plenitude
I want to go back
and rap it as milk, jism, cinnamon,
when it might be a quick blow-job
in a 6-motel,
or a small fear just
in a small town
in Ireland or someplace.

And yet it would be mistaken to read this representation of casual sex as a simple repetition of Muldoon's concerns, not least because the myths Paulin is playing with are those of the Protestant community, as the references to the Tain and the Red Handshake should alert us. One poem which does, however, seem to ask for comparison with Muldoon and McGuckian is Paulin's own version of the Irish motherland myth, 'The Maiden that is Makeless'. Like many of the poems in *Fivemiletown*, 'The Maiden' foregrounds what Paulin takes to be a precarious opposition between the pleasures of the aesthetic (here associated with a Catholicism rooted in the soil) and the formal rigours of enlightened Protestant faith. As I will argue, Paulin is far too ready to theologize, and hence confirm, a distinction between the aesthetic, bound up with tradition and custom, and the civic domain. Thus, despite his desire to dismantle the opposition between Enlightenment and Romanticism, and his awareness that Enlightenment values are equally bound up with custom and tradition (a major theme in *Fivemiletown*), his work too often suggests the need for a synthesis of opposing world-views. A related difficulty lies in the fact that Paulin tends to view politics primarily as a struggle between romanticism and republicanism, and as a result he is unable to acknowledge the political force of issues such as women's rights. His edition of the *Faber Book of Political Verse* was sadly lacking in representations of feminist, or other alternative political, voices, a prejudice which is reflected in his poetry in muted fashion. For while Paulin is often willing to use sexuality as a metaphor for the struggle between public and private realms (as these correspond to the arenas of public or civic duty and private conscience) the importance of sexual politics itself is denied in his work. Concomitantly, the emphasis on sexuality and pleasure, which he attempts to balance against the claims of reason, remains limited to the expression of masculine desire.

From the first lines, 'The Maiden that is Makeless' alerts us to the fact that it is dealing with Paulin's stance towards Southern Catholicism, and to the South more generally, where he is hitching a ride:

> I was sitting on a wall
> in Co. Clare:
> dew brish on the grass
> and the light knocking
> each drop of it
> into the coldest of lead colours—
> magenta and chill purple,
> quicked blues that broke
> on queasy greens—
> all beautiful and base
> like the rings of Saturn,
> or the style a platinum blonde
> who'd skimmed in a jet
> from Connecticut
> flipped *aluminum* to me
> through a hi! smile
> one hour before
> she took me apart
> down a creashy lane.

The maiden that is 'makeless' in the fifteenth-century lyric is the Virgin Mary, who is makeless both in the sense of being matchless and mateless; her virginity is protected by the fact that Christ's coming is described in the poem 'As dew in April that falleth on the grass'.[6] And of course the significant fact about this

[6] 'I Sing of a Maiden that is Makeless', *Medieval English Lyrics: A Critical Anthology*, ed. R. T. Davies (London: Faber and Faber, 1963), 301.

maiden is that because of the dew she becomes Christ's mother. In contrast, the narrator's maiden is makeless in Paulin's poem not because she is virginal but because he cannot make it with her, and this despite her figuration of the metallic lustre given by the dew. One reading of the poem suggests that the narrator's difficulty in responding to her sexuality is perhaps that he sees her *as* metallic (her hair platinum and her teeth filled with aluminium) rather than simply clothed in those colours like the landscape.[7] While this may be what attracts the narrator to her (her style is 'beautiful and base' like base metal), as a representative of speed and technology (she 'skimmed in a jet') the American woman has a merely superficial relationship to the environment in which she lands.[8] It is in part her ungrounded and meretricious nature which renders her 'makeless'. However, this reading of the lines depends on a negative connotation accruing to the superficial and metallic qualities of the girl, a connotation which is denied by the pleasure the narrator takes in the beauty of the landscape which for him reminds him of the blonde. The poem does not contrast one with the other, but equates them, a fact which is emphasized by a comparison of Paulin's poem with Elizabeth Bishop's 'Seascape'. Paulin has written in *Minotaur* of Bishop's characteristic method of identifying natural phenomena with human and technological processes, and he contrasts her celebration of the 'beautifully flimsy and deracinated and benign' with Heidegger's conservative espousal of authenticity, rootedness, and tradition:

> Heidegger celebrates the apparently natural and traditional in order to naturalize a violent politics—a strategy based on European culture's fallacious distinction between nature and society. Bishop refuses to recognize any such distinction, and delights in presenting organic images as artificial consumer objects.[9]

[7] The American spelling of 'aluminum' echoes Elizabeth Bishop, as I discuss below.

[8] As I discuss below, in the final lines of the volume this opposition between technological and 'grounded' experience is linked, via the description of the school which is constructed out of the 'melt of hot metal' (and specifically aluminium) from a Second World War plane, to Heidegger's distinction between building and dwelling.

[9] Tom Paulin, *Minotaur: Poetry and the Nation State* (London: Faber and Faber, 1992), 203.

Bishop's 'Seascape' describes a 'celestial' and 'immaculate' scene from a cartoon by Raphael, 'with bright green leaves edged neatly with bird-droppings | like illuminations in silver'. But the heavenly nature of the picture cannot be acknowledged by 'a skeletal lighthouse standing there in black and white clerical dress'. For the cleric such beauty in art (and by implication also in the metaphorical language of poetry) is a threat to the stark truths of religion:

> Heaven is not like flying or swimming,
> but has something to do with blackness and a strong glare
> and when it gets dark he will remember something
> strongly worded to say on the subject.[10]

In addition to the analogy between the landscape and the figure of the woman, perhaps Paulin's most significant revision of Bishop's poem is the substitution of the Calvinist (as Paulin categorizes him in *Minotaur*) with a Catholic priest. The second stanza draws a parallel between the absence of coitus between the narrator and the woman (he melts in her hand), and the dispersal of desire on the arrival of the priest:

> This wet, fresh place
> was all amethyst and jism,
> and as I had in her hand
> it melted in me
> the second I slung myself
> into the priest's black Morris—
> what a grand day it was, sure,
> and didn't that mountain
> of pure, bare stone,
> though it struck me then
> like a pap next a missal
> beyond the dark jacket,
> have a special position
> to his way of thinking.

The place beneath the mountain is described as 'jism': God's dew has fallen rendering the landscape fertile and full of colour. But this beauty, and the creativity it gives rise to in the narrator is threatened by the arrival of the sterner lessons of religion. It

[10] Elizabeth Bishop, *The Complete Poems, 1927–1979* (London: Hogarth Press, 1984), 40.

dissolves or disappears as he climbs inside the black world of the priest (which denies the sexual pleasure the narrator has been fantasizing). However, the poem implies that the dissolution of colours, the melting of lead to pure black, is of the narrator's own construction. The speaker draws an analogy between the pure, bare stone of the mountain and the bulging breast of the priest, caused by his missal pocketed under his jacket. In other words he traces the landscape on to a masculine body. But on what does this correspondence depend? In one sense the similarity may turn on the fact that just as the priest's swollen breast is a 'fake', since it has been inflated by Catholic rhetoric, so too has the mountain which has been overlaid with the rhetoric of maiden and mother Ireland. To the priest's (Catholic and celibate) way of thinking the land is the maiden that is makeless, the pap is a woman's, and she is mother of both the nation and the Southern Catholics. (The priest's maiden is thus quite literally 'grounded' in contrast to the rootless woman of the first stanza). More to the point, she is mother of the nation in so far as it is comprised of Southern Catholics, which is the difficulty as far as Paulin's secular Republican vision is concerned. The poem plays with the parallels drawn in nationalist rhetoric between Mother Ireland and the Virgin Mary which I have noted in the Aisling poems; in contrast Paulin's 'wet, fresh place' suggests feminine sexuality as opposed to the maternal. But the analogy Paulin is drawing here may have a further, and rather different point. For the narrator *misreads* the priest's relationship to the landscape in terms of his 'protestant faith in the printed text' (p. 57) which depends upon the literal 'pure, bare', and plain words of the Bible, rather than the metaphorical, image-bound, and analogical language of the first part of the poem. The distinction here may be between the puritan's directly personal response to the Bible, which he reads in terms of the free and individual conscience, and the Catholic emphasis on tradition (and, Paulin might argue, superstition). In this regard it is significant that the narrator imagines not a Bible under the jacket but a missal, a secondary product constructed out of layers of ritual and tradition. But the poem also implies that, contrary to what the narrator thought then and unlike Elizabeth Bishop's cleric, the priest welcomes the poetic and analogical method in which Paulin also takes pleasure. Both, in fact, enjoy the erotics of dressing up the mountain.

In addition to its focus on sexuality the poem is at a deep level concerned with questions of politics and aesthetics. There is an abiding conflict throughout Paulin's work between the pull towards a lyrical romanticism, and a conviction that delight in the workings of the poetic imagination can be politically suspect. Bernard O'Donoghue has argued that Paulin's imagination tends 'towards the burgeoningly romantic' but if 'Throughout his work, concern for social responsibility and answerability occurs side by side with assertions of the artistic freedom of the individual', it is important to emphasize that this tension is played out on the level of language and poetic form itself.[11] Paulin's essay on Bishop makes it clear that he is disturbed by the alliance within European aesthetics between conservative ideas of tradition and poetic language. For example, he abhors the connection in Heidegger's philosophy between arguments for the superiority of traditional rural life, the elevation of the poet to the role of leader, and a mythic nationalism:

> the essential concept of rootedness is one which many readers bring to poetry. And for Heidegger, poetry is the essence of language. It is 'where language *is*, where man is *bespoken*'. Language is 'the house of Being. Man dwells in this house.' Those who think and those who create poems are 'the custodians of the dwelling'. But the house, the dwelling, isn't an abstract concept—it is a Black Forest cottage whose walls are impregnated with race memories.
>
> Is it possible to contemplate such an image without smelling the burnt flesh that clings to certain German place-names? And—to push the question further—doesn't this exaltation of the poet reflect two centuries of *European* aesthetics? If it does, how can writers come to terms with this tainted cultural inheritance?'[12]

It is important to realize that, despite the loaded terminology of this passage (and the problematic suggestion that it is solely the German nation which has been guilty of such crimes against humanity), Paulin is not arguing in favour of a 'pure' cultural inheritance. Indeed it is exactly the dissonances and discontinuities within so-called contemporary British culture which he wants acknowledged. His concern centres on how it is possible to

[11] Bernard O'Donoghue, 'Involved Imaginings: Tom Paulin', in Neil Corcoran (ed.), *The Chosen Ground: Essays on the Contemporary Poetry of Northern Ireland* (Bridgend: Seren Books, 1992), 177, 175.

[12] Paulin, *Minotaur*, 200.

work within the European aesthetic tradition, which he believes is 'tainted' precisely in its drive towards purity. The idea of the aesthetic as a separate realm has historically been associated with a conservative politics (within the English literary tradition Paulin's example would be the hegemony of T. S. Eliot's High Anglican aesthetic). Hence his refusal to condone such a separation in the *Faber Book of Political Verse*. But, as Terry Eagleton has pointed out in his discussion of this anthology, Paulin's espousal of a radical republican tradition of poetry carries with it certain contradictions, not least of which is the antipathy of the dissenting imagination towards the mystifications of aesthetics:

> The clear bold light of republican rationalism, and the intimate affective depths of the poetic, have been constructed by the dominant culture as directly antithetical; and it is here, not just in the repressing or re-writing of this or that radical poet, that the true difficulty lies.[13]

Eagleton notes that the same stress informs Paulin's poetry (and *Liberty Tree* in particular), which evidences 'a notable tension between the virtues of rationalist republicanism . . . and a more dense, inward, organic sensuousness which is really more endebted to the conservative tradition from Shakespeare to Hopkins and Hardy.' Undoubtedly Paulin's interest in the 'thickness' and sensuousness of dialect words, particularly in *Liberty Tree*, is intended as a radical and democratic means of undermining that conservative tradition. As I have discussed, it is sorely mistaken to read this exploration of dialect and the vernacular as in any sense 'tribal'. Rather than a preservation of dialect words and non-standard English as the true mark of identity of a subject people, Paulin argues for the elevation of dialect to the same level as 'standard' English, and for its institutionalization. One might argue then that the refusal to separate literary and vernacular registers in the poetry is one way of rejecting the idea of aesthetic purity, divorced from politics.

However, there is, I believe, a difficulty with Paulin's recurrent notion of formal resolution, or the synthesis of the opposing forces of rationality and sensuous particularity (signified above all by the 'form that's classic and secular'). Paulin strives to 'institutionalize' local diversity so that it does not remain at the level of

[13] Terry Eagleton, 'The Poetry of Radical Republicanism', *New Left Review* 158, (1986), 125.

the picturesque, or Heideggerian romanticism. Yet one might legitimately question whether the politics he champions bears the transformative imprint of its new subject-matter. Rather than construct an alternative politics able to acknowledge the differences of Irish Catholic tradition (such as vernacular linguistic traditions, folk culture, and so on), his model of the political remains weighted to cultural institutions such as the printed text and the dictionary, which have their roots in the Protestant tradition. Moreover, as I argued in Chapter 1, such a view can suggest, erroneously, that political and economic difficulties have cultural solutions; indeed, despite Paulin's commitment to a political poetry, the drive to go beyond political conflicts through increased cultural and historical understanding is particularly marked in *Liberty Tree*. As I shall argue below, Paulin's ideal of synthesis and resolution can be traced partly to his interest in Hegel's theory of the modern state as the optimal vehicle for overcoming the clash of opposing 'civic' and 'tribal' rights (for example, in his reading of the *Antigone* which Paulin relies on in *The Riot Act*). Hegel's theory has obvious attractions for anyone hoping for a solution to the situation in Northern Ireland, yet there is a danger both that the irreconcilability of political differences will be glossed over in the ideal of synthesis or resolution, and that such differences will be polarized into the by now familiar distinction between tradition and modernity, or, more problematically still, between Protestantism and Catholicism.

While the opposition between sensuous particularity and 'the clear bold light' of reason may have been clear at least to readers of *Liberty Tree*, in *Fivemiletown* that tension has been taken up as a structuring principle of the poetry itself. As I will argue, *Fivemiletown* opens up these areas of conflict without trying to resolve them to the extent that Paulin's earlier poetry tended to do.

The tension between the wish to speak plainly and the metaphoricity and ambiguity of words, felt as a desire, is a central concern in *Fivemiletown*, and it relates both to the possibility of a free experience of sexuality and to Paulin's conception of the boundaries between public and private discourses. For the question of the relation between aesthetics and politics is linked to the division between public and private spheres. Paulin has stated in rather general terms that poetry is political in Eastern Europe because there there is no private life, and throughout his poetry he insists on its public reference. However, the ideal of the *res publica* or civic virtue is not possible in a highly stratified society which aims for universal political emancipation—what constitutes public life for the ordinary individual in Britain or Ireland? As I have argued, the rise of the 'social' should not be interpreted in wholly negative terms, since through the expansion of the closed political group (and the consequent alteration of the division between private and public spheres) all sorts of private issues become matters for public concern. Sexuality, and the whole area of reproduction is a case in point. Sexuality is perhaps an area of experience which should ideally be experienced privately (in some sense the pleasure depends on intimacy), but in actuality it is colonized by the public domain; legislation and societal expectations govern all aspects of sexuality from the constitution of sexual identities, to conception, child-rearing, and so on (and this is particularly the case for women, whose bodies are treated as a national resource). Undoubtedly this public interest in sexuality is marked in advanced capitalist secular societies as well as those in which Church and State are not separate. Nevertheless, the public side of sexuality is experienced differently by Protestants and Catholics.

'Now for the Orange Card' sets up a division, similar to that in 'The Maiden that is Makeless', between Protestant and Catholic thinking on matters of coitus and contraception; it therefore announces itself as dealing with the public face of sexuality, its legislation. In comparison with Muldoon's 'Quoof' the poem's subject is quite literally a contraceptive, and perhaps also a prophylactic. As Alan Robinson points out, in addition to being 'sent off' the title alludes to Lord Randolph Churchill's anti-Home Rule strategy: 'if the G.O.M. went for Home Rule, the Orange Card would be the one to play. Please God it may turn out the ace of trumps and not the two . . .'[14] More particularly, as the final page of the volume reminds us, 'Free State Referenda' are one of the subjects of this collection and we are surely asked to consider the referenda on abortion and divorce as further opportunities for the Unionist community to play the Orange Card.

[14] Churchill, letter to FitzGibbon (16 Feb. 1886). Quoted in Alan Robinson, *Instabilities in Contemporary British Poetry* (Basingstoke: Macmillan, 1988), 120–1.

Here that card seems more preoccupied with Roman Catholic dictums against contraception: the availability of condoms in the Republic is severely restricted by the Church's insistence that they should only be used for conjugal sex. In contrast, in the poem french letters are described as 'enlightened, protestant and *juste*'. Paulin questions these associations, however, implying they are more fitting for the French letters of 1798 than the contemporary version of enlightened sexual mores which are both violent and patriarchal. He compares the trademark on the condom packet to masonic symbols and the truths of geometry, but while such values might signify the civic virtues of Thebes, as in the epigraph to the volume, here they have been perverted:

> Each time I take a look
> it reminds me of a signet ring
> on a butcher's finger:
> blood and coins,
> the metric rod,
> and a girl crying
> 'I don't like it now.'[15]

The invocation of Thebes is important to an understanding of the poem since in *Liberty Tree* and his version of *Antigone* Paulin interprets the conflict between Creon and Antigone as in part representative of that between civic duty or the State and familial or tribal loyalties in Northern Ireland. In his article on Conor Cruise O'Brien, Paulin objects to O'Brien's reading of the play as one in which it is Ismene who represents the principles of 'common-sense and feeling for the living'.[16] In opposition to O'Brien's reading, Paulin returns to Hegel:

> According to Hegel, for whom *Antigone* was 'the perfect exemplar' of tragedy, the sacred laws which Antigone revered are 'the instinctive Powers of Feeling, Love and Kinship, not the daylight gods of free and self-conscious, social and political life'. As Hegel shows, in the play 'neither the right of family, nor that of the state is denied; what is denied is the absoluteness of the claim of each'. It is in the clash of these opposing

[15] Robinson also notes the allusions here and in the 'stamped sun' of the second stanza to Blake's 'Visions of the Daughters of Albion': 'Stamped with my signet are the swarthy children of the sun: | They are obedient, they resist not, they obey the scourge; | Their daughters worship terrors and obey the violent' (*Instabilities*, 121).

[16] Conor Cruise O'Brien, quoted in Paulin, *Ireland and the English Crisis*, 27.

'rights' that the tragedy resides. Antigone represents the absolute assertion of family against the state . . .[17]

As I have suggested, Paulin implicitly accepts Hegel's implication that in the modern state the conflict and tension between these two views may be eliminated; it is here that Paulin's claims for the value of formal institutions and his optimistic view of rationality's role in resolving conflicts are most problematic. As Martha Nussbaum has argued with reference to Hegel's reading of the *Antigone*, faith in the reform of civic order as a way of overcoming such tensions is misplaced:

Furthermore, we already have reason to think it a dangerous reform, one that involves us in a risk of neglecting some of the richness of the world of value and the separateness of each separate claim within it. From our study of the two protagonists we might infer that to do justice to the nature of two distinct values requires doing justice to their difference . . . requires seeing that there are, at least potentially, circumstances in which the two will collide. Distinctness requires articulation *from*, bounding-off against. This, in turn, entails the possibility of opposition—and for the agent who is committed to both—conflict.[18]

It is precisely this level of conflict which cannot be acknowledged in the model of aesthetic resolution. It would, however, be mistaken to infer from Paulin's discussion of the *Antigone* in *Ireland and the English Crisis* that the Hegelian structure works in a similar way in *Fivemiletown*. Indeed, in the Introduction to *Minotaur* he acknowledges the partial nature of Hegel's theory of the state, which fails to account for its repressive nature. His description of the essays in *Minotaur* as 'attempts to combine immediacy with the historical sense Nietzsche and others have decried' could equally well be applied to the poems in *Fivemiletown*.[19] Indeed, I would argue that the inclusion in the centre of the volume of Paulin's translation of the 'Ode of Man' chorus from the *Antigone* stands as an ironic gloss on Hegel's faith in the power of rationality to resolve conflicts. Nussbaum interprets the lyric as an assertion of the impossibility of avoiding conflict: 'the statement of human triumphs through reason turns

[17] Conor Cruise O'Brien, quoted in Paulin, *Ireland and the English Crisis*, 27–8.

[18] Martha Nussbaum, *The Fragility of Goodness: Luck and Ethics in Greek Tragedy and Philosophy* (Cambridge: Cambridge University Press, 1986), 68.

[19] Paulin, *Minotaur*, 16.

out to be also a compressed document of reason's limitations, transgressions and conflicts. It suggests that the richer our scheme of values, the harder it will be to effect a harmony within it.'[20] And in keeping with this reading, it is hard to read Paulin's fiercely ironic lines, 'We call this progress and it shows | we're damned near perfect', as anything other than a condemnation of the coercive power of the state's alliance with technology.

While in *The Riot Act* Creon's misuse of state power seems loosely analogous to the British rule of law, in 'Now for the Orange Card' the daylight gods are more clearly associated with Northern Unionism which has perverted the values of the Enlightenment. Those things which were meant to symbolize freedom, and in sexual terms the freedom to enjoy erotic pleasure without binding it to the family and to reproduction, have been debased to the sordid activities of an 'Achilles strapped in leather, | a pushy jerk | on his night journey'. Protestant sex is private in that it is removed from State regulation, but public in that it is civic, an open book; yet freedom from Church or State regulation of sex does not also entail freedom from the violent misuse of power against women. The Enlightenment sets nature, as human nature, in opposition to clan loyalties and tribalism (and perhaps in this context more particularly the requirements of the family), but the poem asks what is lost in that process—and, despite the fact that erotic enjoyment might be thought to be enhanced by breaking the link between sex and reproduction, the answer seems to be pleasure.

Pleasure in its turn depends on language and thereby points up a further contradiction within the system of civic values. For the language of sexual freedom countermands that of civic freedom. In choosing to dispense with the condom the narrator sets himself against a world in which 'the roads are straight and secular, | everyone says what they mean'. His desire is for 'what's natural', but the problem is that he cannot tell whether what he wants—to allow his seed to go unwasted, to 'belong'—is a natural desire or one formed by his wish not to play the 'orange card'. The narrator may simply be accepting the ideology of sex in the Republic where, through the dictates of the Catholic Church which firstly celebrates only reproductive sex and secondly restricts access to

[20] Nussbaum, *Fragility of Goodness*, 75.

contraception to married couples, family and State are not separate. The last lines enact this tension in the use, whether intended or not, of highly ambiguous language which, like the play on the meanings of french letter, proves that it is impossible to say what you mean:

All I want
is to snatch a sleaked song
till a wetness slicks and grows
on your dagged black hairs
—but what nature is
and what's natural
I can never tell just now.

Paulin's desired song, his song of desire, is 'sleaked', shifty, or fly—the opposite of an open book, and it also sets itself against the enlightened Protestant values of the rest of the poem in imaging sex without a condom, semen finding its home. And yet this may not be the Catholic ideal of reproductive sex after all, but another version of sex for pleasure's sake, since 'dagged' can mean both wet with dew or rain, and also soiled with dung.[21] (Anal sex can be simultaneously sex for pleasure and a form of contraception.) The suggestion of anal sex here is substantiated by the reference to the branding of the 'steer's bum' in the first stanza, and also by the image of Heidegger 'dagging' (presumably cutting the soiled and tangled wool off sheep) in 'The Caravans on Lüneberg Heath'. Moreover, given the initial spread of AIDS in the West in the gay community, and the importance of the condom for safer sex, it is surely one of the ironies of the poem in its search for 'what's natural' that, despite its historic links with the values of the Enlightenment, Northern Protestantism shares with Southern Catholicism a ferocious homophobia.

As in 'The Maiden that is Makeless' there is a complex tension in the poem between pleasure and politics. The freeing of per-

[21] The *OED* notes that 'dagged', meaning to be cut in ragged points, derives from 'dagging', cutting the excreta-soiled wool off the hinder parts of sheep. A further echo suggests an allusion to Hopkins's poem 'Inversnaid': 'Degged with dew, dappled with dew | Are the groins of the braes that the brook treads through | . . . Let them be left | O let them be left, wildness and wet; | Long live the weeds and the wilderness yet.' I am grateful to Elaine Jordan for pointing this out.

sonal desires is associated with a metaphorical image-bound and analogical use of language, yet the possibility of such freedom is offered by the open, unmetaphorical, and geometric principles of the Enlightenment. Privacy offers the possibility of experiencing natural pleasure outside of state interference, and is thus the place of desire, but at the same time it is repudiated, as collusive in the conservative attempt to separate public from private life, and thereby render politics opaque. Yet it is important to emphasize that in the poem this problem is approached linguistically and formally, as the poem enacts in language the difficulty of saying what you mean.

The relation between the need for true or plain speech and the course of personal and national histories is most clearly delineated in 'Sure I'm a Cheat Aren't We All'. The poem interweaves personal and public events through Paulin's characteristic analogical method and through a careful use of tense, as it begins by dating itself in Oxford (where the narrator is researching in the Bodleian Library) on the day that Stormont was suspended, 24 March 1972. We start with something that is 'for real': the filing-card box whose trademark he graphically renders on the page. It is perhaps the only thing we can count on in this poem about cheating, lies, and betrayal. For Paulin is first of all a pretended Anglican and a pretended scholar (in a room full of ironically 'real' ones). The poem draws a parallel between the narrator's sham status as a member of the Anglican community, and Stormont's fake parliamentary nature, its failure as a representative institution:

> so I began dropping cards into my new box
> my stamped plastic box a fawn one
> and it was like filling in ballot papers

The similarity may lie in the fact that both activities are mere empty procedure, or that both have an equally skewed relationship to the community at large, but Paulin seems to intend a more precise link through the notions of judgement and consensus. For, as he argues in *Ireland and the English Crisis*, the credo of the Bodleian Library is inextricably bound up with a politics:

> Although literary criticism is said to lead ultimately to an ideology or a theology . . ., it could be that the critic's position must always begin with a definite civil and cultural affiliation. The idea of balanced judgement

which is, or used to be, such a strong feature of English literary criticism has obvious links with Anglicanism and English political history.[22]

As the inheritor of that political history, Anglicanism is reflected in politics by a parliamentary system based on tradition and compromise rather than the principles of liberty, fraternity, and equality. Paulin goes on to describe his own mature affiliation to precisely these latter ideals in the form of a secular republicanism, but in the poem his subject is his uneasy, youthful, playing of a role. And just as the narrator feels himself, albeit obscurely, to be unfitted for the literary task assigned him, so the Northern Irish Parliament eschewed both the principles of balanced judgement and consensus as the Civil Rights Movement sought to show (although the subsequent imposition of Direct Rule imposed a bureaucratic rather than democratic form of government, and was thus equally unrepresentative). If it is firstly in failing to be 'the real thing' that the personal situation of the narrator/Paulin-figure resembles the predicament of the public institution of the Northern Ireland Parliament, as the poem progresses it becomes clear that there is a further point of connection: both the narrator and the Ulster Protestants feel betrayed, abandoned by their partners for the Catholics, and the implication is that both respond with equally immature and destructive behaviour—in this case, pretended love:

> though I wasn't in the least happy
> because you'd fallen for this young priest
> he was a loiner Tim Ryan that's a lie
> and driven with him July a heatwave
> all through the West the East Riding
> some harbour Hornsea Spurn Head it's pathetic
>
> you were in cheescloth he'd green shades I could scream still
> the Society of Jesus White Fathers it's invisible
> as that day the same day she and me
> we made a heavy pretence of love
> I mean we'd a drunken fuck in the afternoon
> after a dockland lunch the Land of Green Ginger
> its smell of sex herrings desire

[22] Paulin, *Ireland and the English Crisis*, 17. See also his introduction to the *Faber Book of Political Verse*: 'The idea of balanced judgement is a reflection of consensus politics, and in a polarized society with high unemployment such a concept is bound to appear comically irrelevant' (Tom Paulin (ed.), *The Faber Book of Political Verse* (London: Faber and Faber, 1986), 46).

and I fell asleep with the blinds drawn
waking up like a Cretan
after a dish of leveret and black olives

clammy stunned
a caked lie on my lips
and no pattern in the thing at all

or maybe only I was boxed in
maybe that sappy something we call experience

The final lines of the poem, which return us to the filing-card box, are characteristically ambiguous and open-ended; are we to assume that he *as opposed to* anyone else was boxed in, or that he was *merely* boxed in? Does 'sappy' connote something life-giving (or perhaps 'real') or something foolish? In other words, is the sappiness of experience opposed to, or aligned with, the reality of the box? Overall the lines seem to imply that both narrator and Unionism need to break out of their enclosed and inward-looking provincialism, they need to think in terms other than those dictated by their experiences at the hands of others, in order to be able to create for themselves the 'real thing' rather than an inferior copy. The structure of the poem is significant here since it is a retrospective about the inability (in March 1972) to gain a mature and reflective distance on one's past experience (of July 1971?), in order to create an alternative future. And in this context one of Paulin's favourite citations, from Eliot's 'Little Gidding' is relevant:

A people without history
Is not redeemed from time, for history is a pattern
Of timeless moments.

Paulin gives these lines a Northern Irish gloss in *Ireland and the English Crisis* where he laments the 'non-historical' nature of the State:

It must therefore be one of the tasks of the self-conscious historian to seek out those timeless moments and form them into a pattern. If Northern Ireland were to become a genuinely independent state then it's likely that a historian connected with the UDA would offer an epic account of the formation of that state, but as Northern Ireland is merely an administrative entity like the Borough of Hendon or South Humberside it can only—at least from the Unionist point of view—possess a kind of parish history. For the Official Unionist, who believes that Northern Ireland is permanently part of the U.K., history is static and therefore parochial, while for the republican it is a developing process which aims at the establishment of a full cultural identity.[23]

However, in contrast to this insistence on the necessity for historical pattern, on another level the poem seems to be asking who is it that decides what is a lie and what's 'for real'? The implication is that fake goods lack pattern, the stamp of a genuine trademark. But the books filed in the library suggest that the world is far from stamped and orderly, but arbitrary, false, a riddle, or mystery. For example, Schopenhauer's theory in *Die Welt als Wille und Vorstellung* might be summarized as that there is indeed 'no pattern in the thing at all'. Where then does the possibility of open, rational debate lie? The style of the poem too suggests a high degree of scepticism as to the possibility of realizing a truly representative institution, and the true language it could use as a democratic 'house of speech'. The poem attempts through rigorous use of language to hold things down to the truth ('that day the same day'—the day in July rather than March). The narrator keeps trying to find other ways of saying what he means: 'suspended prorogued done away with', 'I mean we'd a drunken fuck', 'parliament a house of speech'. As in 'The Maiden that is Makeless' and 'Now for the Orange Card' it seems far from possible to speak plainly for a new civility. To probe the issue further, we might consider the nature of the link between the inherent duplicity or ambiguity of language and the failure of representative politics in Northern Ireland. The connection turns on the necessity, both in representative politics and poetic representation, for dialogue and consensus, neither of which can be initiated from a position of pretence. The narrator tries his hand at constructing the grounds for such a dialogue at the beginning of the poem, by utilizing a plain, conversational style, signalled by gestures of inclusion ('of course you know Broad Street'). This gesture, like almost everything else in the poem, is a sham, simultaneously announcing itself as a poem from one Oxford graduate to others, and undercutting that cosy identification with reference to the Protestant martyrs. Paulin calls both aesthetic and democratic forms of representation into question since both lack the moral and rational consensus necessary as a precondition

[23] Paulin, *Ireland and the English Crisis*, 141.

for communication. So the poem is about the *failure* of the public arena, and consequently of a public political poetry which would address it.

The three poems I have discussed in this section are in part acknowledgements of the need to include desire, sensuousness, and particularity within the classical Enlightenment ideals of reason and justice. Much recent feminist theory has approached the same issue, looking primarily at the gender blindness of the universalist tradition (I have discussed this debate in relation to figures of the motherland and to the exploration of maternity in McGuckian's work). But for Paulin the problem with his classical, secular vision is not its exclusion of women, but the arena of pleasure and affectivity, and custom and tradition in general. (As I have suggested, the lack of sensitivity to women's concerns damages the model of synthesis Paulin utilizes; rather than attempt a thorough transformation of the civic ideal, his model of politics remains weighted towards the masculine, Protestant, Enlightenment tradition). As he remarks in the opening poem of *Liberty Tree*, of the failed history of eighteenth-century republicanism in Ireland, 'Maybe one day I'll get the hang of it | and find joy, not justice, in a snapped connection'. But while he may simply want to augment such abstract universalist ideals with the inclusion of matter from 'lived experience', the poetry itself suggests that the ideals themselves are inadequate to the self-understanding of both individuals and communities. Once the Enlightenment model is embodied within language (rather than geometric symbols), it becomes twisted upon itself, confounded by ambiguity and contingency. Paulin's exploration of the limits of the eighteenth-century political ideal in part derives from his awareness of the ways in which the republican model of justice and equality has failed, or been driven underground, in contemporary Protestant culture in Ulster, and his appreciation of the need to recognize the mythic and non-rational aspects of Unionist culture. And on a more general level the very fact that he wishes to explore in his work the self-understanding of a particular community within the nation-state undermines any commitment to purely universal values, since Paulin acknowledges the importance of historical and cultural contingency.

Nevertheless, it remains unclear to what extent Paulin believes it is possible at some point to slough off the accumulated myths and prejudices of a particular culture, in order to overcome a provincial and partial political understanding. One might legitimately enquire what would then be left, as a position from which to claim and struggle for justice? Is he arguing that it is possible not to be boxed in? *Liberty Tree* has a tendency to suggest it is simply a matter of time before the light of reason must dawn, and shows a related desire to smooth out the tensions between sensuousness and formal discipline. The metaphor of the organic growth of the liberty tree is crucial to this move in many poems, particularly 'The Book of Juniper', 'Under Creon', and 'Presbyterian Study', which insists that the 'dream of grace and reason' is a 'free', a 'natural', and not a 'formal' ideal:

Memory is a moist seed
And a praise here . . .

Hardly a schoolroom remembers
Their obstinate rebellion;
Provincial historians
Scratch circles on the sand,
And still, with dingy smiles,
We wait on nature . . .[24]

Fivemiletown offers a bleaker vision, born of the conviction that historical self-understanding conditions the possibilities for change in Ulster. 'The Red Handshake' suggests a very different form of organic growth, rooted in loyalist ideology: 'a man called Bowden Beggs | wrapped in black plastic, like a growbag, | and breathing "mind, It can get no worse"'. As Bernard O'Donoghue has pointed out, in addition to the Ulster Protestant community, Paulin is accusing *himself* of provincialism here, as in much of the volume. Awareness of Paulin's self-examination in this volume unlocks, at least partly, the significance of the parallelism he draws between his own personal history, and the historical understanding of Ulster Protestants. For like Muldoon and McGuckian, Paulin's exploration of sexuality is also a means of exploring the relation between personal and public histories, and the way in which understanding of a personal or national past impinges on attitudes to possibilities in the present. As I will argue in the following section, *Fivemiletown* is concerned with the

[24] Tom Paulin, 'Presbyterian Study', in *Liberty Tree* (London: Faber and Faber, 1983), 49–50.

ways in which Paulin himself is implicated in the myths and historical memories of Ulster Protestantism, and reveals an awareness that, until this aspect of the culture is acknowledged, his ideal of secular equality will remain a fiction.

The Besieged City

For Paulin much of Ulster Protestant culture is beset by a disabling provincialism, a confused and contradictory identification with 'the British way of life'. In opposition to those sections of Ulster which see themselves as the last outpost of the British Empire, Paulin is keen to rescue the dissenting tradition from historical obscurity. While in *Liberty Tree* he treated of that tradition more directly, *Fivemiletown* emphasizes the complex split ideology within contemporary Unionist thinking. Rather than look solely for the signs of degeneration, Paulin investigates the ways in which contemporary Unionists build on and preserve their radical puritan heritage, finding the marks of this altered radical tradition in the conventions of personal testimony, oral witness, and the refusal to separate the activities of reading and writing (interpretation) from political understanding. It is a presentation of this complex and contradictory heritage which forms the basis of his selection 'Northern Protestant Oratory and Writing' in the *Field Day Anthology*.[25] Paulin looks outside official Unionist culture for the signs of the dissenting tradition's contemporary life, and surprisingly finds them embedded in the most uncompromising loyalist ideology. Contemporary orators such as Ian Paisley thus share with eighteenth-century republican thinkers such as William Drennan, not only 'an intense commitment to the right of private judgement and a belief in a value they term "energy" or "the dynamic of heaven"', but also a profound ambivalence to their own Britishness. He notes, for example, how Unionists such as Edward Carson and Ian Paisley have taken pride in the contribution of Ulstermen to the framing of the American Declaration of Independence, and used it to warn British politicians not to alienate the citizens in Northern Ireland:

[25] Tom Paulin, 'Northern Protestant Oratory and Writing', in Seamus Deane (ed.), *The Field Day Anthology of Irish Writing*, iii (Derry: Field Day Publications, 1991), 314–79.

This pride in the Ulster presbyterian contribution to the American Revolution was echoed during the 1980s in publications associated with the Ulster Defence Association, the chief loyalist paramilitary organization, and it issues from those contradictory emotions and beliefs that form the basis of loyalist culture. Distrusting traditional definitions of Irish identity, that culture often aggressively presents itself as being simultaneously British and anti-British.[26]

The crucial event in defining the contemporary loyalist attitude to Britain is the signing of the Anglo-Irish Agreement in 1985, which gave the Irish Government a consultative role in the administration of the Northern Irish State, in return for increased co-operation in the struggle against terrorism. Several poems in *Fivemiletown*, notably 'An Ulster Unionist Walks the Streets of London' and 'The Defenestration of Hillsborough', attempt to articulate the traumatized feelings of exclusion and betrayal which many Unionists experienced at that time. The poems rework the public reactions of politicians such as Ian Paisley and Peter Robinson (of the Democratic Unionist Party) and of Harold McCusker (deputy leader of the Official Unionist Party at the time of the Agreement). The poems emphasize the importance of personal testimony and of biblical and historical analogies in articulating the experience of a community that exists in a marginal relation to the nation-state, that feels it has been betrayed by one nation into the hands of another. For example, Paulin notes, in the Introduction to *Minotaur*, the puritan habit of interpreting the Bible as though it were of direct relevance to Ulster Protestants, and he mentions in particular Paisley's citation of the story of the Three Hebrew Children (from the Book of Daniel):

This story of 'peoples, nations and languages' related hermeneutics to state authority, political power and nationhood. Nebuchadnezzar's Babylon was Britain in post-imperial confusion, Daniel was the loyalist imagination which sits 'in the gate of the king', identifies with the British sovereign and holds a British identity. To read the story in this way was to read both personally and communally, but the process of recognition also carried an awareness that such intensely direct interpretation was boxed in and parochial; it could be of no interest to anyone outside a community that now felt it was a minority within Ireland.[27]

[26] *The Field Day Anthology of Irish Writing*, iii 314.
[27] Paulin, *Minotaur*, 15.

It is important to realize, however, that this examination of Ulster Protestant thought is not merely an ethnographic exercise, but also a self-examination. In 'Why The Good Lord Must Persecute Me', it is Paulin himself who finds in *The History of Received Opinions*, 'a missing chapter | that tells what you can't rub out | however much you might want to'. In some ways the volume acts as a form of personal self-discovery, allowing him to be 'born again' into his British school in the last pages, if not cleansed of his 'received opinions' at least very much more aware of them. Many of the poems in the volume signal themselves as dealing with childhood experience in Northern Ireland during the post-war years. Education in history, language, and sexual difference is the theme variously of 'Where's this Big River Come From?', 'Mythologies', 'Rosetta Stone', 'Peacetime', as well as the final section of 'Caravans'. This childhood education feeds into poems about adolescent experience, particularly sexual experience, such as 'Waftage: An Irregular Ode' and 'Breez Marine'. But as I have discussed, the poems characteristically work on the level of political allegiances at the same time (hence the 'tin | of panties | coloured like the Union Jack' in 'Waftage'). The Protestant youth of Ulster were nourished on British history, both imperialist and monarchist in its concerns, and also on the history of European Protestantism. One of the aspects of contemporary Ulster Protestant culture which Paulin is keen to explore is the historical sense which links them to the history of European Protestantism, and which sees the battles between Protestants and Catholics in Europe as being as central today as at the time of the Thirty Years War. Such a perspective is at once cosmopolitan and at the same time boxed in and parochial, and it is a perspective which has left its mark on Paulin himself.

> Like the loyalist leader who cited the Defenestration of Prague in order to express his anguished sense of being forced out of the British nation, I studied the history of the Thirty Years War within the Northern Irish system of State education. This necessarily conditions my reading of Hopkins ['Wreck of the Deutschland']. I say 'conditions' because with hindsight I can see that the school syllabus was designed to reinforce a Protestant identity and to submerge the Catholic population of the province within those dominant values.[28]

[28] Ibid. 16.

In what follows I wish to examine the ways in which these issues inform the final long poem in *Fivemiletown*, 'The Caravans on Lüneberg Heath'. The poem is difficult to interpret, not only because of the many interwoven historical reference points throughout, but also because, as in Muldoon's work, the stance of the poet towards his material is hard to evaluate. As the 'chorus' says at one point in the poem, '*Simplex says he's going now* | *You can read this anyhow*'. This refusal to offer clear guidelines to the reader is characteristic of Paulin's more recent work and, as I have argued, it undermines the claim that his poetry, because it professes its own political engagement, is reductive in its sympathies and allegiances. Paulin's abiding concern is to find an aesthetic form which can accommodate the political (as opposed to the tribal or rooted). In keeping with this aim 'Caravans' searches for an alternative to the dominant European Romantic aesthetic which, while claiming it is above or beyond politics, reinforces a conservative ideology.

Like 'Madoc', 'The Caravans on Lüneberg Heath' interweaves several historical narratives with the present story of events in Northern Ireland. Paulin's poem has two principal historical reference points—the Germany of the Thirty Years War and of the Second World War. Like Muldoon, Paulin approaches these moments through literary and philosophical texts rather than direct historical analysis. The texts he chooses, by Simon Dach, Günter Grass, and Martin Heidegger, are all concerned with the need and desire to find in German culture alternatives to a strictly political definition of the nation or nation-state. But whereas the cultural moments described by Dach and Grass were attempts to offer alternatives to the cultural desolation and the destruction of Germany at the end of the Thirty Years War and the Second World War, Heidegger's poetic philososphy fed into, rather than opposed, the political and racist ideology of National Socialism. The long poem by Simon Dach, 'Lament over the Final Demise and Ruination of the Musical "Pumpkin Hut" and the Little Garden', was written in 1641 towards the end of the Thirty Years War. The poem laments the loss, to the growth and modernization of the city of Königsberg, of the pastoral idyll built by Dach's friend the composer and musician Heinrich Albert; an informal literary society known as the Cucumber Lodge used to meet in a bower in Albert's garden overgrown with cucumbers and other gourds. There in the midst of the turmoil of the war writers and musicians attempted to create a cultural space, 'a dwelling for love and friendship'. The poem is striking for the way it interweaves a personal story—the loss of the cucumber bower—with the story of Europe's cataclysmic experience of the Thirty Years War. It begins as Dach's personal testimony and becomes a contemplation of the nature of political convulsions, the cyclical nature of time, and the inevitability of decay.

The poem was first published in 1936, which is significant in linking it to the period of the consolidation of Nazi power, and in particular to the consideration of Heidegger's compromised political position on the 1930s. This connection between the cultural politics of the seventeenth and twentieth centuries is emphasized in a further text used by Paulin, Günter Grass's historical *roman-à-clef*, *The Meeting at Telgte*. The novel is set in 1647 when Germany was nearing the end of the Thirty Years War; it recounts the events occurring at a fictional meeting of German writers initiated by Heinrich Albert and Simon Dach:

> It was arranged that in the forty-seventh year of the century (after twenty-nine years of war, the peace negotiations had not yet been concluded), a meeting should be held somewhere between Münster and Osnabrück, for the purpose of giving force to the last remaining bond between all Germans, namely, the German language they held in common, and—if only from the sidelines—uttering a political word or two.[29]

Grass's novel (which reprints Dach's 'Lament') is a thinly veiled analogue for the broadly leftist cultural project of the Gruppe 47, set up by Hans Werner Richter in 1947 in order to foster possibilities for cultural renewal in Germany at a time when the divisions between the Western zones of occupation and the Soviet zone were hardening. Emphasizing above all the social and political responsibility of the writer, the group met every year to read their work and discuss ways of re-creating a German literature in the wake of the Nazi regime.[30] The complex historical interrelationship brought into focus in Grass's text is one explanation for

[29] Günter Grass, *The Meeting at Telgte*, trans. Ralph Mannheim (London: Secker and Warburg, 1981), 17.

[30] After the crushing of the Prague Spring by Soviet troops in 1968 the group suspended its meetings until Czechoslovakia should be freed; they met for the last time in Prague in 1990.

the confusion over the names of places in central Europe in Paulin's poem. Dach's Königsberg has become the closed Soviet military base of Kaliningrad by 1947, just as the Pregel has been renamed the Pregolya. The poem refuses to consider the territorial wars over the lands of central Europe in separation from one another, as the narrator's historical memory collapses events into one another:

> how many years back were Slavata and Martinitz
> pushed out of that window?
> at what hour of the night was it in Ruzyn
> or Hradcany Castle they hanged Salnsky?
> thousands of statements dropped from the presses
> and the day I read Kant's starry sentence
> on a bronze tablet in Kaliningrad
> my protestant faith in the printed text
> turned back on itself

Grass describes the meeting at Telgte as an attempt to bring together representatives of German intellectual and literary life in order to offer an artistic solution to the fragmented state of German political culture. In addition to their deliberations on the German language (what should pass for High German and what should be allotted to the dialects), they draw up a poets' manifesto for peace (here the difficulty of persuading the writers to agree on a plain, unadorned style for their address has clear resonances with Paulin's concerns). However, it is significant that in Grass's text the meeting fails; factional fighting combines with practical problems such as the difficulty of finding sufficient food and accommodation for the writers as the war continues around them. Just at the point when a manifesto for peace has been agreed, the building catches fire (or is set alight) and the group breaks up in disorder. As Leonard Foster points out in the Afterword to *The Meeting at Telgte*, 'the pen rising triumphant out of the rubble of the destroyed cities was Richter's achievement, not Dach's'. Dach's primary difficulty in Grass's novel is to overcome the faction fighting within the group of writers he has invited. None the less, despite their disagreements it is significant that all those he has invited are Protestants (primarily Lutherans)—it is impossible to contemplate a truly egalitarian and secular cultural renaissance, and it is perhaps in this sense that the Cucumber Lodge is a 'besieged city' as Paulin comments in the notes to the poem. Most reviewers understood the reference to the besieged city to apply to the Ulster Protestants' conviction of being under siege from the Irish Republic after the signing of the Anglo-Irish Agreement. However, it is hard to avoid the inference that at one level the poem is also concerned with the cultural project of the Field Day Company to create a 'fifth province', a cultural space non-aligned to either the nationalist or Unionist agendas.

The cultural revival planned in *The Meeting at Telgte* betrays tensions similar to those I have discussed in relation to the abstract ideals of the Enlightenment and the requirements of sensuality, private life, and the family. Here they focus on the opposition between the imposition of a shared language and culture, and the preservation of dialects. There are clearly resonances between the German poets' drive to remake their language, to fit it for a transformed political situation, and Paulin's commitment to a shared linguistic and political culture in Ireland. However, as I discussed in Chapter 3, Paulin evidently has no sympathy with any attempt to separate a national language from its dialects. For him the role of literature (and literary criticism) should be to undermine the divisions between vernacular and traditionally literary language. This was his purpose in his selection for the *Field Day Anthology* which disregarded traditional definitions of the literary in order to include letters, political speeches, and so on, and in his edition of *The Faber Book of Vernacular Verse*. More particularly, the link between the linguistic work on the German language and the process of state formation is disturbing, for, like the imposition of any national standard, there is the danger that it will fail to allow space, linguistic or otherwise, for the marginalized elements within a national community to participate in the public arena. But as Leonard Foster argues, it may at certain times in history be necessary to purge a language of ideological taints: 'The purification of the German language in 1647 meant the elimination of foreign words (mostly Latin and French); in 1947 it meant the avoidance of Nazi terminology and Nazi-tainted concepts: in both cases the creation of a new idiom.'[31] There are obvious echoes here of Paulin's arguments for a dictionary of Irish-English—but again there is a tension between the

[31] Leonard Foster, Afterword, in Grass, *Meeting at Telgte*, 136.

need to move away from 'tribal' language, and the wish to preserve historical and cultural particularity through dialect. As Paulin states in 'A Nation, Yet Again' (alluding to Mallarmé and echoing his own project), the aim is 'to file | a delicate, a tough, new style | that draws the language to the light | and purifies its tribal rites'. Here the suggestion that what is needed is a pure as opposed to a tainted cultural inheritance is deeply problematic, and recalls again the Hegelian ideal of synthesis discussed earlier. It points to an unresolved tension in Paulin's work between the desire to explore conflict and differences of value in Britain and Northern Ireland, and the far more tendentious attempt to overcome political differences through cultural and linguistic projects.

Despite the political wrangling over the true heart of the German nation at Telgte, the final version of the manifesto is a plea for tolerance in matters of religion and politics; moreover it is written in a deliberately unadorned style:

> No ultimate truth was proclaimed. In plain, simple language the assembled poets entreated all parties desirous of peace not to scorn the preoccupations of the poets, who, though powerless, had acquired a claim to eternity.[32]

Similarly Paulin finds in Dach's lament an acceptance of the necessary relationship between literature and political life (including war), but at the same time a refusal to place art in the service of nationalist renewal. The second and fourth sections of 'Caravans' are contemporary versions of Dach's poem:

> I don't believe God is much interested
> in this or that country what happens or doesn't
> and after twenty odd years breaking lives like firewood
> is there anything can shock us now?
> the Virgin of Magdeburg charred in a ditch
> the sleeping girl they shot because she married out
> why give a shit if what you write doesn't last?
> could you feel could you really feel any joy
> watching the nation states rising up like maggots?

In addition to his spirit of mingled commitment and tolerance, Paulin's sense of an aesthetic project shared with Dach (who is directly invoked several times in 'Caravans') relates also to the

[32] Leonard Foster, Afterword, in Grass, *Meeting at Telgte*, 126.

pastoral form of the lament, and to the description of the 'pumpkin hut' in particular, which differs markedly from post-romantic descriptions of the rural idyll. The importance of the pumpkin hut can perhaps be more easily understood through a comparison with Martin Heidegger, who is the main subject of the second half of the poem. To some extent the shadowy reference to the activities of the Gruppe 47 in post-war Germany appears as an ironic gloss on those of Heidegger, who appears in the poem 'digging trenches on the Rhine' in 1944 and offering apologias for his uncritical stance towards the Nazi regime during the 1930s. In 1933 he was made Rector of the University of Freiburg, and in his Rectoral Address he welcomed the National Socialists as a realization of the historical destiny of the German people (a view he repeated, albeit ambiguously, in his *Introduction to Metaphysics* where he speaks of 'the inner truth and greatness of this movement (namely the encounter between global technology and modern man)').[33] As Paulin notes in his poem, he also dropped the dedication of *Being and Time* to his former professor Edmund Husserl, who was a Jew. As I have discussed, Paulin is profoundly disturbed by the political implications of Heidegger's philosophy, particularly his arguments for the superiority of the Germans, and the intrinsic philosophical superiority of the German language. His celebration of the tribal and Germanic qualities of rural peasant life was able to feed all too easily into the ideology of the German people put forward by the Nazi regime.

While 'this old smooth fuck | tried stare through history | at the very worst moment', his philosophical examination of the nature of the German language and of poetry itself serving to buttress a totalitarian regime, Paulin asks whether it is possible to construct poetic artefacts which do not repeat the romantic and exclusivist idea of the nation, which do not elevate the poet to the role of seer. How can poetry break its ties with such mystifications in order both to register the inherently political nature of the acts of reading and writing, and also to articulate the marginalized elements within the nation-state? In his essay on Elizabeth Bishop, Paulin argued that the elevation of the poet to the 'custodian' of Heidegger's racial idea of dwelling and

[33] Martin Heidegger, *An Introduction to Metaphysics*, trans. Ralph Mannheim (New Haven, Conn.: Yale University Press, 1959), 199.

groundedness is reflected in the history of post-Romantic aesthetics, and he asks 'how can writers come to terms with this tainted cultural inheritance?' It is in connection with this issue that the full relevance of the comparison between Dach and Heidegger is revealed. For Albert's pastoral pumpkin hut does not partake of the conservative politics associated with post-Romantic celebrations of the rural and traditional. Whereas for Heidegger certain forms of modern and technological structures belie man's true 'dwelling' in the world (included in 'Caravans' is Heidegger's claim in 'Building, Dwelling, Thinking' that 'bridge and hangar | stadium and factory | are buildings | but they're not dwellings') Paulin is keen to discover the poetic in all forms of human activity, including those least admissible within traditional aesthetics. In *Minotaur* he protests against the post-Romantic idealization of nature as a refuge from the political world. It is precisely this distinction which is undercut in Dach's description of the pumpkin hut. First it is created out of the war-torn land through the natural processes of growth and cultivation ('Vor war es eine Warte | Der wilden Kriegesmacht, ietzt muss es seyn ein Garte, | Der Ruh und Frewde bringt;').[34] In the same way, Paulin as 'witness' to the signing of the truce on Lüneberg Heath notices 'three brown buds on a twig | all gummy and glycerine', signalling the possibilities of new growth out of the detritus of war. The seventeenth-century writers meet and converse within a structure which does not respect the divisions between nature and culture, since the pumpkins and cucumbers create the roof and walls. Moreover the fruit itself defines the nature of the written word, as the writing on the gourds is transformed by the organic process:

we cut our girls' names on pumpkins and melons
—*Arsille Rosita Emilie*
the letters distorted as they grew
and our writing stopped being ours.

But perhaps the most relevant aspect of the pumpkin hut for Paulin is its impermanence; it is destroyed during building work

[34] Simon Dach, 'Klage über den endlichen Untergang und Ruinirung der Musicalischen Kurbs-Hutte und Gärtchens, 13 Jan. 1641', in Günter Grass, *Das Treffen in Telgte* (Darmstadt: Sammlung Luchterhand, 1985), 202: 'Before it was a look-out post for the wild powers of war, now it shall be a garden which brings peace and joy'.

in Konigsberg, and in the course of his lament Dach learns to accept the inevitability of change and decay. If, as Heidegger argues, 'Poetic creation, which lets us dwell, is a kind of building', Paulin is determined that that building need not be constructed out of centuries of romantic tradition.

The final lines of 'The Caravans on Lüneberg Heath' bring together the themes of historical education, dwelling, and aesthetic practice. The poem itself seems to be an attempt by Paulin to remake himself by working through the historical memory which has formed him, sending himself back to school in the final section of the poem: 'now I can get born again | as a square of tracing paper | in A B or C block'. Having stood as a disembodied witness at the signing of the truce on Lüneberg Heath that ended the Second World War ('you'll find me Simon an idea only | where five khakhi caravans are parked on a heath'), he is freed into the force of private judgement which he celebrates in his homage to Jackson Pollock, 'I Am Nature'.

And it is significant that the school into which he is reborn, despite its ideological underpinnings in British imperial history (the names of the four houses are those of generals during the war: Dill, Alexander, Montgomery, Alanbrooke link 'each pupil' to the event on Lüneberg Heath), has none of the permanence or groundedness that Heidegger held necessary for true dwelling or being in the world. Like those in Elizabeth Bishop's work this building is impermanent (the reference to the plane and aluminum recall 'The Maiden that is Makeless'):

> onestorey partitioned
> tacked out of hardboard
> and scrap fuselage
> this aluminum school
> is split in four sections

This is perhaps the point of the characteristically ambiguous final lines which insist on the purely ideal and ungrounded nature of Paulin's artistic dwelling:

> and if you ask my opinion now
> I'll tell you about our musical *Kurbishutte*
> then hand you a cucumber
> and say it doesn't exist

Conclusion

Throughout my reading of Paulin's work I have emphasized the drive towards overcoming the opposition between Enlightenment rationality and Romantic or 'tribal' affiliations. In *Fivemiletown* Paulin seems intent on uncovering the elements of custom, tradition, and historical self-understanding which condition the political responses of the contemporary inheritors of eighteenth-century radical republicanism. The implication is that only through an investigation of the cultural history of Northern Protestantism can the people be 'born again' into an alternative self-understanding. And hand in hand with such a project lies the recovery of aesthetic pleasure and creativity in the radical puritan tradition—the creative witness of a Jackson Pollock or an Ian Paisley. This process in turn is clearly related to Paulin's attempt to find an alternative to the fear of the political associated with traditional post-Romantic aesthetics.

As I have suggested, however, despite Paulin's commitment to an exploration of the elements of custom and tradition, pleasure and dialect, within contemporary Protestant culture, his poetry slips too easily into an acceptance of the opposition between rationality and the aesthetic. Despite his attempt to produce a 'puritan poetic', in his work the aesthetic is repeatedly associated with linguistic confusion and mystification which, he suggests, are problematic for the unfettered workings of reason. There are a number of difficulties with this position; firstly the suggestion that it is possible to cleanse language of ambiguity mistakes not only the nature of poetry but of linguistic reference in general. As I discussed in my reading of 'Sure I'm a Cheat', Paulin acknowledges the inherent duplicity of language, its ever-present capacity for betrayal. None the less he continues to suggest that a rational language—plain speech—is both possible and desirable. In political terms he makes the fundamental error of assuming that rationality inheres in a kind of speech, rather than in the fact of engaging in discussion, however partial and necessarily inadequate to the 'truth' that discussion must be. But a far more fundamental difficulty with Paulin's position is the over-theologized nature of the division he draws between Enlightened and Romantic conceptions of identity. Not only does he suggest that these two traditions correspond to genuine social modes of understanding (which can then be synthesized through culture), but in his work the traditions harden into a distinction between radical puritanism—associated historically with the fight for freedom, equality, and democracy—and a Catholicism bound to hierarchy and tradition. What this dichotomy obscures is the fact that in contemporary Northern Ireland both religions meet not as opposing world-views but as religions which already exist side by side within a secular polity (albeit a neo-colonial one).

The real danger of Paulin's analysis is the tendency to include 'the other side' as primarily a cultural other, offering local colour, but not really an alternative (or complementary) politics. Despite Paulin's ostensible commitment to a progressive alteration of the division between public and private spheres, he fails to take sufficient account of the need to construct an alternative vision of the political—and his blindness to the progressive aspects of the destruction of the public space of politics, and the civic ideal, by a 'social life' more broadly conceived, is one sign of this failure.

5

Medbh McGuckian: The Intimate Sphere

Poetic material has no voice. It does not paint and it does not express itself in words. It knows no form, and by the same token it is devoid of content for the simple reason that it exists only in performance. The finished work is nothing but a calligraphic result of the performing impulse. If a pen is dipped into an inkwell, the work created, stopped in its tracks, is nothing but a stock of letters, fully commensurable with the inkwell.[1]

IT is hard to imagine a neutral response to Medbh McGuckian's poetry. The densely textured material of the poems, the complex and well-defined grammatical structure which holds in place a seemingly dizzying collection of kaleidoscopic images, may conjure excitement at the possibilities opened up for imaginative exploration, or defensive condemnations of poetic egoism and the lack of identifiable meaning, but never indifference. Rather than beginning by taking sides in this debate, this chapter explores some of the ways McGuckian self-consciously thematizes the issues of the obscurity of her work and the relationship between personal and public reference. I will argue that she constructs a mode of operation in which the achievement of authority in an Irish or European poetic tradition depends precisely on the poetry's semantic impenetrability and resistance to paraphrase, as these become associated in the work with the possibilities of the plantation of new life in an altered poetic and political climate in Northern Ireland. My discussion will touch on the relation of the poet to tradition and her construction of a lineage in the future; imaged as the 'living tongue' of the child/poem, McGuckian implies her posthumous legacy will be created both for and by her descendants.

And yet from where does McGuckian derive the authority to make her bequest to the nation? As in her earlier work poetic

[1] Osip Mandelstam, 'Conversation about Dante', in *Selected Essays*, ed. Sidney Monas (Austin, Tex.: University of Texas Press, 1977), 44.

legitimization is imaged through familial relationships—those of daughter, mother, and son. I have discussed elsewhere the poetic function of tropes of motherhood in *The Flower Master* and *Venus and the Rain*. My argument centred on the ways in which McGuckian uses images of reproduction, and specifically the authority a mother has over her children, to construct alternatives to the control of the Catholic Church and its representation of perfect motherhood.[2] The Catholic ideal of femininity is in turn related to the nationalist myth of Mother Ireland, and McGuckian undercuts both by translating the public image into the 'private' discourse of the changing contours of her body. It is of course this 'privacy', signalled by a self-conscious obscurity of reference, which has given rise to condemnations of her work as obsessed with the internal workings of the female self. Yet a curious double response should be noted in hostile critics who reveal contempt for what they designate the primarily 'domestic' and autobiographical subject-matter of the poems and at the same time frustration at the way that subject lies veiled beneath a complex linguistic code.[3] An alternative argument would maintain that the highly developed metaphorical structure of the poems creates an asymmetrical relationship between the poet's self and her poem, and moreover that the disassembled, veiled 'self' presented in the work is often an analogue for something quite different from autobiography. However, this reading is constructed to some extent against the grain of the overt message of the poetry, which seems to encourage the reader to investigate the hidden self beneath the metaphors.

[2] See Clair Wills, 'The Perfect Mother: Authority in the Poetry of Medbh McGuckian', *Text and Context*, 3 (1988), 91–111.

[3] The most notorious example of such an attack is Patrick Williams's review of *On Ballycastle Beach*. Williams criticizes McGuckian for thinking her language can present what is 'really happening' while at the same time condemning her for representing 'pseudo' rather than actual femininity. Since he believes that 'true' poetry deals with the representation of 'worthwhile human experience tellingly conveyed', he is incapable of responding adequately to a type of writing which puts into question the very category 'experience'. McGuckian's belief that a language sufficiently complex can represent the 'truths' of femininity is strictly irrelevant to any analysis of what the poems actually *do*. Moreover a careful reading of the poems reveals McGuckian's own ambivalence concerning the possibility or desirability of poetic language acting as a representation of the self. See Patrick Williams, 'Spare that Tree!' *Honest Ulsterman*, 86 (1989), 49–52. See also the reply by Catherine Byron, ibid. 87 (1989), 87–9.

Wary of the use of tropes of femininity as analogues for the state of the nation, McGuckian is concerned not to create another image of womanhood which can simply be appropriated and reduced by being placed in the service of a different narrative. In contrast to a celebration of the disembodied national-maternal, McGuckian's work emphasizes the bodily and corporeal nature of the meanings of motherhood. And yet, as I discussed in Chapter 2, whatever McGuckian's own description of her activity, the importance of this move lies not in the poet's representation of the truths of womanhood in opposition to stereotypical images of femininity, but in its consequences for the relationship between poet and community. In other words, for the way in which it allows McGuckian, as a woman writer, to take on the role of poet in Ireland. There has been much discussion of the problematic authority vested in the representation in Catholic and nationalist ideology of Ireland as a woman—an identification which, in the social arena, has contributed to the severe restriction of women's rights in Ireland. I have argued that, in the literary tradition, the trope of the motherland fulfils a particular function in enabling the poet to act as spokesperson for his community, public voice of the muted land. In opposition to this public image, the privacy (as opposed to personalization) of McGuckian's troping of motherhood is signalled by the obscure, 'veiling' language she employs, and this obscurity has a particular function in legitimizing her poetic activity. To take her place in an Irish poetic tradition in some senses enabled by the troping of motherhood as a public image, McGuckian must divert the tradition through the domestic, since the discourse of sexuality is the only public language to which, as a woman writer, she has legitimate access.

Nevertheless, in a seemingly contradictory move, McGuckian's representations of femininity *do* construct more or less veiled political analogues. Poems such as 'The Heiress' and 'The Soil Map' are not content with translating the feminine image out of the sphere of politics and into that of personal experience, but attempt to hold both in tension. There is a danger, as I argue in relation to the poem 'Dovecote', that such a strategy will merely serve to reconfirm the tropic association of the body of the Irish woman with the Irish polity, with all the political implications which follow. However, McGuckian characteristically emphasizes the body as a place of struggle, and the mother not as a home or guarantee of a secure identity but as alien and strangely undomesticated. Rather than representing the continuity of generations, maternity for McGuckian is associated with historical discontinuity, bodily disruption, and loss. Moreover, in addition to her figuration of the maternal, McGuckian also investigates the whole range of familial or domestic relationships. In their emphasis on the importance of the daughter rather than the mother, her collections *On Ballycastle Beach* and *Marconi's Cottage* seem to offer an alternative to the myth of the motherland, with its inevitable stress on the binary relationship between Ireland and England. In a striking development from her earlier work McGuckian mentions and alludes to a diverse community of 'European' Romantic and Modernist poets. In addition to Yeatsian echoes the poetry nods towards Frost, Coleridge, Shelley, and Byron (all confirmed Europeans), as well as Pasternak, Tsvetaeva, and Mandelstam. And significantly her construction of a 'Common European Home' for poetry relates not merely to her poetic antecedents, but also to the possible future she envisages for Northern Ireland, side-stepping the relationship with the authoritative father/husband figure, England. The chance for a new political framework for the North is again imaged through the reproduction of both words and children in a new 'Plantation' which will have the power to undo its predecessor. One might read this as McGuckian's poetic version of a 'Europe of the Regions', with its suggestion that, by emphasizing regional identity, Northern Ireland can avoid 'the national question'. Yet McGuckian's primary emphasis lies elsewhere, in an investigation of the fissures of the national body. In acknowledging these historical fractures and tears she avers not only to the complexities of the contemporary Irish community, but to the continuing force of Ireland's fractured history in the present.

The Enigmatic Body

I see my audience very much as male. The voice is female, speaking mostly to be understood by men . . . I don't want men to underestimate women ever. I feel that if they do they will put us in a lower category where they have always put us. And I can only make them understand us, not by competing with them but by baffling them . . . and if they think they know the truth, I say, but the opposite is also true.[4]

McGuckian's use of language as a veil to both shield and represent an enigmatic femininity is brought into focus by a consideration of the poem 'Venus and the Rain'.[5] The poem is set out like a riddle; the various interpretations of the term 'Venus'—an ideal world of love and womanhood, an inhuman place unreached by man—jostle each other for predominance, until the equivocation almost produces the question 'What am I?' in the final stanza. The poem attempts a reversal of the usual relation of black ink to white page typical of the 'eternizing' Elizabethan sonnets: Venus paints 'White on white', is always pregnant, never producing her final statement. McGuckian describes the cloud of white vapours which obscure Venus from Earth:

White on white, I can never be viewed
Against a heavy sky—my gibbous voice
Passes from leaf to leaf, retelling the story
Of its own provocative fractures, till
Their facing coasts might almost fill each other
And they ask me in reply if I've
Decided to stop trying to make diamonds.

She (the speaker), is opening up something that from a distance seems complete, and setting it into a narrative, temporal brokenness—seducing or provoking the reader by fractures or gaps, promises of future significance. The discourse (or the speaker) on the one hand advances, discloses, and on the other holds back, conceals. Thus the poem becomes a dramatization of what McGuckian sees as the mystery of womanhood, which, like the planet Venus, cannot be encompassed by man. The planet can hardly be seen although it is more than half full, ('gibbous'); the pregnant woman empties herself of the male life-giving, contaminating water (she becomes 'less moon' as in the poem 'Next Day Hill'), as the planet moves behind the trees. Alternatively, passing 'from leaf to leaf' could be an image of raindrops dripping through the leaves of a tree. Moreover, her voice spreads across the pages (leaves) of the book, 'retelling' the narrative of

[4] Medbh McGuckian, personal interview (20 Nov. 1986).

[5] Medbh McGuckian, *Venus and the Rain* (Oxford: Oxford University Press, 1984), 31.

its wounds, as childbirth has torn the vulva, or events have fractured the consciousness. This narration may be retold in relation to a previous speaker who told a different story, or told and retold through the poems in the book. It is a process of healing, so that the lips of the vulva/the sides of the fractures on Venus may come together, and 'fill each other'. The speaker is awash with the effects of the rain (gendered male throughout the volume *Venus and the Rain*) which makes her pregnant with a child or the idea of a poem. The bringing forth of the child or poem (narration), acts as a release, allows Venus to close off from the male in order to report her experience. While this fusion of the 'facing coasts' seems to be fulfilling, it necessitates an end to the inner creation of 'diamonds', i.e. children or poems, which require a place for inspiration to enter, and which must be dug up or mined, causing fracturing:

> What the female part does is shut itself off from the male influence, in order to produce the created object. But once she's done that she needs to open herself to male influence in order to become impregnated with the poem.[6]

For McGuckian that shutting off is consonant with a masculinization of the woman. Again, in relation to 'The Rising Out' she speaks of the influence of the male on the woman (through pregnancy) as one which inhibits all creativity, and yet is the necessary seed which will produce the poetry in the end:

> You know, this whole poem was about the baby—my dream sister—it's about the poet being kindled in you, because I didn't write any poetry during the third pregnancy, and I felt that until the baby was born I wouldn't write again. So maybe I felt that the baby was turning me into a complete storm before I was ready or something. I was totally woman at that point, totally sea perhaps, and I had no link with the male world.

The masculinization of the woman might then be interpreted as her returning independence, or recovered autonomy, but it is an autonomy whose rationale is to present the female 'in all its complexity' to the male world, with which the woman now feels she is allied more closely. The second stanza of 'Venus and the Rain' presents an experience in hermeneutic terms (a miscarriage perhaps, or parturition). The personal experience is there to be

[6] McGuckian, personal interview (20 Nov. 1986).

interpreted, but its meaning is distanced by the poetic language. Moreover in a riddle the grammatical 'I' is not the real 'I', but the second stanza closes this distance. It is a 'real' riddle since the mystery seems to concern the speaker, not an external object:

> On one occasion, I rang like a bell
> For a whole month, promising their torn edges
> The birth of a new ocean (as all of us
> Who have hollow bodies tend to do at times)
> What clues to distance could they have,
> So self-exited by my sagging sea,
> Widening ten times faster than it really did?

'Distance' here may refer to the distance between the lips of the vulva, and the distance between men and the planet or woman Venus. The reader attempts to match each unit of the poem with a referent, but remains baffled by the idea that the 'sagging sea' can widen faster than it 'really' does (perhaps one referent here is the time difference between Earth and Venus), especially since this body seems to be 'hollow', not full of productivity. Any attempt to place a definite meaning on the lines (do they perhaps refer to thwarted or unfruitful inspiration?), necessarily entails omission of one element or another. The difficulty with pronouns and referents is compounded in the final stanza where it is unclear whether the 'rivers' are children, or perhaps menstrual blood.

> Whatever rivers sawed their present lairs
> Through my lightest, still warm rocks,
> I told them they were only giving up
> A sun for sun, that cruising moonships find
> Those icy domes relaxing, when they take her
> Rind to pieces, and a waterfall
> Unstitching itself down the front stairs.

Do the rivers make their way in or out of the body? The final stanza could perhaps be interpreted as an unsuccessful attempt to become pregnant again. Hence fluid (menstrual blood) leaves the body, in contradistinction to the first stanza in which Venus is 'gibbous' and full of male influence. This shedding entails giving up on the hope of a 'son', perhaps in order to have a relation with the sun outside the body—Apollo, god of poetry?—a drying, hence masculinizing influence. Venus admonishes the rivers for leaving her 'still warm' body, and reminds them that 'cruising moonships' (the investigatory male phallus, exploring the depths beneath the surface of the female moon, or ships which shine with the light of the body's internal sun?) find both that the 'icy domes' relax in their presence, and that they can relax in that realm, having passed through the external 'rind' of the planet/woman. They also seem to 'find' a waterfall, which may refer equally to orgasm or parturition. In one reading, the male entry of the body takes her 'to pieces' after her careful suturing of the body following childbirth, and this 'unstitching' produces a waterfall much greater than the slow dripping from leaf to leaf experienced earlier. Yet perhaps this excess of water is too great to allow Venus to narrate as she had been able to do during her return to independence and autonomy in the first stanza. In this case the rivers which saw their way out to the heat of the sun would finally be more productive.

It is plain, however, that this interpretation can not come near to the meaning of the poem, as it raises as many questions as it answers. Throughout the poem specific denotation is avoided; the reader is presented with a sequence of provocative half-truths or truths which seem to contradict one another, so that he or she is tempted to name the object without being able to do so. As Roland Barthes points out: 'A powerful enigma is a dense one, so that, providing certain precautions are taken, the more signs there are, the more the truth will be obscured, the harder one will try to figure it out.'[7] In this enigma, however, the solving of the mystery is not merely continually, but perpetually delayed. The 'truth' of woman is that, although she can be charted (as the planet Venus has been), she cannot be 'known' and thereby appropriated. The alternative narrative in McGuckian's poems is not perhaps a means of expressing female experience, but a way of resisting invasion. In poetic terms it consists of a resistance to objectification; the object remains elusive—as the moon changes—so it can not be fixed or 'killed' by an author-owner.

However, by setting herself up as the object for investigation, the mystery to be solved, is the woman not colluding in her own fetishization before the male gaze? The representation of woman

[7] Roland Barthes, *S/Z*, trans. Richard Miller (London: Jonathon Cape, 1975), 62.

'in all her complexity' for a male readership surely necessitates a re-presentation or alteration of the traditional images and symbols which normally surround her. As Irigaray points out in terms echoing Barthes's theory of hermeneutic 'veils':

> We must go on questioning words as the wrappings with which the 'subject', modestly clothes the 'female'. Stifled beneath all those eulogistic or denigratory metaphors, she is unable to unpick the seams of her disguise and indeed takes a certain pleasure in them, even gilding the lily further at times . . . For the imperious need for her shame, her chastity—duly fitted out with the belt of discourse—of her decent modesty, continues to be asserted by every man.[8]

Does the mere appropriation (and representation) of what Freud called the 'masquerade' of femininity disrupt and call into question the values which have been accredited to the female, or does this disruption depend on the intention of the female speaker? This touches on the problematic force of irony in McGuckian's work. Is the term 'diamonds' in 'Venus and the Rain' to be read as an ironization or subtle distancing of the proverbial woman's treasure, or perhaps as presenting the answer to the riddle of the 'truth' of femininity? As implied, an answer seems impossible to find, suggesting that a 'truth' or essence under the masquerade of femininity is illusory. The reader is invited to gaze, but the treasure is never handed over.[9]

My reading of 'Venus and the Rain' implies a tension in McGuckian's work between her wish to represent the self in order that it be more perfectly understood, and her wariness of opening herself up before the public. However, interpretations of McGuckian's work which focus exclusively on the autobiographical nature of the poems tend to ignore the extent to which McGuckian is restructuring the relationship between public and private narratives. The personal narrative becomes a metaphor

[8] Luce Irigaray, *Speculum of the Other Woman*, trans. Gillian C. Gill (Ithaca, NY: Cornell University Press, 1984), 142–3.

[9] For Irigaray, of course, it is precisely the representation of these terms from the standpoint of the object which sets the terms into question. In some respects her theory of 're-accenting' language by placing it in the mouth of the other, the woman, could be read as analogous to Bakhtin's concept of dialogism. For both theorists, parody is the relocation of someone else's words in a new frame, which makes visible the material base from which it springs. See Luce Irigaray, 'Is the Subject of Science Sexed', *Cultural Critique*, 1 (1985), 73–88.

for a public and political one. I will examine the way this coded, symbolic system works, by reading 'Dovecote' in the way that McGuckian has suggested in interview. By reading it in terms of a translation of private into public, I do not want to suggest that this is adequate to the meaning of the poem, but rather to show how this translation is *intended* to work, and to point out the obscurity of the metaphorical relation. McGuckian has stated that the poem is about the attempt of a woman to recover self-definition in body and mind after giving birth to the child which had occupied and to some extent 'taken over' her body. But she says it is also about the attempt of the Catholic community in Northern Ireland to recover or nurture its sense of self-definition during the Hunger Strike at Long Kesh in 1981:

> I built my dovecote all from the same tree
> To supplement the winter, and its wood
> So widely ringed, alive with knots, reminded me
> How a bow unstrung returns again to straight,
> How seldom compound bows are truly sweet.
>
> It's like being in a cloud that never rains,
> The way they rise above the storm, and sleep
> So bird-white in the sky, like day-old
> Infant roses, little unambitious roads,
> Islands not defecting, wanting to be rescued.
>
> Still I liked their manners better than
> The summer, I kept leaning to the boat-shaped
> Spirit of my house, whose every room
> Gives on to a garden, or a sea that knows
> You cannot reproduce in your own shade.
>
> Even to the wood of my sunflower chest,
> Or my kimono rack, I owed no older debt
> Than to the obligatory palette of the rain,
> That brought the soil back into tension on my slope,
> And the sea in, making me an island once again.[10]

Like a bow, the dovecote's beauty masks its ugly purpose. It is built in order to 'supplement' the winter, i.e. the doves are being fattened for slaughter. The dovecote becomes a symbol both of the woman's body which after childbirth 'returns again to straight', and of the desire of the woman, and the Irish community, to be

[10] Medbh McGuckian, 'Dovecote', in *Venus and the Rain*, 39.

'one' and undivided: it reminds her 'How seldom compound bows are truly sweet'. McGuckian has spoken of the hunger strikers at 'the mercy of their own people',[11] who used them in order to feed the patriotism which confirmed Ireland in its island, or 'boat-shaped' isolation. Here she describes the doves as innocent victims, continually circling in on their treacherous home, rather than taking their own direction (in a revision of the story of Noah's ark). The retreat into self-hood in the final stanza after the splitting of the body and the spirit in pregnancy, is imaged in terms of a rainfall (perhaps waters breaking), which enables her body to return to its former well-defined and self-sufficient shape.

But this recovery of self-definition is of course at the expense of the doves whose hovering trustfully over the dovecote was described as a 'cloud that never rains'. Self-definition for both the woman and the Catholic community is achieved by 'letting go' of the child/Strikers who were dependent on them for nurture. (In fact there is an asymmetry in the metaphor here since 'compound' in terms of the woman refers to the existence of the child within her, and in terms of the political narrative it seems most likely that it refers to the coexistence of Catholic and Protestant communities in Northern Ireland. Thus the sacrifice of the prisoners in Long Kesh in order to confirm the Catholic community in its nationalism is not an exact analogue of the letting go of the child in order to confirm the woman in her self-sufficiency—there is no third party in the case of the pregnant woman.)

The poem implies, among other things, that it is impossible to view public events except through the prism of subjective experience—the response to the events surrounding the Hunger Strikes is inseparable from the understanding of the personal experience of childbirth. In this way the private experience becomes generalized into a symbol for a more obviously 'public' experience (although, of course, the experience of childbirth is not absolutely particular, but one shared by many women, and in that sense it is already 'generalized'). However, there is a danger that the metaphor will not only work to translate a personal story into public and political terms, but that it will also work the other

[11] Medbh McGuckian, personal interview (10 Jan. 1986).

way around, to subjectivize the political events, thereby emptying them of their historical significance. But a still more intractable difficulty for both the poet and her critics is the fact that 'Dovecote' is not generally read as a poem with political subject-matter at all; it is only able to be read as commenting on the Hunger Strikes because of McGuckian's explanation of the political content of the poem, as there is nothing within the poem itself which would determine such a reading. Perhaps more in the case of McGuckian than in other less obscure poets, the meaning of her work depends entirely on how people are prepared to read her—more specifically her poems tend to be read in terms of a division between personal experience and public statement which they in fact are working to undermine, (i.e. they are judged in terms of criteria they are attempting to change.)[12] McGuckian's desire to explain the political content of her work in interviews and discussions may be viewed as the result of seeing the significance of her work limited by her audience's insistence on reading it purely in terms of its representation of personal and private experience. For both 'private' and political readings are determined, either by audience expectation or authorial explanation.

♀ and ♂

All my doors are entrances, with no exits. Understand?[13]

The repeated assertion of the poet's inability to disentangle personal and national histories may hinge on the ease with which the woman's mind and body can be invaded. This colonization of the woman, McGuckian implies, takes place not only on the level of political and mythic discourse (Ireland as a raped woman) but also on the level of familial relations where the woman's self is in continual danger of annihilation through fulfilling the needs of parents, husband, and children. Rarely, in her collection *On Ballycastle Beach*, are the doors into and out of her body pulled

[12] See Alan Jenkins, 'Hearts in the Right Place', rev. of Medbh McGuckian, *On Ballycastle Beach*, in *Observer* (10 July 1988), 33.

[13] Marina Tsvetaeva, letter to Boris Pasternak, in Yevgeny Pasternak, Yelena Pasternak, and Konstantin M. Azadovsky (eds.), *Letters Summer 1926: Correspondence between Pasternak, Tsvetayeva, Rilke* (Oxford: Oxford University Press, 1988), 179.

shut. 'Ill-closed doors' let in 'Brown Guests' of sensuality, as well as the thoughts and dreams of which new poems are made.[14] And while such openness is a guard against sterility of thought ('None of my doors has slammed like that') the gestation of those thoughts requires closure. In 'The Time Before You' the body's mouths are shut against invasion by 'foreign bodies' as much as against emissions in order that 'new' communication may take place:

> I wish they could hear
>
> That we lived in one room
> And littered a new poetry
> Long after both doors, up
> And downstairs, shut.[15]

All this might imply that women have a harder time of it in clearing a 'space' in which to create, and thus open McGuckian to the charge of a naïve biologism. But she is at pains to point out the positive aspects of what she designates metaphorically the 'rooted' nature of women's creativity.

Throughout *On Ballycastle Beach* McGuckian notes a gender difference in the political and poetic relationship of the writer to his or her place. She sees in this difference the sign of two diverging aesthetics, which she relates to a sociological and cultural difference between male and female. The poem 'For a Young Matron' (which she says was written for Paul Muldoon's American wife, the poet Jean Hanff Korelitz) notes the difference between Muldoon's 'leavings' (which are both metaphorically important in his poems, and also biographically important since he has left the North of Ireland first for the Republic followed by a brief stay in England, and then emigration to the United States), and the more 'grounded' nature of a woman's creativity, imaged in terms of plantation and growth. The poem contrasts the continual return of the woman to an image or a language with which to make a 'space' for creativity, with the phallic aero-

[14] In the same way it is the sexual activity of the sea whose 'carpentry' saws the ship open in 'Lighthouse with Dead Leaves'. The lighthouses which 'spring to mind' appear then both as phallic symbols and as saviours from the sea of sensuality.

[15] Medbh McGuckian, *On Ballycastle Beach* (Oxford: Oxford University Press, 1988), 45.

plane's ability to transport space inside it to a new place (in Muldoon's case, this might refer to his importation of images from his home town, the Moy, into the more cosmopolitan traditions of British and American poetry):

> Why not forget this word,
> He asks. It's edgeless,
> Echoless, it is stretched so,
> You cannot become its passenger.
>
> An aeroplane unlike
> A womb claims its space
> And takes it with it.
> It says, Once it wasn't like this.
>
> But wood grows
> Like the heart worn thin
> Within us, or the original
> Spirit of October.[16]

In part this opposition between the circle of home and the linear trajectory of leaving is an ironic commentary on the gendered nature of poetic exile. As in 'Balakhana' the arrows and circles suggest male and female symbols, colonizing sperm, and receptive wombs. Significantly, in the light of many of the poems in *Venus and the Rain* these symbols were originally the astrological signs for Mars and Venus.[17] But despite the biologistic metaphors, the poem, and the collection as a whole, may be arguing not that the woman's link to place is necessarily dependent on her sex, but that because of her social position (as a mother with young children) the tradition of exile among male Irish writers is not available to the female writer. Exile is not the way for her to create new possibilities—hence her continual return to the same images, to her own body, as the place from which new things can grow. For though women may occupy a displaced position in relation to ownership of land and language, they are none the less tied to their place through their families.

[16] Ibid. 41.

[17] It seems that the characteristics of the planet Venus which largely contributed to the fact that she was gendered female are her whiteness, and the fact that she disappears during the day, to appear only at night and in the morning (as McGuckian notes in the poem 'Scattering'). Her female gender then is defined in terms of sexual activity, rather than her capacity to mother. In fact Venus the goddess was a notoriously bad mother.

As McGuckian wryly points out, 'None of my removals | Was in any sense a flight' (p. 42). Perhaps then the only option for women seeking authority is to plant 'seeds' and wait for them to grow. McGuckian's often repeated metaphor of growth and plantation works ironically to suggest a wholly female mode of repossession of land lost to the indigenous population during the Ulster Plantation.

Dream-Language

i
Your tongue has spent the night
In its dim sack as the shape of your foot
In its cave. Not the rudiment
Of half a vanquished sound,
The excommunicated shadow of a name,
Has rumpled the sheets of your mouth.

ii
So Latin sleeps, they say, in Russian speech,
So one river inserted into another
Becomes a leaping, glistening, splashed
And scattered alphabet
Jutting out from the voice,
Till what began as a dog's bark
Ends with bronze, what began
With honey ends with ice;
As if an aeroplane in full flight
Launched a second plane,
The sky is stabbed by their exits
And the mistaken meaning of each.

iii
Conversation is as necessary
Among these familiar campus trees
As the apartness of torches;
And if I am a threader
Of double-stranded words, whose
Quando has grown into now,
No text can return the honey
In its path of light from a jar,
Only a seed-fund, a pendulum,
Pressing out the diasporic snow.[18]

[18] McGuckian, *On Ballycastle Beach*, 57.

'For a Young Matron' suggests that the relation to place has not simply biographical importance, but has implications for the construction of poetic method. More specifically, the poem 'Balakhana' asks us to appreciate the relation between McGuckian's rootedness and the growing Europeanization of her work, consonant with the political hopes for the North in Europe. And again it is in woman's openness and receptivity that these possibilities lie: 'The door I found | So difficult to close let in my first | European feeling'. In part McGuckian's interest in poetry's European feelings can be read through her engagement with the theories of Hellenism and poetic method put forward by Osip Mandelstam. Her poem 'The Dream-Language of Fergus' is almost entirely constructed out of quotations from his essays, most obviously 'Conversation about Dante', 'About the Nature of the Word', and 'Notes About Poetry'.[19] McGuckian's conversation with Mandelstam occurs as his phrases, placed in the context of her poem and reorganized by her, are pulled towards new meanings, while still retaining a sense of their original implications. The borrowed material, once 'transplanted', takes on altered significance as Mandelstam's discussion of the nature of Dante's classicism, or the European nature of the Russian language, are placed in the service of thoughts about a child's language acquisition, and the history of language in Ireland. Moreover this process of layering meanings on to phrases, altering their direction by altering their context, constructs at the same time a further layer, concerned with a discussion of McGuckian's habitual circling and inconclusive narratives, and her borrowing, 'translating' method.[20] Her 'conversation' through

[19] See Mandelstam, *Selected Essays*, 3–44, 65–79, 80–4. The references to 'Conversation about Dante' were brought to my notice by Meva Maron's letter to the Editor, *Honest Ulsterman*, 88 (Winter 1989–90), 33–4.

[20] Although she relies on a published translation, McGuckian's repetition of Mandelstam's words performs a 'translation' in the sense delineated by Marina Tsvetaeva as she describes her 'rewriting' of Rilke: 'Today I would like Rilke to speak—through me. In everyday language this is called translation. (How much better the Germans put it—*nachdichten*! Following in the poet's footsteps, to lay again the path he has already laid. Let *nach* mean follow, but *dichten* always has new meaning. *Nachdichten*—laying anew a path, all traces of which are instantaneously grown over.) But "translate"' has another meaning: to translate not only into (into Russian, for example) but also to (to the opposite bank of the river). I will translate Rilke into Russian and he, in time, will translate me to the other world' (Pasternak *et al.* (eds.), *Letters Summer 1926*, 4-5).

images thus becomes not only a dialogue with Mandelstam, and with her child, but also with the reader about how the poems are constructed, and how meaning may be released from them.

A number of the views Mandelstam puts forward in his essays are congenial to McGuckian's poetic method. 'Conversation about Dante', although in part a plea for a less scholarly, more immediate response to Dante's poetry, is also in more general terms an argument against the habit of reading poetry for its semantic value. Rather than an affair of the intellect, poetry happens at the 'crossing of two lines': the manipulation of the 'instruments of poetic speech' (i.e. verbal representations) and that of 'the speech proper' (i.e. intonation). Without a just mixture of these two properties, Mandelstam argues, poetry is reduced either to muteness or to paraphrase. 'Where one finds commensurability with paraphrase, there the sheets have not been rumpled; there poetry has not, so to speak, spent the night.'[21] Mandelstam's insistence on the marriageability of form and content relates to his argument about poetic 'convertibility' or 'transformability', which he finds exemplified by Dante's method in *The Divine Comedy*. Poetic speech is not linear but characterized by swift indirect motions; one image grows out of another, creating a crystallographic structure rather than one of preconceived form. It is in this context that Mandelstam introduces his resonant images of complex, non-linear jouneying, such as a ship's tacking course, or, more famously, his prefiguration of the space shuttle:

> It is only by convention that the development of an image can be called development. Indeed, imagine to yourself an airplane (forgetting the technical impossibility) which in full flight constructs and launches another machine. In just the same way, this second flying machine, completely absorbed in its own flight, still manages to assemble and launch a third—the assembly and launching of these technically unthinkable machines that are sent flying off in the midst of flight do not constitute a secondary or peripheral function of the plane that is in flight; they form a most essential attribute and part of the flight itself.[22]

Both the warning against the impulse to paraphrase, and the description of the swift convertibility of images, which are yet integral to the whole, are useful tools with which to approach a

[21] Mandelstam, *Selected Essays*, 3. [22] Ibid. 19.

reading of McGuckian's poetry. The importance of meaning arriving by oblique and circuitous routes is crucial to an understanding of even her earliest work, which continually stresses the inappropriateness of 'naming' or fixing the poetic object in language.[23] On a more literal level, it is clear that Mandelstam's images of planes and ships have an important function throughout the volume *On Ballycastle Beach.* And yet reading 'The Dream-Language of Fergus' in terms of Mandelstam involves the critic in a contradictory exercise. For Mandelstam argues against precisely this habit of digging for meaning by tracing literary allusions or symbolic equivalences, while ignoring the poem as 'event'. In the reading of the poem which follows I suggest that McGuckian situates meaning 'between' the source text (which is in fact an argument against tracing a semantic 'thread' in poetry), and the 'new' text, her own poem.[24]

In addition to his stress on the internal construction of Dante's poem through the convertibility of images, Mandelstam lays emphasis on the labial nature of the Italian language, the way in which the poetry as speech draws attention to the tongue against the lips, and pressed against the roof of the mouth. And he relates this to the 'infantile quality of Italian phonetics, its beautiful childlike quality, its closeness to infant babbling, a sort of immemorial Dadaism'.[25] It is, he claims, this rhythmic quality which allows Dante to experiment with 'transsense' (*zaum*) language. McGuckian's poem takes the hint about the relationship

[23] e.g. the poem 'Catching Geese' is built around a series of circlings and disappearances. The title is a reference to the difficulty of holding things down long enough to 'catch' them in language, as it echoes the phrase 'If you wish to write, first catch your goose' (meaning you need a quill pen). The speaker faces a similar difficulty in holding things down when it comes to the actual objects in her poem, but she is brought to the rescue by Gertrude Stein's theory of metaphor, as the poem gestures towards the famous sentence 'A rose is a rose is a rose'. Clear definition of this 'letter-perfect rose' is achieved by writing 'about', i.e. around, it: 'All I had to do to hold the sentence still | Was paint it on the circumference of a plate | And every sound of you crying could be heard.'

[24] This is a general strategy in McGuckian's work. She continually posits a tension between what is inside or outside the subject. The poems imply a private meaning, which may be unlocked by finding the key to certain correspondences between body and polity, or by discovering the source (such as Heaney or Yeats) to which the text alludes. But, as in 'Dovecote' the veiled meaning is often the one with obvious public relevance.

[25] Mandelstam, *Selected Essays*, 5.

between the living word of poetry, the enunciating mouth, and a child's language, and places Mandelstam's phrases within the context of a poem about the 'dream-language' of her third child, Fergus. Yet the dream-language presented in the poem is her own, and so the words become a disquisition on her 'transsensual' or 'paralogic' poetic method. And in a further move (like a plane launching another plane), the phrases relate to the question of the dispossession of Irish Catholics and the loss of the Irish language as a 'living tongue'. As Freud describes the mechanism of the dream-work, McGuckian's poem brings together divergent ideas and phrases, displacing them from their original meaning and context, and condensing layers of meaning in a single word.

The link between the child's language acquisition and the history of the language in Ireland is prepared for by a poem earlier in *On Ballycastle Beach*, 'A Dream in Three Colours'. The title suggests at first the tricolor, but the words of the Irish language exist in 'scattered rooms', 'like pearls that have lost their clasp'. The language has no 'hold' and it appears that the child's dream will be shattered by introduction into the syntax of the English language, symbolized by the three colours red, white, and blue:

> Far more raw than the spring night
> Which shook you out of its sleeve,
> Your first winter sheds for you
> Its strongest blue, its deepest white,
> Its reddest silk lapel you can let go
> Or hold, whichever you love best.[26]

The child will learn an 'alien' mother tongue, and thereby experience a separation by implication greater than that in which he was separated from her body in childbirth. And yet the final lines suggest that the child retains an element of choice in relation to his mother tongue. Even if the discourse of the tricolor has lost its hold, the child can choose whether or not to reject the Union Jack. McGuckian has said that she feels a sense of lack of power in relation to the English language: 'I'm very aware that I'm using a kind of foreign language, or that I'm using it in a colonial way'.[27] But the poem suggests that future generations (perhaps by being more European) may have the opportunity to side-step

[26] Medbh McGuckian, 'A Dream in Three Colours', in *On Ballycastle Beach*.
[27] McGuckian, personal interview (20 Nov. 1986).

the monologic power and authority of the imposed English language.

In 'The Dream-Language of Fergus' the child's muteness is related, via the Mandelstam texts, to the muteness of paraphraseable poetry, and to the question of the interpenetration of languages, texts, and images. While for Mandelstam the 'unrumpled sheets' suggest a lack of poetic speech, in McGuckian's poem it is speech itself which is absent from the 'cave' of the mouth (or possibly from the mouth of the body still lying in the 'cave' of the womb). A dream-language is by definition silent, but the language which is absent is not merely missing, rather it has been banished, 'vanquished', and 'excommunicated'. In this sense the Irish language is 'Roman' (Latin) because of its association with Catholicism. To be excommunicated means losing your link with Rome, a link which the poem attempts to reconstruct through the use of Roman numerals. And yet the notion of excommunication from language has a wider resonance in Mandelstam's essay 'About the Nature of the Word' (which is also directly quoted from in the third stanza of McGuckian's poem). Mandelstam employs the term in his discussion of the Hellenic nature of the Russian language—the force of the word in poetry lies not in its denotative capacities (as the Futurists maintain), nor in its ability to stand as figure for something other than itself (as the Symbolists argue), but in its status as image or verbal representation. And the ability of words in the Russian language to act as humanized domestic 'utensils' rather than functional 'objects' arises from its complex and rich history, the depth and multiple branching of root meanings in Russian. So, for the poet, 'Excommunication from the language has for us a force equal to that of excommunication from history'.[28] The notion of a breach in the continuity of Irish history due to the suppression of the Irish language has of course been a resonant one in Irish poetry. In McGuckian's poem the lost mother tongue is given almost literal representation in the mute tongue

[28] Mandelstam, *Selected Essays*, 70. In other words the Hellenic or Classical (for which McGuckian seems to read 'European') nature of Russian arises not out of its ability to translate the Classics, but precisely out of its Russianness. So McGuckian's poem directly contradicts her source which states, 'It is untrue that Latin sleeps in Russian speech, untrue that Hellas sleeps in it . . . Only Russian speech sleeps in Russian speech' (p. 82).

of the child, and yet the conversation which the poem presents is in part a dialogue with the child, suggesting that communication does take place and the poem itself can act to suture that historical breach. (In this sense the poem, like 'For a Young Matron' constitutes not a rejection so much as a reinflection of the traditional trope of femininity, the motherland, as the true linguistic home of the Irish poet.)

In addition the poem may well nod towards Seamus Heaney's theorization of 'The Government of the Tongue' which also draws on Mandelstam's essay 'Conversation About Dante'. Heaney explains his title as concerned with poetry 'as its own vindicating force. In this dispensation, the tongue (representing both a poet's personal gift of utterance and the common resources of language itself) has been granted the right to govern.'[29] Yet the tongue is also 'governed', both politically and personally, through poetic reticence. McGuckian draws together this notion of poetry's power to create new possibilities in the realm of language and imagination, dream-language which may represent a different order, with the notion of the government (domination and submission) of international tongues. And in the brilliant resolution to her poem the possibility which the poetic tongue prefigures is the creation of a new mother tongue for the child.

The majority of the phrases in the second and third stanzas are 'borrowed' from 'Conversation About Dante'. And in this sense McGuckian seems to have taken on not merely Mandelstam's ideas about the construction of poems out of circling images rather than a semantically ordered narrative, but also his belief that in order to create poetry for the future artists must return to the past by a sensitivity to the philological weight of words (since philology necessitates tracing the path of a word's meaning through the quotation and citation of previous texts). Her poem is thus a double-stranded conversation with the previous author. But as my analogy with the dream-work suggests, it is misguided to look for an interpretation (as opposed to a reconfiguration) of Mandelstam's prose in McGuckian's poem.

The complexity of McGuckian's 'transplanting' method may

[29] See Seamus Heaney, *The Government of the Tongue* (London: Faber and Faber, 1988), 92. See also the essay 'Osip and Nadezhda Mandelstam' in the same vol., 71–88.

be revealed by examining in detail the origins and final destinations of the phrases in the third stanza. The first phrase directs us to Mandelstam's interpretation of Dante's 'cave' at the beginning of Canto 10 of *The Inferno*: 'Every effort is directed towards the struggle against the density and gloom of the place. Lighted shapes break through like teeth. Conversation is as necessary here as torches in a cave'.[30] On one level the poem transmutes Mandelstam/Dante's cave into the cave of the child's mouth in the first stanza; the absence of language is symbolized by the absence of teeth which dates the age of the child. The simultaneous growth of teeth and language is gestured towards in the images of pearls which echo in several poems. So the 'pearls' of language in 'A Dream in Three Colours' reappear in 'The Sky Marshall':

> At the stress-points of a shell
> Grows a little grey pearl
> The shape of a child's tooth
> Aged sixteen months and asleep.[31]

Teeth, then, represent both the growth of a child and the importance of the performing impulse in poetry, the speaking mouth. In addition McGuckian's dream-language may be read as overlaying Mandelstam's image of the necessary distance and definition produced by the conversation of images, with her own activity as Writer in Residence at Queen's University, Belfast. And yet the phrase 'familiar campus trees' is itself 'borrowed' from the essay 'About the Nature of the Word', as is the notion of the poet as 'threader' of words. McGuckian sews Mandelstam's text together like a patchwork, but following through the implications of the 'dream' construction of the poem necessitates an investigation of the underlying thought represented in these words. In the original they are associated with notions of domesticity, privacy, and the intimacy of poetic style, as well as an interest in philology and the history of the language (through references to the writer Rozanov). Mandelstam writes,

> Literature is a social phenomenon; philology is a domestic phenomenon, of the study. Literature is a public lecture, the street; philology is a university seminar, the family. Yes, just so, a university seminar where five

[30] Mandelstam, *Selected Essays*, 8.

[31] Medbh McGuckian, 'The Sky Marshall', in *On Ballycastle Beach*.

students who know each other and call each other by first name and patronymic listen to the professor, while the branches of familiar campus trees stretch toward the window.[32]

To continue the catalogue of allusions, McGuckian seems to be bringing together Mandelstam's notion of the timelessness of Dante's metaphors, with his emphasis on the living text. Mandelstam describes the way in which Dante's art contributes to 'the standing still of time. Its root is not in the little word how, but in the word when. His quando sounds like come.' This timelessness is also conjured forth in Mandelstam's reference to Foucault's pendulum. Of the density of the musical timbre of Canto 33 of the *Inferno* he states, 'There exists no power on earth which could hasten the movement of honey flowing from a tilted glass jar', and of Dante's visual perception he notes 'the really remarkable staged experiment with the candle and the three mirrors, where it is demonstrated that the return path of light has as its source the refraction of the ray'. Finally Mandelstam makes a distinction between 'cereals which are eaten and done away with' and 'a seed-fund which is reserved, inviolable, and which constitutes as it were, the property of a time that is unborn but must come'.[33]

Having 'placed' the phrases of McGuckian's poem in Mandelstam's text, they must now be 'replaced', sewn back into the poem. The interest of these passages for the critic of McGuckian lies not primarily in their significance for the argument of the source text, but in their function in the new lines. And yet the function cannot be entirely dissociated from its source. For Mandelstam is arguing that the semantics of poetry should centre on the depth of 'the word' rather than the narrative. The necessary 'domesticity' of the Russian language for poetry derives from its rich and complex family history, a genealogical tree which is to be traced through the quotation and citation of texts. There is thus a similarity between the word in philology and the language of dream, as both depend on the layering and condensing of meaning in a single image. There is an interesting parallel here with Roland Barthes's theory of modern (post-1848) poetry (which I discuss in greater detail in relation to Muldoon's work). Barthes similarly argues for the depth

[32] Mandelstam, *Selected Essays*, 71.

[33] Ibid, 42, 36, 31, 29, 27.

and 'density' of the word in poetry, but for him it is precisely the absence of relations (familial or otherwise), the fact that it has cut its ties with its antecedents, which lends the word its freedom: 'Fixed connections being abolished, the Word is left only with a vertical project, it is like a monolith, or a pillar which plunges into a totality of meanings, reflexes and recollections.'[34] In a more general sense, however, there is fundamental agreement between these theories of the poetic word. For it is precisely because the structure of the narrative, or relational discourse, in which the word is set has receded in importance, that other relations come into play. McGuckian's poem, and her work as a whole, constructs this kind of semantics—the word must be investigated at a variety of different depths, and its complexity depends on the reader's awareness of its meaning in other texts and contexts. This is not to say that the words do not achieve self-sufficiency—McGuckian translates Mandelstam's image of the domesticity of poetic language into the arena of actual family relationships, a conversation between mother and child. The notion of a reserve for the future seems to be incarnated in the child in McGuckian's poem which works as a principle of condensation, a figuration of the living text. Yet despite the implication that the true text exists only in performance, that poetic material has no voice on the page, McGuckian's conversation with Mandelstam through and between images *does* take place through a text (and the child's voice remains silent). In this sense McGuckian's text *is* a 'seed-fund', a nursery where new seedlings are grafted on to old roots to create a new plantation.

One reading of McGuckian's reworking of the diverse strands of European culture into an alternative vision of generation in Northern Ireland might claim she is putting forward an argument for a more comprehensive national identity—one determined by boundaries other than Ireland's binary relationship with England. Yet it would, I believe, be mistaken to associate her position too closely with postmodern discussions of the fragmentary nature of the Irish community. For the recurrent implication of McGuckian's work is not so much that contemporary social changes will be instrumental in overcoming entrenched

[34] See Roland Barthes, *Writing Degree Zero*, trans. Annette Lavers and Colin Smith, ed. Susan Sontag (originally published 1953; New York: Hill and Wang, 1968), 47.

differences between alternative cultural traditions in Northern Ireland, but that the conflictual history of those traditions can work as a disruptive force in the present. Hence her emphasis on the women of the past, such as the figure of the grandmother, who stands both as a sign of historical continuity, and as a reminder of the radical possibilities inherent within the arena of domesticity. As in 'Dream-Language', in the early poem 'The Seed Picture' new plants are formed from old (linguistic and familial) roots. Seeds are gathered from many and various sources, but this diversity is not offered purely as a result of contemporary social changes since it grows from the disparate and eclectic elements of the past; moreover, in order for it to continue, the link with the historical body must be mantained:

> Was it such self-indulgence to enclose her
> In the border of a grandmother's sampler,
> Bonding all the seeds in one continuous skin . . . ?[35]

Historical continuity is predicated on dissonance, and, as I will argue below, that dissonance is in itself found to be integral to the corporeal and social world of women.

Plane Sailing

Throughout my reading of McGuckian's work I have emphasized her representation of the maternal body, and the mother's relation with the child, as a form of corporeality which can be mapped on to history. The temptation might be to interpret this as a representation of feminine continuity which can reveal the gender gaps in the nationalist interpretation of history; however, rather than purity or wholeness, maternal and familial relationships in McGuckian's work are associated with violence, loss, and discontinuity. Familial, and by implication national, communities are stitched and sewn together out of the fragments of torn and dislocated bodies. Thus the poetry is claiming far more than that the narratives of Irish women in history need to be taken into account (though it is also claiming this); indeed, it suggests that

[35] Medbh McGuckian, 'The Seed Picture', in *The Flower Master* (Oxford: Oxford University Press, 1982), 23. See also 'Sabbath Park' (*Venus and the Rain*, 54–5), in which the woman again finds liberation in 'growing' through the embroidered flowers of the Victorian woman's buried garments.

the maternal and national relations mirror one another in their fragmented structure. But if the relationship between mother and child is characterized above all by *lack of connection*, how then is the viewpoint of the child to be included in the picture?

'Dream-Language' seems to some extent to undercut the opposition set up in 'For a Young Matron' between the grounded, circular womb-like nature of a woman's creativity, and the stabbing 'exits' deemed characteristic of male productivity. Circling back on the past, through quotation and repetition, may also be the means to create for the future.[36] Here again, the emphasis is on the links between maternity and the structure of Irish history. Yet the poem raises the problem of the poet's abdication of a place in the tradition for the sake of the child. There is a danger that all hopes and possibilities will be invested in the future; the woman will resign her place in a transformed nation in favour of her children. One recent poem which seems to reverse this pattern, symbolizing legitimation and authoritative repossession for the daughter rather than the mother is 'On Ballycastle Beach'.

The volume *On Ballycastle Beach* is divided into two parts; the first seems preoccupied with the characteristics of sea and sky, while the second is more concerned with the twin themes of travel and territory. But what at first sight seems a radical shift in concerns is in fact more of a progression since sea and sky are 'homes' to planes and ships. So the book is both a two-part mirror, which folds the meanings up inside itself ('my sky-blue portfolio'), and it can also be read for its oblique narrative, which progresses through the two halves. The story charts the course of a woman/ship; the first poem evokes 'ships and their wind-blown ways' and these often indirect ways are followed until the ship sails 'in to harbour' in the title poem at the end. Here the words 'homeless' and 'homesick' suggest that this constitutes a return, a reclamation of the land:

> I found you wandering round the edge
> Of a French-born sea, when children
> Should be taken in by their parents,

[36] In the same way in the poem 'Balakhana' it is her message which flies while her body stays put. The title means 'mezzanine' or 'in between place' suggesting a compromise between the security of an enclosed and inward-looking world, and simply leaving it for another.

I would read these words to you,
Like a ship coming in to harbour,
As meaningless and full of meaning
As the homeless flow of life
From room to homesick room.[37]

As the words 'taken in' imply, this reconstruction of home is facilitated as much by the children's gullibility as by the parents' tolerance. The ship's steadfast journey is opposed, throughout the volume, by the sudden, sharp flights of aeroplanes, wings, and birds, symbolizing breaks in the circle of place and home: 'the sky is stabbed by their exits'. The concatenation of flights through the book contains an ironic gesture towards that (this time an escape) of the Earls, which left the land free for the seventeenth-century plantation of Ulster:

And one arrangement of matter
Is the castle where O'Neill slept

His last night in Ireland, the other
Is the view at which Byron
Never tired of gazing.[38]

Byron, a true European, chose to join, and died for, a republican cause which was not his own; on the other hand, if the Earls fled or 'flew' by ship from the Continent to the north coast of Ireland, McGuckian is sailing determinedly back to it to plant a 'seed-fund' of words. She has said of the poem 'On Ballycastle Beach' that it was written for her father who comes from that coast in the far north of Ireland, but has been displaced and urbanized through the move to Belfast. The title may also contain an ironic reference to Yeats's play *On Baile's Strand*. It is on the beach that the seemingly childless Cuchulain kills his own son who has sailed to Ireland, thereby ensuring his inheritance will be broken up.[39] In contrast, in McGuckian's poem it is the daughter who arrives (from a 'French born' sea, i.e. from the land to which the Earls fled), to reclaim her father's inheritance. Again it is through the domestic, familial relation, but this time as a child

[37] Medbh McGuckian, 'On Ballycastle Beach', in *On Ballycastle Beach*.

[38] Medbh McGuckian, 'The Bird Auction', ibid.

[39] See W. B. Yeats, *On Baile's Strand*, in *Collected Plays* originally published (1934; London: Macmillan, 1953), 247–78.

rather than as a parent, that McGuckian will plant the seeds of the new European polity.

Lyrical Waves

The integral relation between poetic voice (sound and music) and the bodies of mother and child is at the heart too of McGuckian's most recent collection, *Marconi's Cottage*. As in *On Ballycastle Beach* the voice is represented as corporeal and grounded, but none the less as European rather than exclusively Irish. Engaging with the tradition of European lyric poetry is clearly of abiding importance to her, but whereas in *On Ballycastle Beach* this signalled, through the language of flags and national tongues, the political possibilities for Ireland outside a relationship with Britain, *Marconi's Cottage* is more concerned with the nature of the poetic gift and the value of poetry itself. The Europeans most in evidence are Tsvetaeva (the poet who, in spirit if not in form, McGuckian most resembles), Mandelstam, Rilke, and, of course, Marconi, who is to some extent given honorary status as a poet in this volume. Why Marconi? Well, his mother was half-Irish, and he married an Irish woman, but, more importantly, in 1898 in a two-roomed rudimentary cottage in Ballycastle, he experimented with sending radio waves across the sea to Rathlin Island. The cottage, then, is not symbolic but real, and McGuckian really owns it. And why a poet? Much of the symbolism in this book is again concerned with images of seas and houses: chaos and nature as opposed to civilization, order, art, and meaning. Marconi's harnessing of electro-magnetic waves suggests a means of communicating between these two principles, as also between body and spirit, and from soul to soul. To some extent the wave theory is offered ironically as a kind of technological advance on Tsvetaeva's 'lyrical wires', through which, while in Germany, she dreamed of communication with Pasternak in Russia. Many of the poems in *Marconi's Cottage* are concerned with the possibility of dreams and intuitive understanding between women—one of the striking departures for McGuckian in this book is the prevalence of female addressees—foetus, daughter, mother, and other writers.

The collection can be roughly divided into three parts: an initial sequence of poems focuses on the conflict between motherhood and artistic creativity—the claims of differing types of fertility. This is followed by a sequence celebrating the birth of a daughter, and a series of uplifting poems asserting the productivity of both types of creation and affirming the mutual articulation of the poetic and the quotidian. Any interpretation of these complex and difficult poems will necessarily be partial and subjective, but guidelines are given, not only through the by now familiar use of a shaping, albeit plastic, symbolism, but also through what appear to be certain key references. Among others, there are pointers to Patrick Kavanagh, to Sylvia Plath, to Mandelstam's poem 'Silentium' and Rilke's 'Requiem for a Friend'.

To take this last example, Rilke seems to be important partly because of his own ambiguous sexual upbringing (his mother dressed him in skirts and called him Sophie until he was two), and partly because of his sympathy with women artists, 'handicapped' by their femininity. 'Requiem' was written in memory of the artist Paula Modersohn Becker, who died in childbirth—in it the death of the true artist is imaged as the breaking of a mirror through motherhood, rendering her unable to 'close' herself and re-create the perfect, disinterested reflection of the world back to itself. McGuckian discusses the complex gendering of the artist in several poems (for example 'Visiting Rainer Maria' and 'To Call Paula Paul'), and laments the damage that fertility can do to the mirror: 'A thin rain borrowed my silver', rendering her mere glass. But she also tries to count the cost of the preservation of the circular, self-reflecting mirror which cannot countenance the woman's desire to become a mirror for others, specifically by bearing children. So 'Journal Intime' (a kind of bodily diary) images the womb as Plato's cave containing an imagined child, or perhaps an as yet unconceived foetus:

I am a Platonic admirer of her
Flowing Watteau gowns, the volume
Of Petrarch in her lap. It is so
Unthinkable she should look outward
From the depressed, pink light of her
One-time nursery, if only to dilate
Upon the same two faces, if only, upon the snow.

In a child's first (and most satisfying)
House, where everyone is repeated

In everyone else, the door that is so light
To her, so dark to us, is wise enough
To dream through. Her voice fills the mouth
Of her own mirror, as if she were a failure:
As if, what is lifelike, could be true.

As is clear from these lines, McGuckian's poem is a 'translation' in more ways than one—not simply of Rilke's images into her own terms, but of ordinary objects and everyday events into an 'otherworldy' realm. Not only the poet's body, but the objects with which she engages (which she mirrors) are given back to the world as strangers, foreign bodies, or unrecognizable reflections. The charge that this is narcissistic or self-obsessed writing, interested only in the vagaries of the lyrical 'I', needs therefore to be put into perspective. It cannot be denied that McGuckian likes to 'explain' her poems as the pages torn out of a diary, or as personal letters sent to those around her, and in particular to other poets (hence her interest in 'lyrical waves'). But the poetry itself steadfastly refuses to be read in such a way, not only because it repeatedly signals its creative engagement with the tradition of European poetry, but also because the self, which is deemed to structure the work, is in fact all but destroyed by it. McGuckian's lyrical 'I' is continually changing shape, parcelled out in a dialogue between mother and child, masculine and feminine principles or parts of the self (German and Russian help her here, because of their linguistic gendering of objects), even between a heart on the left and one on the right, since pregnancy gives a woman 'two hearts'. While all this could be construed simply as the exploration of a divided psyche, at a more fundamental level questions are being posed about the nature of home. Home may indeed be where we start from but, for McGuckian, it is always insecure, invaded, and disrupted: 'a horizontal cutting | That has always already begun.' To read this as autobiographical poetry, obscurely concerned with domestic life, mistakes the extent to which the home, the family, the mother tongue, and the nation are each torn away from their traditional representations and scattered into wild and undomesticated elements. The continual discovery of improper behaviour and impure forms within the very foundation of these structures (the mother's body) requires us once more to rethink the opposition between groundedness and exile. Rather than a celebration of maternal nature, the reader is continually confronted with the prior colonization of this space, as the discovery of an origin is perpetually delayed. Moreover, the overwhelming tone is one of affirmation of this internal exile, and a refusal to ignore its violence. 'The Unplayed Rosalind', for example, reminds us that 'I have lived on a war footing'. The poem finds the bloody evidence of that war, as well as culture's other product, writing, in the most natural, the most intimate of spheres—the womb:

> The room which I thought the most beautiful
> In the world, and never showed to anyone,
> Is a rose-red room, a roseate chamber.
> It lacks two windowpanes and has no waterjug.
> There is red ink in the inkwell.[40]

McGuckian shares with Muldoon a deep-rooted suspicion of myths of origin, but where Muldoon undermines their power by substituting for them multiple possible origins in language and culture, McGuckian emphasizes the internally disrupted nature of the first relation—the child with its mother. The 'natural' or 'whole' state eludes even the womb, which is bound up with representation from the start. The oppositions between nature and culture, house and sea, order and chaos are never stable; the interpenetration between them is recognized in the triumphant title-poem, with its glancing reference to Marconi's work: 'It is as if the sea had spoken in you | And then the words had dried'. The house, a place of meaning, is both formative of, and formed by, the inchoate disorder of the waves. Electro-magnetic waves are an apt image for McGuckian here since not only do they represent a kind of dry fluidity (avoiding the problems of becoming awash with rain or sea) but they also carry sound—the music and voice from which poetry is created. Many of the poems contain images of the substance of the atmosphere, and the tangibility of sound—the new-born child is 'deluged with the dustless air', and in 'Oval of a Girl' the child,

> might just as well have been water
> Breaking and mending with a dark little movement,
> A kind of forlorn frenzy leaking over into sound . . .[41]

[40] Medbh McGuckian, 'The Unplayed Rosalind', in *Marconi's Cottage* (Dublin: Gallery Press, 1991, and Newcastle upon Tyne: Bloodaxe Press, 1992).

[41] Medbh McGuckian, 'Oval of a Girl', ibid.

The emphasis throughout the volume on waves also suggests a reconfiguration of the symbolism of Venus, who appears here as Aphrodite born from the waves, through a reference to Mandelstam's poem 'Silentium'. For Mandelstam the birth of Aphrodite represents the birth of sound, and Mandelstam's poem seems to be a plea for her to remain unborn:

> She hasn't yet been born,
> she's word and music both,
> thus the unbreaking link
> Of everything that lives . . .
>
> Remain foam, Aphrodite,
> and word, turn into song,
> and heart be shy of heart
> merged with life's origin.[42]

There is debate about how the poem's first lines should be translated, an ambiguity which McGuckian refers to in the final lines of 'Visiting Rainer Maria': 'The it of his translation may mean silence, | But the she of mine means Aphrodite'. In its reference to 'virgin months' and the experience of being 'not his', McGuckian's poem seems to refer to a failed or estranged relationship, or perhaps the failure of conception (the title echoes the unfulfilled pact made between Tsvetaeva and Pasternak, 'What would you and I do if we were together? . . . we would go and see Rilke').[43] But the unborn feminine element is given life later in the collection, as the child herself whose birth is heralded in 'Breaking the Blue' ('You utter, become music, are played'), and as one part of the creative process.

Venus, then, seems to represent the female child as much as the mother, but also the elemental quality of creativity which needs to be harnessed and structured to form art. There are clear analogies with Virginia Woolf's concept of androgyny here, and as with Woolf one must ask whether the emphasis on the balance between opposing forces ensures in effect a containment of disruptive elements. One might wish to read the architectural

[42] Osip Mandelstam, 'Silentium', in *Works in Two Volumes*, i, ed. P. M. Nerler (Moscow: Khudozhestvennaya Literatura, 1990); trans. Angela Livingstone, to whom I am grateful for pointing out the reference to the poem in McGuckian's text.

[43] Pasternak *et al.* (eds.), *Letters Summer 1926*, 61.

symbolism as an analogy for the relationship between form and content—rooms and walls act primarily as a kind of scaffolding for the feminine 'foam, aura and melody'.[44] Thus, rather than separating into their constitutive elements, body, house, and land expand to contain the fissures and fractures within. However, rooms, walls, and spaces are very far from acting as simple enclosures; they are as liable to emerge from within as to function as external boundaries. Moreover, bodies and buildings bear the signs of a history of distortion and discontinuity, as the beautiful poem 'Branches' attests:

> This window, clumsily inserted,
> Was originally a door.
> So am I detached
> From the fabric which claims me.[45]

Similarly it would be mistaken to suggest that McGuckian is advocating a marriage of masculine and feminine elements since not only is the sea gendered feminine, but so too is the house. (Significantly, unlike Woolf, her building is a cottage not a phallic lighthouse.) In orthodox psychoanalytic fashion, rooms signify parts of the female body, yet for McGuckian they are also places of cultivation and meaning, as in 'The Book Room' or 'Flowered Sitting Room'. The body, the home, and the family are thus not outside culture, but the very place where society's battles are staged. There are clearly analogies here with the Catholic and nationalist attempted use of the female body to confirm a sense of national integrity, but also with the violent and disruptive forces of colonial and neo-colonial culture. Moreover, by locating these forces 'always already' within the body McGuckian rejects conventional representations of the division between the private and domestic sphere and the public realm of culture and politics. Indeed, it is in the most intimate of signs, in the body's scar tissue, that the history of the violence of our civilization, as well as its artistic culture, may not only be seen but read.

[44] See the poem 'From the First Underworld', in *Marconi's Cottage*, 86–7. In keeping with this emphasis on balance, order, and architecture, many of the poems are less syntactically complex and demanding of the reader's time and ingenuity than earlier work. They are also more formally diverse, experimenting with verse forms and framing narratives such as the fairy tale and dream vision.

[45] Medbh McGuckian, 'Branches', in *Marconi's Cottage*.

Conclusion

I have argued that the work of contemporary Northern Irish poets cannot be properly understood using established definitions of the relation between poetry and politics, maintaining that the poets construct an alternative relation between public and private registers, in which a work's political responsibility no longer derives from its public or communal reference. The work of all three writers I have chosen to discuss forces a recognition that such public address is impossible in a complex modern society, in which the poetry speaks to both a local and an international audience. Like Muldoon and Paulin, McGuckian asks us to acknowledge the diverse nature of the contemporary Irish community, which is riven both socially and politically, but in McGuckian's case a distinction must be made between modern society in general, and the situation of women in Ireland. I have argued that the obliqueness of McGuckian's work is in part the result of her desire to write about the domestic environment, and its intersection with public and political matters. The poems offer not representations of the truth of feminine experience, but a private language whose rationale is in part the maintenance of secrecy. One consequence of this strategy of concealment is a foregrounding of the problematics of poetic address across different sections of the local and international community.

What is said in the poems works differently at different levels of address, whether to other Irish women, or Irish readers in general, or to an international audience, representing differently to each in turn. Importantly, however, the poetry foregrounds this element of disarticulation, leaving itself open to different levels of meaning and interpretation. Thus, despite the intimate focus of the work, poetic form in McGuckian's work is very far from acting as an aesthetic refuge, instead it serves to challenge redemptive approaches to everyday life. Indeed, as I have argued, the poems lack a fundamental ingredient of the refuge—a stable and secure centre, a grounding for the authenticity of personal experience. The implications of her exploration of the impropriety of the maternal body extends to the improper past—the colonial history—of the Irish nation, which has ensured that internal exile is part of the cultural condition of Ireland, rendering the very concept of private or personal space deeply problematic. Thus, just as McGuckian's work foregrounds the intimacy of personal relations, it emphasizes the fact that such intimacy is both constitutive of and constituted by public, or more significantly, national political discourses.

Albeit in different ways, both Muldoon and Paulin explore the disrupted nature of community, and the discontinuity of personal and national identity in overtly historical and political terms, including in their work references to the history of global colonization, Irish republicanism, and sectarian warfare. In McGuckian's work that historical material, though present, is muted, radically 'privatized', and filtered through the screen of poetic tradition, and of maternal and familial experience. Her poetry is thus far more obviously allegorical in its focus on the relation between familial and national communities. It is important to emphasize therefore that McGuckian is not (as I have suggested of Paulin) using sexuality as a metaphor for the cultural condition in Northern Ireland. For if the maternal body acts as the figural 'ground' of the national narrative, it is also linked to material circumstances peculiar to Ireland's colonial history. And as McGuckian's focus on maternal sexuality attests, placing the figure of woman at the centre of the nation's supposedly rational public iconography cannot fail to destabilize both terms in the analogy between home and nation. Thus the body itself becomes a historical document, which, as Freud explains of the uncanny, contains an 'improper past', always ready to recur in the present.

As my analysis has shown, McGuckian's primary emphasis is on familial relations, whether across the generations—between mother and child, child and grandmother—or the sexual relation between husband and wife. Each are the spur to both historical and narrative generation. Yet, as I have argued, it would be mistaken to interpret this emphasis on generation as an argument for historical continuity, or the stability of personal or national identity. Though 'grounded', McGuckian's allegorical female has no resemblance to purist representations of the integrity of the community or its traditions. Like the maternal relation itself, the national community is built upon loss and separation.

However, despite the dissonance, loss, and violence which characterize the maternal figure in McGuckian's work, one might legitimately question whether the emphasis on the relation between mother and child relies on a form of historical determinism, underplaying the influence of contemporary social movements in questioning the integrity of tradition, and in forcing a reappraisal of the relation between political and personal discourses. One could argue that McGuckian herself could not take the position she does in relation to Irish history, were it not for transformations in the structure of society in the present. For the transformed relation between public and private registers is in part the result of historical factors peculiar to the colonial and post-colonial experience (and the female figure in Irish political discourse is testament to this fact), and in part to the evolution of the modern social arena. New social movements have altered our understanding of the political, and particularly relevant to an understanding of McGuckian's work is the influence of the women's movement in establishing the public relevance of the private sphere of the home. Nevertheless, despite McGuckian's seeming reluctance to admit the pertinence of this aspect of social transformation, her work reveals the complex ways in which national, Catholic, and postmodern discourses about the representation of femininity can be fruitfully articulated together, to question the integrity of both political and literary dominant histories.

6

Paul Muldoon: Dubious Origins

WHATEVER its ostensible subject-matter, Paul Muldoon's poetry is fundamentally bound up with an investigation of the nature of origins, whether biological, familial, 'tribal', or national. These in turn are often figured through an examination of the nature of linguistic origins and etymology. His work can be read as a thoroughgoing rejection of the notion of stable or univocal origins which, as I have discussed in Part I, are linked to a conservative politics, not only in nationalist, but also in neo-imperialist rhetoric. At issue here is the security of our personal and national borders, borders which, Muldoon's poetry implies, are continually breached by 'improper' forms and modes of behaviour, where impropriety consists in being both inside and outside the border at the same time.

In a Northern Irish writer such distrust of the value of borders, and of their success in acting as boundaries, should come as no surprise, and indeed this has been a preoccupation of Muldoon since his very earliest work. The breaching of boundaries is both a thematic and a formal concern; Muldoon's suspicion of the traditional lineaments of family, community, and nation is paralleled by his refusal to respect the outlines of traditional poetic form, which is twisted almost out of all recognition in his hands. (But, as most famously with his 'deconstruction' of the sonnet form, the underlying shape remains as the foundation of the poem.) More tendentiously, perhaps, Muldoon's habit of 'stealing' from other writers also reveals a lack of deference to customary notions of the 'ownership' (or 'propriety') of poetic material, and an understanding of the meaning of 'creativity' which owes little to the post-romantic tradition. The writer is no longer put forward as origin of the work spun out of his own thoughts and experiences, but as a craftsman who borrows, reuses, and parodies elements of literary and historical tradition.

Muldoon's characteristic technique, particularly in his more recent work, could be described as the art of repetition, or, as he puts it in 'The Key', the 'remake'. Clichés from the world of the media, borrowed styles, even borrowed phrases are all represented in his poems. (For example, the sections of '7 Middagh St' are all to a greater or lesser extent constructed out of statements made by the artists themselves. This is particularly true of 'Salvador' which is a patchwork of Dali's declarations culled from various texts.) In 'Madoc—A Mystery' the pretence that this material is anything other than stolen has been dropped, as quotations from Southey, Byron, Lewis and Clark, Chief Red Jacket and George Catlin, to name but a few, are included and acknowledged in the text. It is precisely these practices which suggest that Muldoon's work as a whole is concerned with rejecting traditional notions of personal and national identity, and putting forward in their stead a postmodern identity formation. Yet if this has partly to do with the way in which Muldoon undermines notions of poetic authenticity or romantic sincerity, it also relates to the issue of community. In this interpretation the formally interrupted or discontinuous nature of his work can be read as a reflection of the diverse and heterogeneous nature of the contemporary Irish community, and as an acknowledgement of the fragmentation of the poetic audience across national and cultural boundaries. It is undoubtedly the case that Muldoon's work does register an impatience with traditional constructions of the community which are unable to accommodate contemporary social divisions of class, gender, race, and religion. However, if Muldoon's work emphasizes dissonance and discontinuity, what interests me here are the links between the general contemporary move towards the celebration of fragmentation, and the peculiarly Irish concerns of Muldoon's subject-matter. As I have argued, postmodern forms have a rather different purchase in Ireland (which lies both inside and outside the history of the European Enlightenment) than in metropolitan Europe. Like McGuckian, Muldoon's work continually points us towards the fragmented nature of Irish historical experience, as much as contemporary developments in the social sphere, as the grounds for the inevitable dissolution of origins. But he then goes further, to suggest that such a fragmented and discontinuous history has affected imperial as well as post-colonial cultures (and hence too their forms of cultural politics). The opposition is thus not between the pure and the impure, but occurs within the 'original' hybrid. This hybridity does not only affect a culture such as that of Ireland (or other post-colonial societies, which are both excluded from metropolitan cultures but also help to determine their identity). As Muldoon's work reminds us, the 'centre', whether Britain or America, contains within it the fragmented signs of other cultures, both because of modern processes such as immigration and tourism, and as the result of the history of colonialism (though these processes cannot be separated).

Emboldened perhaps by Muldoon's move from a putatively authentic rural Ireland to the ultramodern world of the United States, it is tempting to read his work as arguing similarly for the abandonment of ideas of 'proper' place and location. But in tension with this aspect of his work lies his emphasis on local narratives, and the particularity of historical events. For Muldoon's work relies significantly on historical knowledge and research, both local (such as the history of the Armagh faction fights in 'Armageddon, Armageddon', or the importance of flax growing and the linen industry in *Meeting the British*, or of the United Irishmen in 'Madoc'), and global (the histories of Native American tribes, or the literary world centring on '7 Middagh St' in Brooklyn in the 1940s). The detailed research Muldoon undertakes as background to his poems seems to belie the ostensible celebration of arbitrariness and fragmentation in the work. If his earlier poetry focused primarily on Irish mythic and historical narratives, more recently his work has taken on American myths of origin, continually emphasizing the complex histories which lie behind the American celebration of the new. (Postmodernism's famed 'fusion' of old and new may therefore be particularly appealing to him.) Origins (both cultural and linguistic or etymological) are offered not as the source of true knowledge, but as a reminder of the historicality of structures and terms deemed natural and universal. So while Muldoon refuses the purity of mythic constructions of the past, his poetry emphasizes the ways myth and history are imbricated with one another, and the fact that myths and fictions (including poetry), while they may be 'ideal' constructions of the imagination, none the less have real effects.

Another way of putting this might be to say that it is not possible to choose finally between the demand for rational truth as political motivation, and the arena of fiction, desire, and affectivity as spurs to real events. (A comparison with Paulin's work may be helpful here; as I have argued, Paulin's more recent poetry attempts a synthesis between these two poles, but always with the ideal of reason paramount. In contrast Muldoon's poetry suggests that the attempt to resolve these competing claims in a general theory is misguided, not only with regard to the poetic, but also the political realm.) But if Muldoon questions the opposition between Enlightenment rationalism and Romantic notions of community, showing how each is infected by its opposite, he also runs the risk of collapsing all distinctions between historical and contemporary values in a generalized relativism. As I will argue below, this risk is self-consciously thematized in the poetry which repeatedly turns on the tension between authentic and counterfeit goods. Having dispensed with the notion of the intrinsic value of a thing, all events and objects may be substitutable, all of equal worth (a process which is suggested formally by the tendency for Muldoon to allow the seeming arbitrariness of rhyme and word association to direct his poems).[1]

The struggle between arbitrariness and the authenticity of the traditional community (or indeed personal identity), is brought out in a consideration of Muldoon's figuration of sex, which frequently turns on a tension between uniqueness and substitutability. As I discussed in relation to the poem 'Bran', Muldoon sets up an opposition (which he then undercuts) between the securities of a rural Irish childhood, and the arbitrary and violent quality of personal relations in the modern, international, and metropolitan world. In my analysis of the trope of the motherland in Chapter 2, I argued that the celebration of a secure and stable origin is associated with a secure personal, and by extension also national, identity. The link between these two very different registers is drawn through the analogy of the 'national family' with the biological one; thus the mother is called upon to offer a secure 'grounding' for the identity of the son, as simultaneously the motherland performs the same role for the national community.[2] Like both McGuckian and Paulin, one of the ways

[1] See e.g. 'Something Else', in *Meeting the British* (London: Faber and Faber, 1987), 33.

[2] For a general critique of such ideas in the field of psychoanalytic theory see Clair Wills, 'Mothers and Other Strangers: A review of Julia Kristeva, *Strangers to Ourselves*', in *Women: A Cultural Review*, 3:3 (1992), 281–91.

in which Muldoon chooses to figure poetic impropriety, the breaching of boundaries, is through sex. The more unpleasant aspects of sexual relations are a particular theme of the volume *Quoof*, but also at work in poems such as 'Quoof' and 'Aisling' is a parody of the desire to use a 'pure' image of (maternal) sexuality as analogue for the purity of the national community.

As in McGuckian's work, however, it is often unclear whether the poet is critiquing the association of family and nation, through the body of the mother, or reinflecting it by focusing on 'improper' forms of sexuality. At issue here is the by now familiar question of the relation drawn in the poetry between public (national, civic, or communal) and private (familial or perhaps individual) registers. I have discussed at length the characteristic association in discussions of Northern Irish poetry of poetic responsibility to the political situation with the poet's ability to open the privacy of the lyric up to more communal concerns. I argued that this process depends on a notion of representativeness which in turn derives from the romantic ideal of poetic authenticity and personal sincerity, which enables the poet to find a voice beyond his or her individual concerns. In Muldoon's work, however, the private sphere remains irreducibly private, it narrows to the point at which it becomes incommunicable, and loses all possible relevance it might have to more public concerns. Indeed, by focusing on sexuality (as opposed to maternality), Muldoon suggests that the private sphere is no longer to be found within the family, but in the individual. This narrowing process is in part the subject of the celebrated poem 'Quoof':

> How often have I carried our family word
> for the hot water bottle
> to a strange bed,
> as my father would juggle a red-hot half-brick
> in an old sock
> to his childhood settle.
> I have taken it into so many lovely heads
> or laid it between us like a sword.

As in 'Bran', Muldoon sets up a seeming parallel between the father's rural childhood, and the son's modern, cosmopolitan experience of personal, specifically sexual, relations—('How often have I . . . as my father would'). But the transportation of the familial word out of its context and into 'so many lovely heads' results in the construction of barriers to communication. The word becomes a sword, which may be used to pierce or break barriers but here is used to create one (so the lack of communication in the first stanza leaves language inert in the second, which contains no verb).

> An hotel room in New York City
> with a girl who spoke hardly any English
> my hand on her breast
> like the smouldering one-off spoor of the yeti
> or some other shy beast
> that has yet to enter the language.

The poem acts as a linguistic prophylactic, guarding against infection and generation simultaneously; yet on a further level it is concerned with language as an agent of colonization. For what is the significance of the girl 'who spoke hardly any English'? Even if she had perfect command of the English language the word 'quoof' would be unintelligible to her since it is a familial rather than a national word. The poem hints at the way language is used to colonize and, conversely, to empower. There are dangers as well as gains in allowing the beast/the hand to enter the language (in this case the language of the girl which is other than English). Like the Indians in the poem 'Meeting the British', the danger in opening up to new forms of communication is colonization, a loss of self-containment. The poem can be read as another version of the traditional trope in which the female represents the land to be colonized by the male; here, however, the woman resists—the poem ends still lacking a verb, the 'entering' unaccomplished. Thus the relation between narrator and woman (or women) refuses to be co-opted into a (nationalist) narrative—indeed it refuses to be generative at all.

Interestingly, despite the poem's ostensible disengagement from narrow definitions of community, it none the less relies for its effect on a notion of personal authenticity, in which the inexpressible particularity of the personal is dependent on the family (and in particular the personal history of the father). Despite the fact that the passage from familial to national registers is interrupted in the poem, the suggestion that the rural community does have access to truths unavailable in the modern cosmopolis remains, precisely because of the inability to translate the familial discourse. (As I will argue below, the abiding nostalgic tone in the poem derives in part from the presence of the father figure—who more than any other figure in Muldoon's work is associated with a lost truth.)[3]

In 'Quoof' the borders between individuals are strikingly not crossed; despite the interchangeability of the woman, the distinction between man and woman, poet and poetic object, remains. In the reading of Muldoon's work which follows I will argue that this tension between substitutability, and an inexpressible particularity is a central issue. I will discuss firstly Muldoon's conception of the nature of poetic reference, and the relation between meaning in 'everyday' and poetic discourse. I will argue that in contrast to the idea of poetic responsibility dependent on the role of the poet within the community, Muldoon's poetry offers an alternative form of accountability which works at the level of linguistic reference. While Muldoon suggests that the poet's role is above all to control the arbitrariness of linguistic reference, the implication of the poems is that it is equally controlled by social context impinging on the reader. Despite the much discussed 'hermeticism' of his poetry, social and historical meanings continually force their way through aesthetic form. Muldoon repeatedly figures the relation between social and aesthetic significance (or public and private reference) as a process of 'trading' meanings, much as languages expand and alter as they come into contact with others. Thus, at the heart of Muldoon's investigation of the nature of personal and linguistic origins, lies a preoccupation with the confrontation between cultures, and their assimilation to each other, an assimilation which too often (as in the case of Native American culture) means the destruction of a 'primitive' society by a more powerful 'modern' one.

The desire to found a poetry which can ignore the cultural context of its tools (such as language), and find an origin outside

[3] Muldoon's poetry repeatedly points to a tension between the idea of sex as a point of origin or generation, and non-reproductive sex, or sex purely for pleasure. The effects of this break on narrative are explored in a series of poems written after *Quoof*, many of which are collected in the pamphlet, *The Wishbone*. Language becomes increasingly rarefied as, in the absence of communication or generation (like the 'would-be children' of 'Pandas'), it is forced to feed off itself. The narrative discontinuity which ensues is formally reflected in absences in the text, such as the historical gaps in 'The Wishbone': 'Sir—or Sir—' (a 'historicized' version of the characteristic Muldoonian asterisk).

society, is one of the principal subjects of '7 Middagh St', a poem which is often read as Muldoon's most direct treatment of the debate over art's social responsibility. 'Wystan' and 'Louis' offer contrasting views on the pull of the poetic ideal as opposed to the claims, not merely of history, but of contemporary events, on the writer's consciousness. I will argue, however, that Muldoon's most recent long poem 'Madoc' takes the issue of the relation between poetry and the political world much further, as it examines various alternative theories of the role and function of the imagination. Above all Muldoon emphasizes the impossibility of resolving the competing claims of fiction (poetry, myth, utopia) and history or the facts, within a general theory.

The poem ostensibly offers us two main paradigms of the function of poetry. Coleridge's preferred ideal 'lofty imaginings' might be described as the power of the creative imagination to collapse the distinctions between words, objects, and even between cultures. This Romantic theory of poetry is distinguished from that which relies on 'story and event' for its purpose and effect (as Coleridge suggests of Southey). However, I shall argue that there is a third paradigm of the relation between poetry and politics at work in 'Madoc', gestured towards by the shadowy presence of Byron.[4] Rather than rely exclusively on the solipsistic creations of the romantic imagination, or alternatively the 'accurate' recounting of narrative history, like Byron, Muldoon creates an epic narrative which defines its seriousness almost entirely in terms of comedy and fantasy. His work emphasizes the importance of particular histories but at the same time forces us to recognize the fact that all histories come to us through fiction, and that this does not necessarily inhibit their affectivity. Byron's work takes a stance that combines concern with factuality in all its aspects, with sceptical awareness of the limitations and problems of appeals to the facts (among them the problem of invoking personal experience, as 'witness' to the facts). As I will argue, Byron's example offers Muldoon a way of creating a 'responsible' poetry which does not fall back on notions of truth, sincerity, and personal authenticity, but instead

[4] Muldoon has traced the genesis of the poem to his rereading of Byron for an edition of the selected poems; Paul Muldoon (ed.), *The Essential Byron* (New York: Ecco Press, 1989).

plays with the humour and deception of 'the society of false faces'.

Responsibilities

I think that the writer should be alert to all these possible readings. And alert to the curtailing of possible readings that are not productive. And I don't care what people say, it's the writer who does that. And the points at which he doesn't do it are the points at which there is confusion . . . Because that's what the process of writing is about. It's about opening himself, or herself to the floodgates, what it's about is discovering the extent of limits, the confinement, the controlling of readings, of possible readings.[5]

Muldoon claims that it is possible for poetic discourse to be harnessed to the particular function of expressing the writer's meaning and intention; the writer's task is to 'control' and 'confine' meanings which words may carry in everyday discourse, by constructing a type of discourse which is closed off from the normal communicative functions of language—a hermetic, poetic 'world'. Such a theory attempts to deny both the role of historical context and change, and the activity of the reader in the process of interpretation, and suggests that it is possible for the writer to 'own' completely the keys to interpretation. By taking words out of circulation the poet can ascribe to them a value of his own.[6] And yet the very fact that artistic discourse is to some extent 'at a remove' from the normal functions of everyday communication may ensure that the writer has less rather than more control over his or her intended meaning. As Roland Barthes claims in his discussion of the 'encyclopaedic' word in modern poetry, once the word is abstracted from social reality the poet's intention can never be fully adequate to its meaning, which now comprises all the word's possible meanings in history and society.[7] He argues

[5] Paul Muldoon, personal interview (2 June 1987).

[6] For a discussion of the way in which the poetic word works actively to negate the history of the word and the object in the world see Mikhail Bakhtin, 'Discourse and the Novel', in *The Dialogic Imagination*, ed. Michael Holquist (Austin, Tex.: University of Texas Press, 1981), 259–422.

[7] Roland Barthes, *Writing Degree Zero*, trans. Annette Lavers and Colin Smith, ed. Susan Sontag (originally published 1953; New York: Hill and Wang, 1968). See also Jean-Paul Sartre, *What is Literature?*, trans. Bernard Frechtman (London: Methuen, 1950), 4–11.

for the 'magical' and 'mysterious' quality of poetic language. In modern (post-1848) poetry:

> poets give to their speech the status of a closed Nature, which covers both the function and structure of a language. Poetry is then no longer a Prose either ornamental or shorn of liberties. It is a quality sui generis and without antecedents. It is no longer an attribute but a substance, and therefore it can very well renounce signs, since it carries its own nature within itself, and does not need to signal its nature outwardly.[8]

Barthes's assertion is that modern poetry deals with the linguistic rather than social relationships between words. It

> destroys the spontaneously functional nature of language and leaves only its lexical basis. It retains only the outward shape of relationships, their music and not their reality. The Word shines forth above a line of relationships emptied of their content, grammar is bereft of its purpose, it becomes prosody and is no longer anything but an inflexion which lasts only to present the Word.[9]

Because of the lack of the necessity for connections, the meaning of the word in 'discontinuous speech' is 'encyclopaedic'—it contains all the possible associations and connotations 'from which a relational discourse might have required it to choose'. Abstracted from the workings of everyday discourse, the syntagmatic relations of the word are suppressed, and it therefore achieves a state possible otherwise only in the dictionary, 'where the noun can live without the article—reduced to zero degree—pregnant with all past and future specifications'.[10] So for Barthes the loss (or the distancing) of the social function of language in poetry ensures that the poetic word forgoes the 'stability of intention'—since it can mean in one moment all the meanings it has ever had. Muldoon's claim to wish to limit readings is all the more strange in that the poetry itself exemplifies to a marked extent Barthes's 'degree zero' writing, a poetry characterized by gaps and discontinuities, where connections are made often only on the level of the signifier. Far from placing writerly control as the central organizing principle of the poetry, he undermines expectations of a stable point of origin in language or intention. Muldoon characteristically fragments narrative continuity; the poems are not held together syntactically (so, for example, he

[8] Barthes, *Writing Degree Zero*, 42–3. [9] Ibid. 46. [10] Ibid. 48.

often uses gaps marked by asterisks to encourage the reader to 'leap' from one fragment to the next), instead different tones and styles are brought together by the 'vertical' relationships between meanings. Reading the poems necessitates shifting between different levels of meaning which act as clues to the narrative 'behind' the paradigmatic structure. Even those poems which seem more obviously syntagmatically constructed, such as 'Immram', 'The More a Man Has', and '7 Middagh St' tend to hide narrative connections, offering the reader instead sometimes heavily disguised repetitions of single words and images with which to 'build' links.

The difficulty of 'holding on' to the meaning of words once abstracted from syntagmatic relations is examined in 'Chinook':

> I was micro-tagging Chinook salmon
> on the Qu'appelle
> river
>
> I surged through the melt-water
> in my crocus
> waders.
>
> I would give each brash,
> cherubic
> face its number.
>
> *Melt*-water? These were sultry
> autumn
> fish hang-gliding downstream.
>
> Chinook. Their very name
> a semantic
> quibble.
>
> The autumn, then, of Solidarity,
> your last in Cracow.
> Your father
>
> rising between borsch
> and carp,
> relinquishing the table to Pompeii.[11]

The speaker stands in the river 'that calls' and tries to arrest the movement of the fish, to name them. But he realizes that so far from being able to place a limit on the salmon, he has even mistaken the meaning of his own activity. The melt-water and cro-

[11] Paul Muldoon, 'Chinook', in *Meeting the British*, 9.

cus waders of spring are out of place in this narrative—these are 'sultry | autumn | fish hang-gliding downstream'. Just as Spring and Autumn are interchangeable in the speaker's memory, so the names are unsuited to the activity of the fish, since when they make their way upstream to spawn it is their 'autumn'. Thus they are not the angelic children the speaker thinks he sees. Similarly the 'sultry autumn fish' are the young, newly hatched. So the meaning changes according to the context of the utterance and the situation of the speaker, just as it changes depending on whether you are a fish or a fisherman. In the same way the very name of the salmon is 'a semantic quibble', since it gathers several meanings to itself—the 'encyclopaedic' nature of words in poetry becomes the very subject of the poem. Apart from the name of a salmon, 'Chinook' is the native name of an Indian tribe on the Columbia river in North America. It is also the name of a creole language which originated in the dealings of the Hudson Bay Company's servants with the Native Americans. It was then used by the Indians as a means of communication between the different tribes and with the colonizers. Moreover the Chinook wind is an ocean wind which is warm in winter and cool in summer (like the Spring/Autumn confusion, the temperature of the wind depends on the temperature of the surroundings—it is contextual. And indeed the wind itself creates seasonal confusion as the warmth of the winter wind heralds a false spring, encouraging plant life to flower only to be destroyed by the 'real' winter.)

But probably the most immediately recognizable reference of the term 'Chinook' for contemporary readers is as a name for a type of military helicopter; the Chinook became famous in news coverage of the Vietnam and, more recently, the Falklands Wars. This usage of the name seems qualitatively different from the others mentioned, since it arises out of a distinctively modern and self-conscious process of naming. And indeed the name for the helicopter does differ in its linguistic relation to the other objects designated by the word 'Chinook'. For although it may be impossible to say which came first, the names for a wind, a salmon, and a tribe are the same because of geographical proximity—they share a contextual, or metonymic relation with each other. In the same way the language Chinook is so named because of its use by the Chinook tribe—the process by which names are conferred in society depends on contextual relations. In contrast, the name for the helicopter arises out of a metaphorical relation between the Chinook wind and the wind made by the action of the helicopter's blades. And the poem as a whole records the self-conscious artistic process by which such metaphorical relations are created. For the activity of 'micro-tagging' the fish is itself a metaphor for designating objects and events in poetry. So the poem in fact records the *difference* between the social process of naming which depends on metonymic displacement, and the metaphorical relation which arises when such naming becomes self-conscious or 'artistic'.

Within the poem all the meanings of the word Chinook exist simultaneously—as Barthes says the poetic word is magically 'whole':

> it shines with an infinite freedom and prepares to radiate towards innumerable uncertain and possible connections. Fixed connections being abolished, the Word is left only with a vertical project, it is like a monolith, or a pillar which plunges into a totality of meanings, reflexes and recollections.[12]

And this totality of meanings is self-consciously harnessed by the poet, so that the 'semantic quibble' becomes productive not disruptive of meaning. At least one of the meanings of 'Chinook'—that of the trading patois—is significant not only within this poem but in the poem 'Meeting the British' (where it is made clear that a language which seems to be a third language, created in order to communicate and more specifically to trade, in fact works as a means of domination over the colonized). In contrast to the patois the nouns in the final two stanzas at first sight suggest stability and untranslatability. 'Borsch', 'carp' and 'Pompeii') are all words which carry a single, identifiable meaning. However, the reason that they do not need translation is that they are already borrowings from one language to another, and in this sense they perform exactly the same function as a patois, a means of representing one culture to another. Just as 'borsch' and 'carp' are words which suggest a stable meaning as well as a country of origin so 'Cracow' 'means' Poland. (And here the false spring born by the Chinook wind may act as a reminder of the Prague Spring, with all the difficulties of holding on to politi-

[12] Barthes, *Writing Degree Zero*, 47.

cal change which it connotes). 'Pompeii' similarly has one meaning although it is not of the same order as Cracow—the word has passed into another realm because of an event, so that it now stands for stasis in movement, or the sudden petrification of events. Solidarity, although translated from the Polish, stands for a political movement rather than an abstract concept, but the displaced concept 'solidity' works on the level of metaphor in the poem. The word works with 'Pompeii' as a symbol of the solidification of events and meanings, due to departure, which the speaker's failed attempt at micro-tagging could not achieve. The speaker, unlike his addressee in the poem has not been able to place a limit on experience by cutting it off at a certain point, and it is for this reason he cannot hold down events in his memory.

The only way out of this impasse for the writer is to be aware of all the possible meanings and readings of his work, but of course this is impossible to achieve. And as if to point this out (in contradistinction to Muldoon's stated belief about intention), the nouns in the final stanza are not as univocal as one might think. For the meanings of 'borsch', 'carp', 'Pompeii', and 'Solidarity' which the poet is attempting to utilize in the poem (Eastern Europe, petrification of events, solidity), are metonyms derived from the associations of places and events, in exactly the same way as the language meaning of 'Chinook' is derived from its designation of a tribe. (So in Eastern Europe 'borsch' designates a type of soup rather than a Russian dish). In the same way, though the word does not change, people understand very different things by 'Solidarity', depending on their political allegiances and personal understanding, i.e. depending on the context which the word inhabits for them. Moreover, the reader takes 'borsch' and 'carp' to be examples of particular types of food—so particular that they do not need to be translated into English. But of course 'carp' also means discourse, argument, and complaint, and thus it shares with 'Chinook' not merely the meanings of a type of discourse and a fish but also a semantic duplicitousness.

In the poem words are undecidable both because of their lexical richness (the entirely different meanings which a word such as 'carp' may denote), and because of the various connotations which the single meaning of a word may carry (just as the fishing scenario depends on contextual interpretation, so the meaning of the final stanzas may alter depending on different understanding of the events in Poland). But the poem reduces the gap between the polysemous word, and the word rich in social connotation by showing that both depend on the same processes. For example, the word 'borsch' (which is in some senses representative of an early stage of development of 'Chinook''s polysemousness) initially begins to carry the different meanings of soup and Russian food because it becomes weighted with a new social connotation (Russianness).

Interestingly my analysis of the poem 'Chinook' which has as its subject the instability and polysemousness of words, has tended to confirm Muldoon's theory of creative writing as the control and limitation of linguistic meaning. Even as the poem emphasizes the number and diversity of meanings of words, the poet must be aware of them all in order to include them in his statement about polysemousness. Such a writing project opens up two methodological difficulties. On the one hand the reader is encouraged to read the poetry in terms of what Barthes has termed the 'fullness' or 'wholeness' of the word in poetry, displaced from its position within a relational discourse. But on the other he or she is constrained by the knowledge that all this has been planned and controlled by the author in order to give the *illusion* of instability. This in turn produces a difficulty for Muldoon; the fragmentation of narrative connections, which encourages words to perform to their 'zero degree', also opens up the way for interpretations which the writer may not have accounted for. (Significantly, the authority of the reader in determining meaning also includes the ability to discover *political* readings, i.e. linguistic polysemousness need not necessarily increase the hermeticism of the poetry but can equally encourage socially responsible readings.) Of course this is all a matter of degree since words can never be absolutely confined to intended meanings. Nevertheless Muldoon's continual destruction of the syntagmatic relations, which serve to some extent to limit the encyclopaedic reference of poetic words, sits oddly with his prescriptivist insistence on his own control of meaning. My analysis of 'Chinook' has highlighted the slippery nature of a discourse which attempts to give voice to the inexpressible particularity of objects and events by naming them, but finds that names themselves become arbitrary and undecidable when released from their contexts. In the following section I will relate this issue of linguistic reference to Muldoon's understanding of his own aesthetic project, and in particular his view of the relation between art and reality.

Roots and Origins

Chinook, the language of trade, is constructed by means of the trading of words, the replacement of words from one context to another where, like 'borsch', they take on an altered meaning in order to represent one culture to another. Yet if the role of the trading language is to translate cultures for each other, its end lies not in translation but in substitution, as objects, cargoes, are exchanged for one another.[13] My analysis of 'Chinook' has suggested the difficulty which arises for the writer in stopping the process of alchemical translation (a one-way process in which objects are transformed into gold) from sliding into one of infinite substitution (when gold itself becomes a means of barter). Once objects are transformed by the Midas touch of poetry, how can the difference which gives them meaning and value in the world be maintained between them?

The distinction between 'everyday' and poetic symbolic processes lies at the heart of 'Sushi', a poem which sets up an opposition between argumentative discourse and a magical, silent alchemical matching of essences. While the two people sit having (or not having) an argument about the lack of productivity in arguing, alongside them the master and his apprentice transform objects into precious works of art:

> I saw, when the steam
> cleared, how this apprentice
> had scrimshandered a rose's
> exquisite petals
> not from some precious metal
> or wood or stone
> ('I might as well be eating alone.')
> but the tail-end of a carrot:
> how when he submitted this work of art
> to the master—

[13] The volume teasingly refers several times to John Masefield's poem 'Cargoes'. See John Masefield, *Poems* (London: Heinemann, 1966), 906.

Is it not the height of arrogance
to propose that God's no more arcane
than the smack of oregano,
orgone,
the inner organs
of beasts and fowls, the mines of Arigna,
the poems of Louis Aragon?—
it might have been alabaster
or jade
the master so gravely weighed
from hand to hand
with the look of a man unlikely to confound
Duns Scotus, say, with Scotus Eriugena.[14]

The carrot becomes a rose which 'might have been alabaster or jade': any material will serve for this mysterious alchemy since 'God's no more arcane' than the indiscriminate list of things displaced from their origins. The activity of the 'volatile' (a name for an alchemical compound) apprentice suggests that arbitrary connections, not systematic analysis, are the fundamentals of creation—the carrot and rose are both red, but there is nothing more essential in their connection. What is strange about the poem is that such an arbitrary, metonymic link between the material of creation and the finished product should be associated with the alchemical search for essences, and the philosophy of Duns Scotus.[15] The poem attempts to find some common ground between the arbitrariness of relations between words, and between words and their referents, and the transmutation of ordinary reality into art, a process which seems to depend on extracting the true 'essence' from the raw materials of creation.

But the linguistic capriciousness of the central italicized section sits uneasily with the master's training in magical and mystical transformation. The name Louis Aragon is a reminder of the surrealist project of juxtaposing opposites in language and image so that perception may be renewed, and of the surrealist mentor

[14] Paul Muldoon, 'Sushi', in *Meeting the British*, 34–5.

[15] Eriugena, or 'John the Irishman' called into question the transcendence of God with respect to the natural world in a sophisticated version of pantheism, whereas Scotists believed that man's intellect has a direct, intuitive knowledge of the singular material object, and not merely an indirect knowledge of it gained by reflecting on the material image. Duns Scotus's theory of 'haecitas', or the 'thisness' of a thing, recurs in altered form in Michael Heffernan's 'quidditas' in 'The Soap-Pig'.

Rimbaud's faith in the 'alchemy of the word'. Rimbaud believed that it was possible to transform existing reality with its limited logic, by effecting free substitution, the miracle of the word. But the very arbitrariness of the substitution undercuts any notion of essence so necessary to the process of alchemy, since the slippage between objects and words ('oregano', 'orgone', 'organs'), implies the impossibility of returning to a 'truth' before the objects existed, i.e. it denies the fact that there is an essence in ordinary reality or everyday language to be extracted and transformed. The alchemical magic is a pretence. This philosopher is a hack—the value of the gold/philosopher's stone has degenerated to that of exchange. In fact Muldoon has gone further than the usual capitalist structure of exchange in which some commodities are more valuable than others. Here everything is exchangeable, since everything is comparable to everything else. The mention of Arigna (the last coal-mining village in Ireland) might suggest to an uninitiated reader the mining of precious metals but in fact Muldoon is less of a prospector who digs deep than a pirate who plunders whatever cargo comes his way.

The cargoes of Masefield's poem are scattered throughout the volume, and the colonizing effects of this imperialist trade are evident in poems such as 'Meeting the British' and 'Chinook'. In both poems trade depends on the ability of a language to translate one culture for another, in other words to erase the difference and unknowability of the cultures enough that they may interact (but not so much that the colonized culture may think of itself as the same or the equal of the colonizers). As the poem 'Profumo' points out ('Haven't I told you, time and time again, | that you and she are chalk | and cheese? Away and read Masefield's "Cargoes"'), difference must be maintained in the interests of hierarchy, a hierarchy which results in the domination of one culture by another. In 'Meeting the British' this asymmetry is imaged in the lack of equality of the objects of exchange—the Native Americans will cede their land and wealth in return for fish-hooks, blankets, and smallpox. It is precisely this difference between objects which Muldoon's plundering method, his association of any word or object with any other, denies. In piracy the trade (exchange) value of the object is lost, it becomes arbitrary as the pure value is exalted. The pirate's cargo brings together all different types of value from different ships and nations, but the notion of value itself must depend on maintaining difference. If everything is equally substitutable the hierarchical value of the commodity is lost. This could be read then as a utopian, anti-colonialist move, in which all the products of imperialism are stolen and stuffed together so that they lose their singularity. But if the capitalist impulse is to substitute a quantitative measure of value for a qualitative, then it is premissed upon everything being the same in a certain way—everything can be judged by the same standard of value. In this case piracy is merely an extension of capitalism's mode of substitutability, for pirates do not work for colonized nations, but hoard wealth for themselves.

As Mick Imlah points out all the end words of the italicized passage in 'Sushi' are variations on the consonantal theme 'rgn':

> This fragment . . . is only joined to the rest of the poem by its rhymes with, again, the first and last lines of the poem—'arguing' and 'Scotus Eriugena'—and with 'erogenous' in the middle. When we find further variants, ('organza', 'Oregon') dispersed through other poems an enigma presents itself; . . . it does make sense if the origin of this rhyme sequence (which like the theme behind the Enigma Variations doesn't itself appear) is the word 'origin'.[16]

But in the end this alchemical mystery, which seems predicated on words being the same, or the same in essence, depends on being able to tell the difference—like the master (who knows that things are not just all versions of the same thing).

As Muldoon has said in an interview, Masefield's poem 'Cargoes' is 'Essentially about one idea: the distinction between the colour, beauty, possibility of the imagination that we associate with far off lands and the down to earth ordinariness of our day to day world of dirty British coasters'.[17] So the imagination does not 'confound' objects and ideas, the real and the ideal, in the way that the central section of 'Sushi' suggests: the distinction between carrot and rose must be maintained. The sight of the

[16] Mick Imlah, 'Abandoned Origins', rev. of *Meeting the British*, in *Times Literary Supplement* (4 Sept. 1987), 946. Something fishy does indeed occur in the poem, for what is 'oregano' doing in Japanese cooking? The 'smack' suggests the 'bad taste' of this addition, which involves imposing Italian on Japanese simply in order to keep to the artificial 'rgn'. It is surely 'origami' (similarly creating art out of cut-up strips of things) which should be present instead.

[17] Muldoon, personal interview (2 June 1987).

carrot through the rose does not amount to a perception of the essence of the work of art (for the carrot is not its referent) or of the rose. But while the referent is the real rose, and this is gestured towards in the work of art, the carrot (the 'root'), the place from which the art has been taken and cut, can none the less be *seen*.

The assertion of absolute relativity between all found objects may in certain contexts be read as a Utopian project which breaks down hierarchical barriers (the essence of postmodernism), but on the other hand, as the poetry shows, a mere declaration of similarity can not affect the determining grounds on which such hierarchies have been built. As Imlah suggests, throughout the book the rhyme words are often joined by little more than the letters they have in common. Like false etymology this process depends on an idea of common but displaced origin—so in '7 Middagh St', 'Auden' speaks of his willingness to return to 'Eden' (Europe), but also suggests that in going to America the emigrants are searching for their origins as they move away from them:

For history's a twisted root
And art its small, translucent fruit

And never the other way round.
The roots by which we were once bound

are severed here, in any case,
and we are all now dispossessed;

prince, poet, construction worker,
salesman, soda fountain jerker—

all equally isolated.
Each loads flour, sugar and salted

beef into a covered wagon
and strikes out for his Oregon.

Here, in an equation of the loss of hierarchy gained in severing class from its social roots with democracy, Muldoon's Auden asserts that just such a move frees art from its roots in the social world. In other words social levelling leads to a type of 'origin' outside the social and political orientation of human beings. Similarly, in the metonymical displacements which the poems effect all words are weighted equally, and, as Freud explains of the dream-work, they lose their hierarchy of importance accruing to them in the dream thoughts. Auden wishes to leap from the England of the industrial revolution 'with its mills, canals and railway bridges | into this great void', wherein words, like the landscape will be empty and ready to be filled with whatever meaning he wishes to assign them. Words then are bereft of responsibility just as they are bereft of any type of effect on history. However, this desire is revealed as a mere fiction in other poems in *Meeting the British* (such as the title-poem) and in *Madoc* which insist that the landscape is far from empty, but populated by the remnants of indigenous populations, as well as those of previous settlers.

Reading Wystan's statement against the grain, however, we are faced with the ironic suggestion that myth and fiction are the spur to events in history, as much as the other way round. For if art is always the fruit of history ('and never the other way round') severing roots in history entails the destruction of art. But the characters here are heading for a frontier, and it is myth or fictional fantasy which pulls them there; so with 'Oregon' as an 'origin', history will be the fruit of art. Similarly as MacNeice/Yeats points out in 'Louis', 'In dreams begin responsibilities'—even the dream where words are liberated from their order in the social world, where words can stand for anything through displacement and condensation, has a social conscience, and social effects.

My analysis has pointed to a deep-seated tension in the poetry between the pull towards interchangeability, or substitutability, and the desire for an authentic standard (which is linked to a notion of stable origin). In '7 Middagh St' this opposition is clearly situated as an opposition between different ways of viewing the relation between poetry and politics, as the writers offer alternative visions of the origin of their work. The search for an origin outside the European social and political world is the spur too to Coleridge and Southey's pantisocratic dream of new life in America—the ostensible narrative which shapes 'Madoc'. The Romantic poets share with Auden a desire to dispense with rootedness (associated in their radical youth with a conservative, monarchist, and hierarchical form of politics) in order to found a new democratic society. Yet one of the lessons of the poem is that historical origins have always preceded them, whether the mythical origins of the Welsh Indians, or the etymological origins of Native American languages, which prove that art like language cannot be invented out of nothing. 'Madoc' reveals the complex history on which the fantasy of rootlessness depends, and also the way that that history is itself the fruit of imagination. The poem considers the relative demands of the ideal fictions of the imagination, against the requirements of historical accuracy or responsibility, as it attempts to construct a form of poetic accountability which depends not on truth but on mystery and fantasy.

Madoc's Mystery

Let us start with the mystery, for there are many to be unravelled in *Madoc*. The title poem conjures a historical fantasy—Coleridge and Southey have travelled to America to fulfill their Utopian pantisocratic dream, where they become embroiled with various historical events, such as the expedition of Lewis and Clark, and federalist and republican political squabbles. Yet what exactly happens to them? Something untoward certainly befalls Sara Fricker, abducted in the middle of the night and kept in a bee-hive but with a gopher for company. The mystery as far as Coleridge is concerned primarily concerns Sara; he spends much of the poem trying to discover her whereabouts among the Seneca tribe of Indians, before he falls in with the Lewis and Clark expedition, and with them moves further and further west. Coleridge is given certain clues—the white dog ceremony, 'a belt of blue beads, and a bow made of horn'. Yet for the reader there are so many further mysteries to be investigated. The beads and the bow, for example, are a clue in quite a different narrative, that concerning the existence of a tribe of Welsh Indians who may or may not be the Mandans (of which more below). Or one might begin with the teasing connections between the first seven poems in the volume, and the long poem which follows them; or focus on the many keys and clues within 'Madoc' itself. Almost every clue has its parallel, as is suggested by Jefferson's poly-graph machine which:

> will automatically
> follow hand in glove
>
> his copper-plate 'whippoorwill'
> or 'praise' or 'love':

> will run parallel to the parallel
> realm to which it is itself the only clue.

In addition to the introductory 'key', the reader learns to look out for 'the teeney-weeney key' which Sara Fricker sends to her sister Edith (and its exactly identical twin), the valise (and its miniature twin inside the pearwood box), the scrap of paper (the letter Coleridge sends to Joseph Cottle), the pair of earrings given to Cinnamond, and the many variations on the word 'Crotona'.[18]

I am not going to attempt to unravel the plot of this complex narrative, but instead try to suggest some reasons why the poem is structured as it is. Perhaps the most immediately obvious conundrum on encountering the poem is the fact that it is 'subtitled' throughout with the names of the major figures in the history of Western philosophy (and some others whose claim on the discipline of philosophy is more dubious). The careful chronological ordering of these thinkers suggests that in part at least what is being offered is a playful 'history' of the discipline. Yet the links between philosopher and poem are often of the most bizarre and tenuous kind. Sometimes the reference is biographical (so '[Augustine]' is set in the hamlet of Carthage in New York, a reference to Augustine's birthplace), sometimes philosophical ('[Kant]': 'it stands to, well, "it stands to reason"'), sometimes the philosopher's name is the same as one of the characters in the poem (Moore, Burnet, the Seneca), and at other times the connection is built on word-play (so '[Bacon]' features a boiled ham, as well as a reference to the way Bacon met his end, and '[Paine]' seems to refer to the pain felt when 'Burr sends a ball through the | kidneys and mighty spleen of Alexander Hamilton').

Given the teasing nature of many of the links drawn between the history of philosophy and the narrative of 'Madoc', we should, I think, read it as Muldoon's ironic candidate for the category of contemporary philosophical poem. What all the thinkers

[18] 'Crotona', the birthplace of Pythagoras, is linked in the imagination of the unconscious 'narrator' South with the letters found on the piece of board left by Sir Walter Ralegh's lost colony on Roanoke Island. The letters CROATOAN are thought to represent the name of a Native American tribe, but South decodes them in '[Pythagoras]' as 'C[oleridge]RO[Bert Southey The S]ATAN[ic School]'. It is this link between Western philosophy and Romantic poetry which is in many ways the motor force of the poem as a whole.

featured in the poem's titles share is their attempts to explain the nature and structure of the world, though often in widely divergent ways. Part of what Muldoon's history is charting is the separation of philosophical enquiry from other forms of knowledge (though one implication of the poem's structure, which begins and ends in the future—opening with the pre-socratics and finishing with Stephen Hawking—is that the separation of philosophy from other disciplines such as science, linguistics, and literature is perhaps at an end, distinctions are once more abolished). The philosophical poem, by its very nature, attempts to break down the separation of philosophy from aesthetics and linguistics, and Muldoon's poem also includes history, geography, and science. The synthesis between philosophy and poetry has been rarely attempted since the Romantic period, and since Coleridge in particular. But while Coleridge sought in the philosophical poem to give expression to new modes of knowledge (in particular through the theory of the organic symbol), Muldoon offers us only old knowledges remade for the present moment. Synthesis occurs in the poem only parodically, not through the bringing together of myth, religion, philosophy, and science in an overarching theory, or aesthetic practice, but simply by adding mythic, historical, and philosophical narratives together. In several respects, then, Muldoon's poem seems to be the archetype of the postmodern work, taking his characteristic plundering method to its extreme, and reusing materials from a wide variety of sources. As 'The Key' which opens the volume suggests, 'Madoc' is a remake, constructed out of many epic tales (by Southey, Lewis and Clark, and Byron among others), and thus it replays events that have gone before. But, as I have argued elsewhere in this book, the general category of the postmodern cannot do justice to the specificity of the narratives Muldoon is employing here. In the reading of the poem which follows I will argue that, despite Muldoon's characteristically ironic tone, the poem emphasizes above all the parallels between imperial and colonial or post-colonial understandings of history, and between Enlightened and Romantic understandings of the nature of community.

The Way of Reason and the Way of Faith

A strange people came to the other side of the river with tools and weapons of metal such as no-one had ever seen. Cautiously the Mandans approached the river bank, to be startled by shouts in their own language. 'We are you', called the strangers, 'You are we. We are the same people'.[19]

This narrative of 'white Indians', reminiscent of that of the poem 'Meeting the British', is one of the aspects of native American Mandan culture which fuelled speculation at the end of the eighteenth century that the Mandans were the descendants of the Welsh prince Madoc, who had discovered America in 1169. It signals the abiding importance of questions of colonialism and cultural interchange to Muldoon's most recent volume. Disillusioned with the political situation at home, characterized by feuding between brothers and inter-tribal warfare, Madoc left his native Wales to sail westwards. There are clearly many resonances in this story for a poet who has left Northern Ireland in order similarly to travel West. The use of the Madoc legend continues Muldoon's interest in legends of voyagers to the Isles of the Blessed, which were central to the volume *Why Brownlee Left*. Yet with Madoc, perhaps more clearly than with the voyages of Bran and Mael Duin, the links between myth, legend, and popular interpretations of history and the enterprise of colonialism are revealed. For Madoc is at one and the same time a national (and nationalist) myth, and an instrument of British imperialism. The history of the transformations of the Madoc legend reveals the complex interrelationship between the history of colonization, myth, and popular history; the legend both feeds and is fed by imperial and nationalist desires. Several of the 'philosophers' whose names subtitle sections of Muldoon's long poem are imperial myth-makers: the inclusion of historians and geographers such as Dee, Hakluyt, Mandeville, Ptolemy (whose geography of AD 150, when rediscovered at the close of the Middle Ages, provided important motivation for the Portuguese voyages of discovery) suggests links with the use in *Meeting the British* of Gerald of Wales's fantastic travel writings about Ireland. Sir John Dee was the first to put the Madoc story to work in the service of

[19] Gwyn Williams, *Madoc: The Making of a Myth* (London: Eyre Methuen, 1979), 12.

Elizabethan imperialism; in 1583 he published a pamphlet promoting English colonization of America by detailing and embellishing the record of the 1169 voyage from the Welsh chronicles. Together with Richard Hakluyt's *Discourse of Western Planting* (1584), which also used Madoc to assert a prior claim to the Americas than the Spanish could muster in Columbus, it led to the launching of the first Virginia colony (Ralegh's Roanoke settlement), and the beginnings of what Dee precociously named 'The British Empire'. Moreover the Madoc legend was also used to justify imperial claims on Ireland.[20] As Gwyn Williams argues in tracing the history of the myth, 'Whatever his original provenance and character, Madoc first effectively entered history as an instrument of imperial conflict. His story henceforth was to follow the ebb and flow of imperialism, trade rivalry and colonial settlement with hypnotic precision.'[21] In later years Madoc changed his political hue considerably; importantly for an understanding of Muldoon's poem, he became a Jacobin, and a mainstay of Welsh nationalist arguments for emigration to the new world. There, so republican Welshmen such as John Thelwall and Iolo Morgan claimed, the Welsh could claim their democratic heritage free from the traditionalist constraints of the British monarchy.[22]

Several of the narratives which Muldoon weaves into his own are directly bound up with the search for the descendants of Madoc (itself moulded by the republican fervour of the late eighteenth century): the lone journey of the Welshman John Evans in search of the lost tribe of Welsh Indians; the Lewis and Clark expedition (Jefferson spoke of his Welsh heritage and instructed Lewis and Clark to find the Welsh Indians); even the narrative of the struggle between federalists and republicans, woven around Aaron Burr, Hamilton, and Jefferson is related, for as Williams points out:

It was by the last decade of the eighteenth century, the dramatic decade, the age of the French Revolution and the struggle for the soul of the

[20] See Meredith Harmer, 'A Chronicle of Ireland', in Sir James Ware (ed.) *The Histories of Ireland Collected by Three Learned Authors* (originally published Dublin, 1633; Amsterdam: De Capo Press, 1971). I am grateful to John Goodby for this reference.

[21] Williams, *Madoc*, 67.

[22] Significantly Southey's interest in Madoc, which culminated in his 1805 epic of which Muldoon's is in part a 'remake', was sparked by Thelwall's republican rhetoric.

new American republic, that people finally realized that the Madocians had gone into the land of mystery up the great and unknown Missouri river, where they enjoyed their golden age as the Mandans.[23]

In other words the eighteenth-century experiments in Enlightened democracy and republican ideals, in Wales, Ireland, and America, were all to some extent bound up with nationalist myths which had once served imperialist ends. And indeed in America they continue to be bound up with the process of colonization.

A re-creation of the fortunes of the Madoc legend is one way of investigating the political hues of early romanticism, and in particular the strange disappearance of Coleridge and Southey's radical youth (as their belief in reason narrowed to a dogmatic adherence to the Christian faith). But beyond historical and biographical considerations, what is the significance of this use of myth and legend, interpreted through multiple narratives? As so often with Muldoon's work, it can be read in various, even contradictory ways: Muldoon has always been interested in the intersections between myth and history, and one aspect of the poem could be read as a critique of historical revisionism's attempt to empty out or deny the mythic aspects of history. Significantly the historical information in the poem is gleaned from a variety of sources, not all of them equally reliable. Muldoon's historical fantasy gives equal weight to personal accounts of events in the period (such as the memoirs of Joseph Cottle, and the Journals of Lewis and Clark), poetic fantasies such as Byron's *The Vision of Judgement*, and historical fictions such as Gore Vidal's *Burr*. One conclusion we must surely draw from the interweaving of mythic and historical material, is that neither myth nor history remains a pure or unadulterated genre. Myth and legend, much as the conflict of nations, are motivated by personal fortunes (as is philosophy), and they motivate historical events in their turn. On the other hand, the presentation of alternative versions of history could equally be read as an endorsement of revisionism's attempt to replace the single, nationalist narrative of Irish history with variety and plural narratives, in a kind of historical prefiguring of cultural pluralism. Nevertheless, we might legitimately question how plural the narratives presented in the poem really are—in

[23] Williams, *Madoc*, 85.

many ways the poem offers us a series of similar narratives running on parallel lines (like Jefferson's polygraph). As much as dissonance and dissimilarity, the poem's importance lies in the connections it draws between American, British, Irish, and by implication French, political battles between republican and monarchist groups. Not only, it seems, are all deeply imbricated with mythic discourse but all are forced to come to terms with the degeneration of their ideals and the loss of cultural integrity which ensues as a result of imperialist and nationalist myths.

One anchor for the meta-narrative in the poem appears in the section subtitled '[Plotinus]':

> The next morning, before they pass under
> the mare's tail of a waterfall
>
> where the Way of Reason
> narrows to the Way of Faith
>
> Coleridge and Southey must pause
> to draw lots.

One referent of this passage lies in the history of Western philosophy. In the first place an attempt to substitute mythic explanations of the world for physical and rational ones (hence the science fiction narrative of the early pre-Socratic sections of Muldoon's poem, which reappears only with the contemporary physicist and philosopher of time, Stephen Hawking), philosophy is fed back into a system of belief through Plotinus, the Neoplatonist philosopher who influenced medieval Christian thinkers. In the poem it is at this point that Coleridge and Southey 'must pause | to draw lots' as they go their different ways. Both, however, depart substantially from the 'Way of Reason' which was the spur to their Utopian dream, the pantisocratic 'experiment in human perfectibility'. To a certain extent the poem as a whole is concerned with the failure of rational and Utopian schemes, not only in their endings, but also in their beginnings. Herein lies the significance of the fact that the Madoc myth was from its inception bound up with imperialist designs on America and rivalry with Spain. The new revolutionary Madoc which inspires Southey's poem—Jacobin, democratic, and republican—becomes similarly tainted by colonialist designs, and imperialist wars between the Americans, the British, the Spanish, and the French over the territories of the Native

Americans. Muldoon's poem charts the demise of the principles of pantisocracy and aspheterism on ground which is very far from Rousseau's ideal state of nature. As Lucy McDiarmid has pointed out, the projected Utopia never gets away from the worldliness of the world at all, as all the members of the band maintain links with the politics of the American frontier, republicanism, and the British literary and political scene.[24] (For example, Sara seals her letter with a coronet seal and is thus connected with the monarchist Anthony Merry.) Moreover, given that the projected Utopian society is centred on Ulster (significantly located downriver from Athens, the heart of democracy), and the date of its inception is given as 1798, it is hard to avoid the conclusion that also at issue here is the corruption of Enlightenment values and the struggle for the equal rights of man in eighteenth-century Ireland. The suggestion is that the dissolution of the hopes of the United Irishmen in sectarian squabbling is analogous to the struggles between federalists and republicans in America (and in this regard it is significant that 'Smith' is an ex-Unitedman 'in the service of Aaron Burr').

In addition to drawing cultural parallels, however, the poem is fundamentally concerned with the processes of cultural exchange and assimilation. As in *Meeting the British* the virgin territory sought by the idealistic emigrants, far from being 'uncultivated since the creation', has already been 'corrupted' and is home to various native societies and strains of settlers. The pantisocratic ideal of cultivating the land for the common benefit of mankind and spending leisure time in intellectual study is thrown into ridicule in '[Proclus]' where it is clear that the emigrants have not escaped society since they are cultivating land next to a stockade. They are surrounded by the signs of British cultural life, as Southey tracks down Cinnamond to Carthage's ale house, while Coleridge is entertained by Joseph Brant's tea and scones and philosophical conversation.

For the Englishmen this appears as a nightmare of assimilation equivalent to sex between the white woman and the Seneca in '[Hobbes]', at which Coleridge turns away 'sickened'. As in Muldoon's earlier work, sex is fundamental to the issue of community, either that of the rural family (as in 'Bran'), or the

[24] See Lucy McDiarmid, 'From Signifump to Kierkegaard', *New York Times* (28 July 1991), 14.

national family (as in 'Aisling', 'Quoof', and 'Christo's'). As I have discussed, the woman's body is all too often called upon to act as the place where ideas of nation and race must be upheld. In Muldoon's work, however, sex tends to figure the disruption, rather than the containment of the national family, as the poetry concentrates on the 'improper' liaison, or those deemed improper by conservative Catholic nationalism. Nostalgia for the ideal rural community and the desire for a secure personal (and perhaps also national) identity does figure in Muldoon's work, however, but importantly in his poems about his father. Poems such as 'The Coney', 'The Fox', and perhaps especially 'Cauliflowers' offer a vision of a lost ideal (and also suggest, *contra* Heaney, the lack of continuity between father and son).[25] In contrast, Muldoon tends to use sex to image cultural exchange and assimilation. But it is important to realize that he is not suggesting that 'traditional' societies are bound by conservative ideas of sexual practice, and that modern and enlightened mores are necessarily linked to a freer expression of sexuality. Far from it, throughout 'Madoc' it is the seemingly enlightened male who is most perturbed by alternative sexual practices, and this because his sense of community depends partly on the ownership (or 'propriety') of women and their progeny. The question of origin thus encompasses not only the tracing of a cultural heritage (as in '[Origen]'), but also biological origins. While York is entertained by a group of Mandan transvestites (undercutting notions of an 'original' gender), Southey attempts to shore up his idea of cultural identity against the dangers of assimilation to another. But as Bucephalus points out in '[Hume]', his efforts are fruitless since the 'enemy' is within their ranks, in the shape of Edith's child:

> September, 1799. They're putting the finishing touches
> to the maze of dykes and ditches
> beyond the live-oak palisade.
> The stone blockhouse is proof against a mortar-blast . . .

[25] See particularly 'The Coney' (*Meeting the British*, 3–4). Alternatively, one could argue that the very formal style of the poems, for example the sestina of 'Cauliflowers', and the numerous literary allusions (to Joyce and Hopkins among others) set the unaccustomed tone of sincerity and authenticity in these poems into relief, and suggest that Muldoon is exploring his relation to his literary, as much as to his biological, antecedents. More recently still he has suggested the need to revise any nostalgic or sentimental tone in relation to his father. See 'Milkweed and Monarch', *The Irish Review*, 11 (1991), 71–2.

And, as always, Bucephalus, niggling; 'Who *owns* the child?'

As we have learned in '[Hartley]', Edith has been raped by the Scots-Irish scout Alexander Cinnamond—thus the child may represent an ironic revision of the rape of Ireland by English soldiers and planters, which gives rise, as Heaney phrases it in 'Act of Union', to a 'bastard fifth column | whose stance is growing unilateral'. Like the besieged Protestant community in Northern Ireland, Southey finds himself building walls in 'Ulster' to protect the illegitimate progeny of an Englishwoman raped by an Irish mercenary. The irony of Southey's increasingly 'Unionist' mentality, and his fear of the surrounding natives, is thus directed as much at contemporary Ulster politics (hence the reference to the mortar blast), as at the failure of the ideals of 1798. Significantly, Bucephalus later goes on to draw an analogy between the presence of the genetically related 'enemy within' and the ravages caused by venereal disease (in '[Foucault]'). Colonization is in this sense akin to trade, involving a two-way traffic, but it is this which Southey would deny in his attempt to create a British cultural island in America. The implication of the analogy is that it is the refusal to adapt and compromise with the indigenous population in Ireland, which led to the founding of the state of Northern Ireland, a state which, like Southeyopolis, was not viable from its inception.[26] At one level, then, the poem can be read as Muldoon's imaginative investigation of the decline of republican ideals and the dissenting tradition in Ireland, to the disabling provincialism and siege mentality of the contemporary loyalist community. If this is reminiscent of Paulin's concerns in *Fivemiletown*, however, where Muldoon differs in his approach is in the repeated suggestion that the Utopian ideals which fuelled the rebellion of 1798 were never pure and 'reasonable', but always a struggle between competing motivations and fissured allegiances.

[26] The directness of the political analogy may seem uncharacteristic of Muldoon's work, yet he has encouraged such a reading: 'I don't want to belabour the point, but the fact that much of the poem is set in a place called "Ulster", and that one of the main characters is a particularly unwholesome Scots-Irish scout, Alexander Cinnamond, whose "theme music", as it were, is the "de dum, de dum" we hear throughout the poem, is scarcely an accident: though I think of *Madoc: A Mystery* as being a ripping yarn with a strong humorous element, I certainly don't discourage its being read as a political poem.' see 'Introduction to a Dramatised Reading of "Madoc–A Mystery"', held in Manhattan Theatre Club (May 1992).

In addition to the specific analogy between the fictional American Ulster and its 'real' counterpart in Ireland, Muldoon seems to be pointing towards more general similarities between the American and Irish situations—and perhaps more particularly drawing analogies between the dispossession of Indians and the Irish in the seventeenth and eighteenth centuries.[27] Indeed the colonization of Ireland served as a template for the subsequent British settlements in America. The idea of 'virgin land' was central to the justification of the early colonizers of both Ireland and America—both were viewed as countries still in a state of nature. The native inhabitants could then be passed over as primitives who would benefit from the civilizing influence of the Christians in the New World and Englishmen in Ireland, who could lead them away from their primitive superstitions.[28] But if Muldoon's poem suggests such parallels, it also undermines any simple correspondence between the situation of the indigenous peoples of Ireland and America, by insisting on the role the Irish played in the destruction of Native America. So the characters of Cinnamond, 'Smith', and Bucephalus emphasize above all the colonialist designs of Irish emigrants. One consequence of the complex relation between Ireland and Native America is that formulaic stories of resistance and oppression are undercut; as in 'Meeting the British', native and agent of colonization become intertwined, allegiances are provisional and accommodations imperative for survival.

The various forms of accommodation made between American Indian tribal beliefs and Christianity is a major theme throughout the poem, primarily told through the story of the ambiguous cultural renaissance of the Seneca under Handsome Lake. As told by Anthony Wallace this is a story of the preservation of a culture through adaptation and compromise.[29] At a time of growing crisis for the tribes in constant contact with European settlers,

[27] For an excellent account of the parallels drawn in colonialist thinking between Native Americans and the Irish, see Luke Gibbons, 'Race Against Time: Racial Discourse and Irish History', *Oxford Literary Review*, 13 (1991), 95–113.

[28] Thus in '[Maimonides]' we witness a 'decline' from Reason to Faith as Coleridge brandishes a Bible at the Mohawk—an action which later proves ironic in that he is led by the Mohawk to Joseph Brant, of whom we learn in '[Wycliffe]', 'In 1786 Brant again visited London. He met with the Archbishop of Canterbury to discuss his new edition of the Mohawk Prayer Book.'

[29] Anthony F. C. Wallace, *The Death and Rebirth of the Seneca* (New York: Vintage Books, 1969).

decimated by smallpox, the steady whittling away of land, and the corrupting influence of whisky, the Iroquois chief Handsome Lake had a series of visions (in one of which, as in '[Pseudo-Dionysius]', he meets his dog). Setting himself up as an emissary from the Great Spirit, (as in '[Seneca]'), Handsome Lake's new religion offered a curious compromise between the values and sober life-style of the Quakers who at that time lived among them, and a reaffirmation of traditional ritual and belief—such as the ceremony of the burning of the white dog. In other words the 'reborn' Seneca religion stemmed from a desire to remain strong and separate, but it was actually built upon an accommodation between Native and Quaker life-styles (in particular the enclosure of land, farming, and the idea of an afterlife):

> The religious renaissance among the Iroquois was essentially a renewal of popular observance of the traditional, communal religious rituals. The major innovation in belief—the idea of divine judgement and an afterlife in heaven or hell . . . was readily palatable and widely accepted because it was similar in form to the old belief in the cosmic bargain between the Good Twin and the Evil Twin.[30]

Part of Muldoon's poem is directly concerned with the debates among the Seneca about the extent of cultural integration advisable. This is the point of the discussions about the white dog ceremony, for example, or this statement by Handsome Lake's rival chief Red Jacket, in '[Spinoza]', showing 'sympathy' with the Christian missionaries for having 'destroyed the son of the Great Spirit':

> Brother, we pity you. We wish you to bear to our friends our best wishes. Inform them that in compassion towards them we are willing to send them missionaries to teach them our religion, habits and customs.

In this regard it is interesting that Muldoon's Coleridge adopts a shamanistic religion ('his familiar is a coyote made of snow'), while Southey goes to the opposite extreme, using violence in an attempt to hang on to a notion of 'British' cultural integrity.

While one turns inward, to contemplate his own visions, and the other depends increasingly on conservative propaganda, nevertheless Coleridge and Southey still share their belief that they have a monopoly on truth, and that truth and 'sentiment'

[30] Anthony F. C. Wallace, *The Death and Rebirth of the Seneca,* 316.

(Edith's last word) are the fundamentals of poetry. Indeed one could argue that the basis of the truth claim is common to philosophies based on both reason and faith, so that neither poet's choice of the conservative way of faith entails a fundamental reconsideration of the nature of poetry. In contrast Muldoon's poem is based not on ideals of truth, but on a rhetoric of anti-sincerity, comedy, and satire. The characteristic absence of any overt direction in how to read and evaluate the poem or any clue as to where Muldoon's sympathies lie has as much to do with impatience with the idealization of writerly sincerity and authenticity, as with a refusal to take a particular stand on the issues. In effect Muldoon distances himself from both Coleridge and Southey through the form of his poem, through which he attempts to find an accommodation between imaginative fantasy and historical fact.

Linguistic Origins

Part of what's going on is the invention of a new language, and the way in which language is a weapon of colonisation. One of the clues as to whether there might be Welsh Indians lies in language for instance.[31]

One of the most striking aspects of Muldoon's poem is its linguistic exuberance. Muldoon's available dictionary is expanded by American Indian words, period discourse, and idiosyncratic spelling—in many respects this continues the concern of *Meeting the British* with semantic and linguistic change caused by the meeting of cultures, and particularly by trade. Language is opened up to more and more varied means of expression, it gains in precision by adding new terms—but, at the same time as a language moulds itself to a new situation, as it becomes particular, it also becomes increasingly particularized, giving expression to an ever more narrow range of meanings. The furthest extreme of this process is represented in the poem by Sara Fricker's private language, a variation on the private or familial word of 'Quoof'. Sara's discourse becomes wholly personalized (and animalistic), a language for a community of one: 'For the only society I have left now | is Bumble-Cum-Tumble and Doggy-

[31] Paul Muldoon, interview with Blake Morrison, *The Independent on Sunday* (28 Oct. 1990), 37.

Bow-Wow.' (The female character's linguistic privation is perhaps suggestive of the restriction of women writers to stories and rhymes for children.) This process is discernible on a more general level, in the search for signs of racial identity in language—what the poem terms winkling 'the semen out of semantics'. There are two contradictory forces working on language in the poem; on the one hand there is an opening up of English linguistic terminology both in the face of new objects and artefacts encountered on American soil (such as the gopher), and as a result of the encounter with American Indian tribes and their languages. At the same time this process is cut across by the search for cultural (and genetic) origins through language. The section subtitled '[Schelling]' is constructed out of quotations from members of the Lewis and Clark expedition on the 'strangeness' of the language of the Mandans, which (along with the habit of living in fortified dwellings, and of making blue glass beads) is taken to be a mark of their Welshness:

> These savages has the Strangest language of any we have ever seen. They appear to us to have an Empediment in their Speech or bur on their tongue. We take these savages to be the Welch Indians if there be any such.

As in 'Becbretha', 'Madoc' ridicules the practice of seeking the signs of racial origins in etymology, such as the derivation of 'penguin' from the Welsh for 'white head' ('Southey wakes in a cold sweat | penguins don't have white heads'), or Bucephalus's nationalist attempt to derive Monadnock from the Gaelic word *cnoc*, a hill.[32]

It is tempting to read the poem's emphasis on the differentiation of meanings (a major theme of *Meeting the British* also) as a version of Coleridge's theory of desynonymy, or the inherent tendency in language towards increased particularity. For Coleridge the progress of language was an index of the progress of humanity for 'the whole process of human intellect is gradually to

[32] As Muldoon has suggested, Bucephalus can be seen as a conduit for some of the more bizarre claims of the Harvard Professor of History, Barry Fell. Among other assertions, Fell claims that the marks found on certain stones in the north-eastern states are examples of the ancient Irish ogham script. See Barry Fell, *Bronze Age America* (New York: Little Brown, 1982), and Muldoon, 'Introduction to a Dramatised Reading of "Madoc—A Mystery"'.

desynonymize terms'.[33] In Muldoon's poem, however, this process of particularization is in part the result of historical 'regression', as the poet returns to archaic meanings and etymology in order to differentiate meanings. Language 'progresses' through an investigation of the past. The contradictory nature of a process in which, in order to point to differences, it is necessary to return to 'origins' is revealed in the teasing 'key' which opens the volume, in which we find the technician Foley attempting to match 'sound to picture' on a remake of the film *The Hoodlum Priest.* There are many wry jokes in this opening sequence—the subject of the film, territorial gang warfare, suggests not only the victims and battles of 'Madoc' but those of its parallel—Ulster. The Muldoon figure at first cannot recognize this, and (in a parody of 'Brock') upbraids the emigrant Foley for abandoning the ancient roots of the Irish, traceable through the etymology of root-sounds!

When he sookied a calf down a boreen
it was through Indo-European.
When he clicked at a donkey carting dung
your grandfather had an African tongue.
You seem content to ventriloquise the surf.

Foley swallowed whatever it was;

Still defending that same old patch of turf?
Have you forgotten that 'hoodlum' is back-slang
for the leader of a San Francisco street-gang?

The implication is that the creation of a new language entails taking on the new world, moving away from that 'same old patch of turf'—which ignores the ways those battles have been played across the world stage. But here again the ambivalent status of the 'new' is revealed, as once more it is seen to depend on the history of international cultural exchange. The dialogue thus points to the importance of the interweaving of a narrative centred on 'Ulster' and one investigating the struggles of the new American republic. As I have suggested, links are drawn through Foley's precursors in emigration—Cinnamond, 'Smith', and

[33] Coleridge, quoted in Paul Hamilton, *Coleridge's Poetics* (Oxford: Blackwell, 1983), 65.

Bucephalus—but also through the parallel lines running through the history of republicanism in both countries.

The problem of matching sound to picture identified in 'The Key' also refers to South's 'retinagraph' from which the historical narrative supposedly 'flickers and flows'. 'Retinagraph' means literally 'eye-writing', a replay of the pictures recorded on the back of the eye, and the inclusion of graphic signs such as diagrams and maps supports this visual interpretation. At a more fundamental level, however, the suggestion that the narrative is based on pictures recorded from the back of the eye (as opposed to pictures created out of the mind) implies a critique of the Coleridgean idea of the philosophical poem. As I will argue the poem is hung between two poles, between a narrative based on the ideal creations of the imagination and narrative as recording device, the recounting of a history.

Coleridge's theory of desynonymy is closely related to his claims for the philosophical nature of poetry, and to his distinction between the primary and secondary imaginations and the fancy (in large part gleaned from Schelling). Paul Hamilton has pointed to the importance of Coleridge's 'primary orientation towards language in his drive towards philosophical understanding', noting that in his search for a philosophy which will provide him with a theory of the imagination, 'he develops the eighteenth-century attempt to emancipate theories of the imagination from the "despotism of the eye".'[34] One of Hume's most fundamental beliefs was that 'our ideas are images of our impressions', but such a theory imprisoned the workings of the poetic imagination within a strictly representational frame. Coleridge's arguments in *Biographia Literaria* can be seen as a direct challenge to the empiricist tradition of philosophy in that he maintains that poetic expression (metaphor and analogy) is irreducible; there is a distinctly poetic use of the imagination which functions at the level of the symbol and gives access to a particular kind of knowledge, and which guarantees the autonomy of poetry. Moreover, poetry, as an untranslatable medium, symbolizes an ideal for desynonymy to aim at.

The debate between figurative and representational theories of the imagination and poetry is clearly of central importance

[34] Coleridge, *Coleridge's Poetics*, 25–9 *passim*.

throughout 'Madoc', where the mystery revolves around the difference between what can be observed and what is in the mind, 'story and event' as opposed to 'lofty imaginings'. The difficulty faced in the poem, that of matching sound to picture, mirrors the attempt to match the ideal and the factual registers of creative writing. This is brought into focus by a consideration of the function of the 'subtitles' (albeit superimposed subtitles) which introduce the events of the poem. In film, subtitles act as a visual (graphic) translation of an aural message, which (for those unfamiliar with the language in which the film is made) must be matched not only with the sound but with another type of visual representation—the picture on the screen. In Muldoon's poem, however, the visual representation of events is also translated into graphic signs, which must be in turn translated back into a visual image. Each poem is a snapshot of an event (or series of events both linked and separated by asterisks)—a fictional fact—which is introduced by a name which stands for both an individual and a body of texts. The relation of the subtitles to the poem's sections suggests the attempt to match an abstract mythic discourse of philosophy with representations of action and event. This structural pattern is repeated within the events of the poem itself, in which various imaginative ideals (the myth of the Welsh Indians, the ideals of pantisocracy and aspheterism) are mapped on to (and motivate) historical events.

Once again the poetry contemplates the complex causal relation between history and myth or fiction. Mythic and Utopian ideals are the spur to the events in the poem, and to a certain extent they motivate the history which ensues, but at the same time this history becomes bound up once again with fiction, as it is relayed through South's poetic and philosophical concerns. The complex relation of cause and effect is mirrored in the structure of the volume itself; it begins, in the first six poems, with the present in the United States, but a present determined by the echoes of the past, and ends with Hawking, who sets time's arrow in reverse. As 'The Key' insists:

> These past six months I've sometimes run a little ahead of myself, but mostly I lag behind, my footfalls already pre-empted by their echoes.

In the poem, the fantasized future is determined by a (bounded) fantasy of the past, which in turn is powered by myths of origin. 'Madoc' asks us to recognize the fact that the ways we perceive and record, construct us and our histories as much as the other way around. Hence the importance of the graphic machines—the polygraph, the retinagraph—which both appear in, and structure, the poem, acting as reminders of the importance of the form in which fictions and histories are relayed. While both machines suggest the need and desire to match elements with one another, they also ensure that the different registers are kept separate—like sound and picture, fictions and history are 'parallel' realms, they cannot interpenetrate, they can only offer 'clues' to one another. Fittingly then, the subtitles stand outside the body of the poem (in other words they are not contained by the ambiguities and polyvalences of poetic language, but stand for bodies of knowledge); the structure of the poem, like a retina, acts as a net, or network, for a variety of possible interpretations. A comparison with 'Chinook' may be helpful here; I argued above that Muldoon attempted to control the variety of interpretations inherent in poetic language by utilizing all possible meanings within the structure of the poem. In 'Madoc' the net-like form ensures that such mastery cannot occur; the poem is a machine for introducing ever new possibilities of meaning and interpretation. For even as the network of meanings attempts to hold representation in place, it is always in danger of disintegrating, freeing interpretation from its laws.

The interpretative network is created not merely out of the parallel lines drawn between sound and picture, but the snapshots taken of texts written by the characters in the poem. Thus, though this history is a fiction, it is a bounded one, it occurs within the limits of the possible in terms of dates and personages (which is not true of the narrative, based in the future of course). The emphasis on historical fiction offers a way of grounding the work, recognizing the force of historical circumstance, without turning to the truths of personal experience, or poetic authenticity. Here again a comparison with Byron may be helpful, for Byron offers an alternative to exclusive reliance either on the ideal fictions of the imagination or the exaltation of fact. As the fates of Coleridge and Southey reveal, both these paths depend (like reason and faith) on a secure grounding in inner or outer truth. Byron's work by contrast insists on the importance of fact, but, rather than use it as the basis of a moralizing truth claim (as he argues of Southey), he admits its necessarily fictional character. As the famous passage from *Don Juan* attests, 'the facts' can be placed in the service of any 'mythic' narrative (and vice versa), when substantiated by claims of personal authenticity or personal witness. But it is precisely this which is always in doubt where Byron (and Muldoon) are concerned:

> If any person doubt it, I appeal
> To history, tradition, and to facts,
> To newspapers, whose truth all know and feel,
> To plays in five, and operas in three acts;
> All these confirm my statement a good deal
> But that which more completely faith exacts
> Is that myself, and several now in Seville
> *Saw* Juan's last elopement with the devil.[35]

This ironic view of the poetic 'eye', and the truths dependent on it, stands in direct contrast to the elevation of the authenticity of poetic voice which I have discussed as a core of arguments for the social responsibility of poetry in Northern Ireland. The 'voice' of the poem (South's unconsciously relayed images), is constructed out of the sum of various histories, principally those of post-Romantic poetry, the colonization of Ireland and America, and the chronicle of Western philosophy. Indeed, as the 'identity parade' in 'The Key' suggests, it is South's meditation on the structures which cohere to produce his identity (in the minutes before he dies) which serve as a clue to the parallel and interconnected narrative of the North.

Conclusion

The significance of Muldoon's characteristic stance of ironic and unreliable witness should not be underestimated in assessing the meaning of his poetic form. Muldoon himself has suggested that 'Madoc' is a political poem, but, as I have argued, the concept of political poetry must be rethought with regard to his work, which is fundamentally concerned with the relative claims of fiction and fact on the writer's imagination. So far from attempting to create a balance between the ideal constructions of the imagination and

[35] Lord Byron, *Don Juan*, ed. T. G. Steffan, E. Steffan, and W. W. Pratt (Harmondsworth: Penguin, 1982), 96.

the requirements of 'real' history, his work continually implies that they cannot be weighed against one another, since they cannot be separated. History is no more true than fiction, since it comes to us filtered through the imagination, which moulds it in its turn. In consequence, Muldoon's work does not depend on a notion of the 'true', a concept he always treats with suspicion. The self-conscious rhetorical form of the work undermines the aura of authenticity and sincerity necessary for the reader's belief in the truth claim inherent in poetic statements. Both vatic and propagandistic theories of poetic discourse are rejected, in favour of membership of the 'society of false faces'. It would be mistaken, however, to conclude that Muldoon's poetry attempts to undermine the distinction between true and false; rather the implication is that the true cannot be assumed like a mantle, nor arise spirit-like from within—both these modes of claiming poetic authenticity result in delusion.

We might compare here Paulin's desire to recover the radical potential in the role of the writer as witness, responding to the dictates of his or her conscience, rather than to the requirements of a conservative and hierarchical tradition. The act of witnessing, Paulin suggests, may be one means to reinvest the historical sense with a feeling of immediacy and directness. For Muldoon such a project is beset with dangers primarily because it privileges objective knowledge and personal experience as the key to the authenticity the poet claims. Paulin also discerns this risk, which he describes as becoming 'boxed in' by personal or communal interpretations of events; however, in order to avoid such a consequence (giving voice to a partial understanding of history, and thus underwriting the prejudices of the Ulster Unionists), he attempts as far as possible to separate the mystifications consonant with poetic language from a historical understanding which can be apprehended through reason. Muldoon faces a similar difficulty, namely that if he is to appeal to facts, he runs the risk of implying that such facts can be disentangled from the ways they are perceived and recorded. So he chooses the opposite path, insisting that fantasy cannot be extricated from our understanding of history, and indeed at certain points it motivates that history. Rather than working from a notion of rational truth which can be located, and which would serve as the basis for a politics and ethics, Muldoon suggests that the 'good' cannot be decided in advance, but must always be argued for in specific contexts.

Nevertheless the rejection of truth claims necessarily involves some difficulties for the political poet, traditionally conceived. Throughout my reading of Muldoon's work, I have emphasized a tension between the drawing of distinctions, and the drawing of parallels. As I have discussed, there is a danger that in pointing to the similarities and parallels in the histories of the colonization of Irish and American territory, and of periods in the history of Ireland (1798 or 1922 for example), distinct cultures and histories will be conflated. More problematically still, however, the recurrent narrative of decline from Utopian ideal to dangerous fiction suggests a cynical view of politics as a whole. Forms of state organization and political processes are ignored as politics is equated with belief, prejudice, or ideal, rendering any alternative vision of the political difficult, if not impossible. Yet conversely, the suggestion that, rather than authentic or natural principles, personal identities and political processes are both equally constructed, dependent on accident and historical contingency for their fabrication, suggests the possibility of changing their structure. Hence, despite Muldoon's suspicion of the value of transformative politics, his own work bears a liberatory potential.

Conclusion

THROUGHOUT this book I have argued that the writing strategies of the younger Northern Irish poets cannot be understood within established paradigms of the relationship between literature and politics. Moreover the poets' attempt to construct alternative political strategies in their work must be interpreted in the light of cultural and theoretical discussions in Ireland about tradition, modernity, and the structure of the contemporary community, and international debates over the status and significance of post-modernism. Within Ireland those arguments are filtered through the preoccupation of cultural critics with the Enlightenment and Romantic traditions in Irish culture—traditions which have been associated respectively with rationality and atavism, modernity and tradition, cosmopolitanism and tribalism, despite the diverse meanings of all these terms. This preoccupation is in turn a reflection of the desire to find some accommodation within the split community in Northern Ireland, as well as coming to terms with Ireland's colonial and post-colonial heritage (and is echoed in a rather different guise in the debates over Irish historiography).

In one very general sense the question being posed in these debates concerns Ireland's position in relation to the legacy of the Enlightenment, a legacy which is experienced only fitfully and partially in a culture where the values of the Enlightenment conspicuously failed to take hold. Yet if it is the case that Ireland was historically the recipient of a 'failed' Enlightenment (offering a rather different gloss on the phrase 'modernity's incomplete project'), in what sense is it possible to discuss the cultural forms in contemporary Ireland as part of the 'post'-modernity which has been defined as the cultural condition of Europe's and America's metropolitan centres? The prevalence in the poetry not only of literary forms associated with postmodernism, but also of thematic concerns informed by post-structuralist ideas (even if these are mostly presented negatively in Paulin's case) poses a difficulty of placing the cultural phenomenon under examination. Similarly, perhaps my own use of theoretical and philosophical material informed by post-structuralist ideas undermines my commitment to a contextualized reading of the work, by relying on ideas forged in very different (post-Enlightenment) cultural conditions.

A number of responses may be advanced in the face of such reservations; firstly it is of course not the case that in the late twentieth century Ireland is, or could be, isolated from international stylistic trends, so that the writers cannot but be part of a First World cultural condition (moreover two of the writers I have chosen to discuss live outside Ireland). However, while I would not wish to deny the importance of international stylistic movements on the poetry, there are I believe more pressing considerations. For Ireland, and more specifically Northern Ireland, is by no means alien to the project of modernity. As Paulin's work repeatedly reminds us, the North of Ireland was the home of the republican ideals of equality, democracy, and the rights of man, even if these later degenerated into sectarianism. But, on a more general level, the fact of Ireland's colonial (under)-development should not be interpreted simply as the underside or reverse of the experience of the modern, for this risks replaying conservative Catholic and nationalist arguments for the traditional rural nature of Ireland, its inherent resistance to modernizing progress.

Thus the alternative argument I have advanced is that, by virtue of its post-colonial status within Europe, Irish culture is in a position to say something unique about the experience of being modern (a position which is similar to, but not identical with, that of post-colonial cultures outside Europe, which are none the less linked to the hegemonic project of modernity both economically and politically). Hence my use of the term 'impropriety', by means of which I distinguish the experience of being inside and outside the project of modernity at the same time. It is here that the post-colonial and the postmodern may look at each other, and see some of their traits reflected in the other, though they will not find there an identical image to their own. So, for example, the fragmentation of historical narrative which is part of the cultural condition of Ireland finds a correlate in postmodernism's valorization of local narrative, its characteristic use of parody and pastiche, and the reuse of historical and literary material.

In this book I have focused on the strategies of representation which arise as a consequence of the experience of the improper—which might be described as not owning or controlling, but being somehow part of the history of modernity's progress. Given the inescapably skewed history of the Enlightenment in Ireland, attempts to portray Ireland as an advanced European state are, I believe, doomed to failure, and along with them those strategies of representation which depend on the division between public and private spheres which seems to hold for metropolitan cultures. As I have discussed, the Enlightenment model of the relation between the personal (or familial) realm and the public and political arena cannot account for the particular relation drawn between these two spheres as a consequence of Ireland's colonial history. From a different perspective Dorinda Outram has argued that Ireland is still locked into a pre-revolutionary culture, 'Missing from Irish political culture was a crucial bearer of history—that of the bourgeois virtuous man' and without him it lacks 'ideals of individualism and autonomy'.[1] This is undoubtedly a normative claim, suggesting that Irish political culture might be better off if it had taken a more central role in European Enlightenment culture. But taken as a purely descriptive statement it suggests the need to look again at the construction of public and private spheres and forms of political rhetoric in Ireland, and hence its forms of literary representation also.

None of the poetry I have discussed is ostensibly based on patterns of neo-Romantic aesthetic enclosure, insulated from the political world, or on the closed linguistic world of the typical Movement lyric. None the less the idea of a separate private sphere which needs to be opened up to more public and communal concerns is common to much Irish poetry. As I have discussed, the valorization of a private or personal space for poetry, and its employment in giving voice to communal concerns are not mutually exclusive—indeed they are often predicated on one another. For it is within the private sphere that the values of authenticity and autonomy deemed essential for poetic responsibility are thought to reside. Strategies of representation which hinge on the valorization of the personal and subjective imply that the representation of a publicly accessible and transparent version of personal experience is able to undo or counteract the

[1] Dorinda Outram, 'Holding the Future at Bay: The French Revolution and Modern Ireland', *Irish Review*, 6 (1989), 5–6.

ways in which the values pertaining to the individual have been codified and truncated in contemporary society. But this ignores the ways in which personal and public experience are already imbricated with one another, and help to constitute each other's boundaries. On the other hand, as I have argued, poetic strategies which fall back on a mythic or symbolic model of representation, as the means to speak for the community, are similarly inadequate to contemporary cultural circumstances in Ireland. In contrast to both these approaches, I have delineated attempts to reconfigure the relationship between public and private arenas, in poetry which reveals the ways in which the private world is never closed off, but improperly breaches the boundaries of public life, at the same time as it is invaded by it.

So far from being associated with personalization, or subjectification, the private in this scheme is a figure for concealment and secrecy, a conspiracy of language. The personal is the locus not of truth value, authenticity, or sincerity, nor of the autonomy of the individual constitutive of the private sphere in its classic liberal definition. The obscure and cryptic relation between the private experience and its public meaning suggests the arbitrariness, or what I have termed the 'uselessness', of personal experience, and the historical contingency of everyday life. This kind of politics differs from classic liberal definitions of the political to the extent that it disrupts clear lines of communication, and the bedrock of instrumental reason. At stake is the inscription of the body, pleasure, desire, fiction, and even faith (as the underside of reason) into narratives about the nature of the community and the structures by which we can make sense of it.

It would, however, be misleading to imply that all three poets I have chosen to discuss are equally committed, or committed in the same way, to a radical questioning of rationality and its concomitant claims to truth. Most obviously Tom Paulin's work takes as its fundamental premises the value of reasoned argument in overcoming differences and forming the grounds of a just state. As I have discussed, Paulin's poetry itself questions many of the premises of his theoretical position, in particular his valorization of 'plain speech' as a means to political understanding; his requirement of a rational language for political and poetic representation is confounded by the ambiguities and mystifications of the aesthetic. Nevertheless, despite his commitment to politicizing aspects of custom and tradition which lie outside the traditional realm of the public, and finding a reconciliation between the opposing poles of romanticism and republicanism, his work seems weighted on the whole towards the Enlightenment model, with the consequence that those aspects which lie beyond it (vernacular discourse, folk culture, pleasure, and sexuality) are included in the poetry at the level of content but do not serve to transform the structure of the politics he advances.

A fundamental premises of my argument has been that the allegedly isolated spaces of the obscure and secretive poetry I have discussed are in fact socially imbricated; despite the seemingly hermetic and recondite nature, of the work, it does lay claim to a form of 'representativeness' fitted to conditions in which the boundary between the public and the private are not so clearly drawn (as in the colonial context). I have discussed this alternative model of representation with reference to the figure of the woman in Irish political and literary discourse, for a central aspect of this model of the political is that it inscribes the body, with its full and varied sexual valency, on public life. Again it is important to understand this partly as a consequence of Irish historical experience for, in the absence of alternative political structures, great emphasis was placed on the figure of Mother Ireland as a focal point for national identification. And while it is important to acknowledge the debilitating effects that the conservative use of the figure of the woman as metaphor for the nation has had in Irish society, the radical possibilities inherent in the figure of the national-maternal should not go unnoticed. As McGuckian's poetry insists, placing the female body at the centre of a nation's supposedly rational structures cannot fail to destabilize both terms in the analogy between private home and public community. The woman's body cannot, it seems, be transported from private domestic home, to public space, without at the same time becoming that of a 'public woman'. Her body therefore acts as the place of disruption of the public/private distinction at the heart of bourgeois social relations, ensuring that the politics of the body is not a metaphor or a substitute for public political concerns, but bound up with them.

Albeit from a more general perspective, such matters have of course been a primary concern of the women's movement, suggesting that here again is a point where political transformations within the contemporary social sphere coalesce with the particular historical and cultural condition pertaining to Ireland. However, the importance of such contemporary movements is very little evident in McGuckian's poetry which tends towards a rather too exclusive reconfiguration of the elements of Irish literary and historical tradition (though this is placed in the context of alternative European histories). Indeed, despite their marked differences, the emphasis on the burden of historical tradition is a trait which McGuckian's poetry shares with Paulin's. In Muldoon's work, by contrast, the significance of the fractured legacy of Irish history is inseparable from contemporary transformations of the structure of the political. The disruption of the Enlightenment faith in reason is related not only to the soured narrative of romanticism and republicanism in Northern Ireland, but to contemporary postmodern developments in the social sphere. Muldoon's case then seems overdetermined—in addition to his focus on the constitutive elements of Irish mythic and historical tradition, he is also, of the three, the poet most obviously postmodern in his concerns. Perhaps more than either McGuckian or Paulin, Muldoon's work serves to undermine redemptive approaches to everyday life, and the idea that the personal world of the individual contains truths generalizable for all. As the analogy (or parallel) of South's fractured and discontinuous identity with the narrative of the North in 'Madoc' suggests, not only are personal and public histories bound up with one another, but they are both equally fabricated, constructed out of the shards of an arbitrary and contingent history. While it is of course inescapable that all personal and national identities are partly the result of accident and chance, Muldoon's work is notable for its refusal to force disparate elements into a coherent narrative that can give meaning to experience. Thus, while he is willing to draw parallels he refuses to draw conclusions. Unlike Paulin's narrative construction in 'The Caravans on Lüneberg Heath', Muldoon's history does not add up to anything larger than itself, least of all to the birth of a consistent historical witness.

One of the implications of the fact that private and public or political narratives mirror one another, not only in their content but also in their dislocated structure, is the impossibility of using private life as a source of redemption, or as a refuge from the inhospitable, mechanistic, and bureaucratic thought of the contemporary world. What is at stake here is not simply the idea that the private world of the individual is the residence of the unique and the authentic (Muldoon implies that while it may be experienced as unique by the individual concerned, that uniqueness is incommunicable and therefore 'useless'), but also the ideal of autonomy on which liberal definitions of privacy depend. For just as the private sphere is shown to impinge on historical and political narratives, at the same time it is invaded by social and political processes. Nevertherless, as I have suggested, the emphasis on the construction, rather than the discovery of the self in Muldoon's poetry (a process which can be traced too in Byron's work) has liberatory potential. It suggests that despite Muldoon's suspicion of political idealism there is indeed an Enlightenment aspect to his work, if one understands the contemporary transformation of an Enlightenment stance to involve a permanent critique of ourselves which 'will separate out, from the contingency that has made us what we are, the possibility of no longer being, doing, or thinking what we are, do or think.'[2]

It is this reinterpretation of the meaning and value of modernity (rather than its rejection) which, I have argued, is of fundamental importance in a reading of the younger Northern Irish poets. Yet, if it is necessary to contextualize their poetry in order to appreciate the significance of their interrogation of the legacy of the Enlightenment, the significance of their work is not limited or bounded by its national context. For the transformation of the relationship between privacy and the public and political world in Ireland necessarily puts in question the hegemonic models of these spheres as they are taken to apply to the metropolitan centre. It requires us to rethink fundamental assumptions about the politics of representation as a whole.

[2] Michel Foucault, 'What is Enlightenment', in Paul Rabinow (ed.), *The Foucault Reader* (Harmondsworth; Penguin, 1984), 46.

Select Bibliography

ADAMS, GERRY, *The Politics of Irish Freedom* (Dingle: Brandon Books, 1986).

ADAMSON, IAN, *The Identity of Ulster: The Land, the Language and the People* (Belfast: Adamson, 1982).

ADORNO, THEODOR, 'Commitment', in Ernst Bloch *et al.*, *Aesthetics and Politics* (London: New Left Books, 1977).

ALLEN, MICHAEL, 'Barbaric Yawp, Gibbous Voice', rev. of Medbh McGuckian, *Venus and the Rain*, in *Honest Ulsterman*, 77 (1984), 59–64.

—— 'Realism Meets Phantasmagoria', rev. of Paul Muldoon, *Meeting the British*, in *Honest Ulsterman*, 84 (Winter 1987), 60–5.

ALLNUTT, GILLIAN, D'AGUIAR, FRED, EDWARDS, KEN and MOTTRAM Eric, (eds.), *The New British Poetry* (London: Collins, 1988).

ANDERSON, BENEDICT, *Imagined Communities: Reflections on the Origin and Spread of Nationalism* (London: Verso, 1983).

ANDERSON, PERRY, 'The Antinomies of Antonio Gramsci', *New Left Review*, 100 (Nov. 1976–Jan. 1977), 5–79.

ANDREWS, ELMER (ed.), *Contemporary Irish Poetry: A Collection of Critical Essays* (Basingstoke: Macmillan, 1992).

ANDREWS, JOHN, *A Paper Landscape: The Ordnance Survey in Nineteenth-Century Ireland* (Oxford: Oxford University Press, 1975).

ARENDT, HANNAH, 'Reflections on Violence', *Journal of International Affairs*, 23:1 (1969), 1–35.

ASHCROFT, BILL, GRIFFITHS, GARETH, and TIFFIN, HELEN, *The Empire Writes Back: Theory and Practice in Post-Colonial Literatures* (London: Routledge, 1989).

ATTRIDGE, DEREK, 'Language as History/History as Language: Saussure and the Romance of Etymology', in *Peculiar Language: Literature as Difference from the Renaissance to James Joyce* (London: Methuen, 1988).

AUDEN, W. H., *Collected Poems*, ed. Edward Mendelson (London: Faber and Faber, 1976).

BAKHTIN, MIKHAIL, *The Dialogic Imagination*, trans. Caryl Emerson and Michael Holquist, ed. Michael Holquist (Austin, Tex.: University of Texas Press, 1981).

—— *Rabelais and His World*, trans. Helene Iswolsky (Bloomington, Ind.: Indiana University Press, 1984).

—— *Problems in Dostoevsky's Poetics*, ed. and trans. Caryl Emerson (2nd edn., Minneapolis: Minnesota University Press, 1987).

BANVILLE, JOHN, 'Slouching towards Bethlehem', rev. of Derek Mahon, *Selected Poems*, and Paul Muldoon, *Madoc—A Mystery*, in *New York Review of Books* (30 May 1991), 37–9.

—— 'Rapture's Menace', rev. of Tom Paulin, *Minotaur: Poetry and the Nation State*, in *Observer* (19 Jan. 1992), 27.

BARRELL, JOHN, *English Literature in History, 1730–80: An Equal Wide Survey* (London: Hutchinson, 1983).

BARRY, SEBASTIAN (ed.), *The Inherited Boundaries: Younger Poets of the Republic of Ireland* (Dublin: Dolmen, 1986).

BARTHES, ROLAND, *Writing Degree Zero*, trans. Annette Lavers and Colin Smith, ed. Susan Sontag (originally published 1953; New York: Hill and Wang, 1968).

—— *Mythologies*, trans. Annette Lavers (London: Granada, 1973).

—— *S/Z*, trans. Richard Miller (London: Jonathan Cape, 1975).

—— *Roland Barthes*, trans. Richard Howard (originally published 1975; London: Macmillan, 1977).

BAUDRILLARD, JEAN, *In the Shadow of the Silent Majorities* (New York: Semiotext(e), 1983).

BEALE, JENNY, *Women in Ireland: Voices of Change* (Basingstoke: Macmillan, 1986).

BECKETT, J. C., *The Making of Modern Ireland: 1603–1923* (originally published 1966; London: Faber and Faber, 1981).

BELL, DESMOND, 'Cultural Studies in Ireland and the Postmodernist Debate', *Irish Journal of Sociology*, 1 (1991), 83–95.

BELL, GEOFFREY, *The Protestants of Ulster* (London: Pluto, 1976).

BENHABIB, SEYLA, *Situating the Self: Gender, Community and Postmodernism in Contemporary Ethics* (Cambridge: Polity, 1992).

BENJAMIN, JESSICA, 'Authority and the Family Revisited: Or A World Without Fathers?', *New German Critique*, 13 (1978), 35–58.

BHABHA, HOMI, 'Of Mimicry and Men: The Ambivalence of Colonial Discourse', *October*, 28 (1984), 125–33.

—— 'Signs Taken for Wonders: Questions of Ambivalence and Authority under a Tree Outside Delhi, May 1817', in Francis Barker *et al.* (eds.), *Europe and its Others*, ii (Colchester: Essex Conference Papers, 1985), 89–106.

BISHOP, ELIZABETH, *The Complete Poems, 1927–1979* (London: Hogarth Press, 1984).

BOLAND, EAVAN, 'The Woman Poet: Her Dilemma', *American Poetry Review*, 16:1 (Jan./Feb. 1987), 17–20.

—— 'The Woman Poet in a National Tradition', *Studies*, 76 (Summer 1987), 148–58.

—— *The Journey and Other Poems* (Manchester: Carcanet, 1987).

BOLGER, DERMOT (ed.) *The Bright Wave/An Tonn Gheal: Poetry in Irish Now* (Dublin: Raven Arts Press, 1986).

BOYCE, D. GEORGE, *Nationalism in Ireland* (Baltimore: Johns Hopkins University Press, 1982).

BOYLAN, THOMAS A., and FOLEY, TIMOTHY P., *Political Economy and Colonial Ireland: The Propagation and Ideological Functions of Economic Discourse in the Nineteenth Century* (London: Routledge, 1992).

BRAIDWOOD, JOHN, *The Ulster Dialect Lexicon* (Belfast: Queen's University Press, 1969).

BROWN, TERENCE, *Northern Voices: Poets from the North of Ireland* (Dublin: Gill and Macmillan, 1985).

—— *Ireland: A Social and Cultural History, 1922–1985* (originally published 1981; London: Fontana, 1985).

BUCKLAND, PATRICK, *A History of Northern Ireland* (Dublin: Gill and Macmillan, 1981).

CAHILL, EILEEN, 'A Silent Voice: Seamus Heaney and Ulster Politics', *Critical Quarterly*, 29:3 (Autumn 1987), 55–9.

CAIRNS, DAVID, and RICHARDS, SHAUN, *Writing Ireland: Colonialism, Nationalism and Culture* (Manchester, Manchester University Press, 1988).

CARDINAL, ROGER, *Figures of Reality* (London: Croom Helm, 1981).

CAREY, JOHN, rev. of Paul Muldoon, *Quoof*, in *Critic's Forum* (BBC Radio 4, 1 Oct. 1983).

—— 'The Stain of Words', rev. of Seamus Heaney, *The Haw Lantern*, and Paul Muldoon, *Meeting the British*, in *Sunday Times* (21 June 1987), 56.

CARSON, CIARAN, 'Escaped from the Massacre?', rev. of Seamus Heaney, *North*, in *Honest Ulsterman*, 50 (1975), 184–5.

—— *The New Estate* (Belfast: Blackstaff, 1976).

—— '*Sweeney Astray*: Escaping From Limbo', in Tony Curtis (ed.), *The Art of Seamus Heaney* (Bridgend: Poetry Wales, 1985).

—— *The Irish for No* (Dublin: Gallery Press, 1987).

—— *Belfast Confetti* (Dublin: Gallery Press, 1989).

CHATTERJEE, PARTHA, *Nationalist Thought and the Colonialist World: A Derivative Discourse* (London: Zed, 1986).

CHRISTIAN, BARBARA, 'The Race for Theory', in Linda Kauffman (ed.), *Gender and Theory: Dialogues in Feminist Criticism* (New York: Blackwell, 1989), 225–37.

CLEAR, CATRIONA, *Nuns in Nineteenth Century Ireland* (Dublin: Gill and Macmillan, 1987).

CORCORAN, NEIL, 'The Shy Trickster', rev. of Paul Muldoon, *Quoof*, in *Times Literary Supplement* (28 Oct. 1983), 1180.

—— 'Flaneur along the Shopfronts', rev. of Paul Muldoon, *Meeting the British*, in *Poetry Review*, 77:3 (Autumn 1987), 44–6.

CORKERY, DANIEL, *The Hidden Ireland: A Study of Gaelic Munster in the Eighteenth Century* (2nd edn., Dublin: Gill and Macmillan, 1979).

COULTER, CAROL, *Ireland: Between the First and the Third Worlds* (Dublin: Attic Press, 1990).

CROWLEY, TONY, 'Bakhtin and the History of the Language', Ken Hirschkop and David Shepherd (eds.), in *Bakhtin and Cultural Theory* (Manchester: Manchester University Press, 1989).

CROZIER, Maurna (ed.), *Cultural Traditions in Northern Ireland* (Belfast: Institute of Irish Studies, 1991).

CULLINGFORD, ELIZABETH, 'Thinking of Her as Ireland', paper presented at Yeats Annual Summer School, Sligo (Aug. 1988).

CURTIN, CHRIS, KELLY, MARY, and O'DOWD, LIAM (eds.), *Culture and Ideology in Ireland* (Galway: Galway University Press, 1984).

—— JACKSON PAULINE and O'CONNOR, BARBARA (eds.), *Gender in Irish Society* (Galway: Galway University Press, 1987).

CURTIS, L.P., Jun. *Anglo-Saxons and Celts: A Study of Anti-Irish Prejudice in Victorian England* (Bridgeport, Conn.: Conference on British Studies of University of Bridgeport, 1968).

—— *Apes and Angels: The Irishman in Victorian Caricature* (Newton Abbot: David and Charles, 1971).

DAVIES, R. T., *Medieval English Lyrics: A Critical Anthology* (London: Faber and Faber, 1963).

DAWE, GERALD (ed.), *The Younger Irish Poets* (Belfast: Blackstaff, 1982).

—— and LONGLEY, EDNA (eds.), *Across a Roaring Hill: The Protestant Imagination in Modern Ireland* (Belfast: Blackstaff, 1985).

DEANE, SEAMUS, 'Irish Poetry and Irish Nationalism', in Douglas Dunn (ed.), *Two Decades of Irish Writing* (Cheadle Hulme: Carcanet, 1975), 4–22.

—— 'Remembering the Irish Future', *Crane Bag*, 8:1 (1984), 81–92.

—— 'Civilians and Barbarians', *Ireland's Field Day*, ed. Field Day Theatre Company (London: Hutchinson, 1985), 33–42.

—— *Celtic Revivals: Essays in Modern Irish Literature, 1880–1980* (London: Faber and Faber, 1985).

—— *A Short History of Irish Literature* (London: Hutchinson, 1986).

—— (ed.), *The Field Day Anthology of Irish Writing*, 3 vols. (Derry: Field Day Publications, 1991).

DENVIR, GEAROID, 'Continuing the Link: An Aspect of Contemporary Irish Poetry', *Irish Review*, 3 (1988), 40–54.

DOCHERTY, THOMAS, 'Initiations, Tempers, Seductions: Postmodern McGuckian', in Neil Corcoran (ed.), *The Chosen Ground: Essays on the Contemporary Poetry of Northern Ireland* (Bridgend: Seren Books, 1992), 191–210.

DOOLEY, TIM, 'Soft Cushionings', rev. of Medbh McGuckian, *The Flower Master*, in *Times Literary Supplement* (29 Oct. 1982), 1200.

DUNN, DOUGLAS, 'Manœuvres', rev. of Paul Muldoon (ed.) *The Faber Book of Contemporary Irish Poetry*, in *Irish Review*, 1 (1986), 84–90.

DUNNE, TOM, 'New Histories: Beyond "Revisionism"', *Irish Review*, 12 (1992), 1–12.

EAGLETON, TERRY, 'Recent Poetry', rev. of Seamus Heaney, *Field Work*, in *Stand*, 23:1 (1980), 76–9.

—— 'Capitalism, Modernism and Postmodernism', *New Left Review*, 152 (July/Aug. 1985), 60–73.

—— 'New Poetry', rev. of John Montague, *The Dead Kingdom*, in *Stand*, 26:2 (1985), 67.

—— 'The Poetry of Radical Republicanism', rev. of Tom Paulin (ed.), *The Faber Book of Political Verse*, in *New Left Review*, 158 (1986), 123–7.

EASTHOPE, ANTHONY, and THOMPSON, JOHN O. (eds.), *Contemporary Poetry Meets Modern Theory* (Hemel Hempstead: Harvester Wheatsheaf, 1991).

ECO, UMBERTO, 'Striking at the Heart of the State', in *Travels in Hyperreality* (London: Pan, 1987), 113–18.

EDITORIAL, *Crane Bag*, 1:2 (1978), 4–7.

ELLIOTT, MARIANNE, *Partners in Revolution: The United Irishmen and France* (New Haven, Conn.: Yale University Press, 1982).

FARRELL, MICHAEL, *Northern Ireland: The Orange State* (London: Pluto, 1980).

FENNELL, DESMOND, 'The Last Days of the Gaeltacht', *Crane Bag*, 5:2 (1981), 8–11.

FLOWER, ROBIN, *The Irish Tradition* (Oxford: Oxford University Press, 1947).

FOSTER, ROY, 'We Are All Revisionists Now', *Irish Review*, 1 (1986), 1–5.

—— *Modern Ireland, 1600–1972* (Harmondsworth: Penguin, 1988).

FRAZIER, ADRIAN, 'Juniper, Otherwise Known: Poems by Paulin and Muldoon', rev. of Tom Paulin, *Liberty Tree*, and Paul Muldoon, *Quoof*, in *Eire–Ireland: A Journal of Irish Studies*, 19:1 (Spring 1984), 123–33.

FREUD, SIGMUND, *The Interpretation of Dreams*, trans. James Strachey, ed. Angela Richards, Pelican Freud Library, iv (Harmondsworth: Penguin, 1976).

GARRAT, ROBERT F., *Modern Irish Poetry: Tradition and Continuity from Yeats to Heaney* (Berkeley Calif.: University of California Press, 1986).

GARVIN, TOM, 'The Return of History: Collective Myths and Modern Nationalisms', *Irish Review*, 9 (1990), 16–30.

GELLNER, ERNEST, *Nations and Nationalism* (Oxford: Blackwell, 1983).

GERALD OF WALES, *The History and Topography of Ireland*, trans. John O'Meara (originally published 1951; Harmondsworth: Penguin, 1982).

GIBBONS, LUKE, 'Montage, Modernism and the City', *Irish Review*, 10 (1991), 1–6.

GIBBONS, LUKE, 'Race Against Time: Racial Discourse and Irish History', *Oxford Literary Review*, 13 (1991), 95–113.

GITZEN, JULIAN, 'Northern Ireland: The Post-Heaney Generation', *Poesis*, 6:2 (1985), 47–64.

GOODBY, JOHN, '"Armageddon, Armagh-geddon": Language and Crisis in the Poetry of Paul Muldoon', in Birgit Bramsbäck and Martin Croghan (eds.), *Anglo–Irish and Irish Literature: Aspects of Language and Culture*, ii (Uppsala: Uppsala University Press, 1988), 229–36.

—— 'Elephantiasis and Essentialism', *Irish Review*, 10 (1991), 132–7.

GRAMSCI, ANTONIO, *Selections from Cultural Writings*, ed. David Forgacs and Geoffrey Nowell-Smith, trans. William Boelhower (London: Lawrence and Wishart, 1985).

GRASS, GÜNTER, *Das Treffen in Telgte: Eine Erzahlung und dreiundvierzig Gedichte aus dem Barock* (Darmstadt: Sammlung Luchterhand, 1985). Trans. as *The Meeting at Telgte*, trans. Ralph Mannheim, Afterword by Leonard Foster (London: Secker and Warburg, 1981).

GRENNAN, EAMON, 'A Whimful, Myopic Book', rev. of Paul Muldoon (ed.), *The Faber Book of Contemporary Irish Poetry*, in *Honest Ulsterman*, 82 (Winter 1986), 58–66.

GWYNN, A. J. (ed.), *The Metrical Dindschenchas* (Dublin: Royal Irish Academy, 1903–35).

HABERMAS, JÜRGEN, *The Structural Transformation of the Public Sphere* (Cambridge, Mass: MIT Press, 1989).

HAMILTON, PAUL, *Coleridge's Poetics* (Oxford: Blackwell, 1983).

HARDY, BARBARA, 'Meeting the Myth: *Station Island*', in Tony Curtis (ed.), *The Art of Seamus Heaney* (Bridgend: Poetry Wales, 1985), 151–63.

HARMER, MEREDITH, 'A Chronicle of Ireland', in Sir James Ware (ed.), *The Histories of Ireland Collected by Three Learned Authors* (originally published Dublin, 1633; Amsterdam: De Capo Press, 1971).

HAUGHTON, HUGH, 'An Eye on the Everyday', rev. of *Faber Poetry Introduction 5* [with Medbh McGuckian], in *Times Literary Supplement* (13 Aug. 1982), 876.

HEANEY, SEAMUS, *Wintering Out* (London: Faber and Faber, 1972).

—— *North* (London: Faber and Faber, 1975).

—— 'Unhappy and at Home', interview with Seamus Deane, *Crane Bag*, 1:1 (1977), 66–72.

—— 'The Interesting Case of John Alphonsus Mulrennan', *Planet*, 41 (1978), 34–7.

—— *Preoccupations: Selected Prose, 1968–78* (London: Faber and Faber, 1979).

—— *Sweeney Astray* (London: Faber and Faber, 1984).

—— 'An Open Letter', *Ireland's Field Day*, ed. Field Day Theatre Company (London: Hutchinson, 1985), 21–30.

—— *Place and Displacement: Recent Poetry of Northern Ireland* (Grasmere: Trustees of Dove Cottage, 1985).

—— *The Haw Lantern* (London: Faber and Faber, 1988).

—— *The Government of the Tongue: The 1986 T. S. Eliot Memorial Lectures and Other Critical Writings* (London: Faber and Faber, 1988).

—— *Seeing Things* (London: Faber and Faber, 1991).

HEDERMAN, MARK PATRICK, 'Seamus Heaney: The Reluctant Poet', *Crane Bag* 3:2 (1979) 61–70.

—— 'Poetry and the Fifth Province', *Crane Bag*, 9:1 (1985), 110–119.

HEIDEGGER, MARTIN, *An Introduction to Metaphysics*, trans. Ralph Mannheim (New Haven, Conn.: Yale University Press, 1959).

HENIGAN, ROBERT H., 'Contemporary Women Poets in Ireland', *Concerning Poetry*, 18:1–2 (1985), 103–115.

HOFMAN, MICHAEL, 'The Recent Generations at Their Song', rev. of Paul Muldoon, *The Wishbone*, in *Times Literary Supplement* (30th May 1986), 585–6.

—— 'Muldoon—A Mystery', rev. of Paul Muldoon, *Madoc—A Mystery*, in *London Review of Books* (20 Dec. 1990), 18–19.

HOLLINGHURST, ALAN, 'Telling Tales', rev. of Paul Muldoon, *Why Brownlee Left*, in *Encounter*, 56 (1981), 80–5.

HOLMES, RICHARD, *Coleridge: Early Visions* (Harmondsworth: Penguin, 1989).

HOMANS, MARGARET, *Women Writers and Poetic Identity* (Princeton NJ: Princeton University Press, 1980).

HUGHES, EAMONN (ed.), *Culture and Politics in Northern Ireland, 1690–1990* (Milton Keynes: Open University Press, 1991).

INGLIS, TOM, *Moral Monopoly: The Catholic Church in Modern Irish Society* (Dublin: Gill and Macmillan, 1987).

IRIGARAY, LUCE, 'Women's Exile', *Ideology and Consciousness*, 1 (May 1977), 62–76.

—— *Speculum of the Other Woman*, trans. Gillian C. Gill (Ithaca, NY: Cornell University Press, 1984).

—— 'Is the Subject of Science Sexed?', *Cultural Critique*, 1 (1985), 73–88.

—— *This Sex Which is Not One*, trans. Catherine Porter (Ithaca, NY: Cornell University Press, 1986).

JAMESON, FREDRIC, 'Postmodernism, or The Cultural Logic of Late Capitalism', *New Left Review*, 146 (July–Aug. 1984), 53–92.

JENKINS, ALAN, 'Hearts in the Right Place', rev. of Medbh McGuckian, *On Ballycastle Beach*, in *Observer* (10 July 1988), 33.

JOHNSTON, DILLON, *Irish Poetry After Joyce* (Ind.: Bloomington, University of Notre Dame Press; Mountrath: Dolmen Press, 1985).

JOYCE, P. W., *The Origin and History of Irish Place Names*, 3 vols. (Dublin: McGlashan and Gill, 1889), i.

KEARNEY, RICHARD, 'Myth and Motherland', *Ireland's Field Day*, ed. Field Day Theatre Company (London: Hutchinson, 1985), 61–80.

—— (ed.), *The Irish Mind: Exploring Intellectual Traditions* (Dublin: Wolfhound Press, 1985).

—— *Transitions: Narratives in Modern Irish Culture* (Dublin: Wolfhound Press, 1988).

—— (ed.), *Across the Frontiers: Ireland in the 1990s* (Dublin: Wolfhound Press, 1990).

KERRIGAN, JOHN, 'The New Narrative', rev. of Paul Muldoon, *Quoof*, in *London Review of Books* (16–29 Feb. 1984), 22–3.

KINSELLA, THOMAS (ed.), *The New Oxford Book of Irish Verse* (Oxford: Oxford University Press, 1986).

KRISTEVA, JULIA, 'Women's Time', in Nannerl O. Keohane, Michelle Z. Rosaldo, and Barbara C. Gelpi (eds.), *Feminist Theory: A Critique of Ideology* (Brighton: Harvester, 1982), 31–53.

KUBAYANDA, JOSAPHAT B., 'Minority Discourse and the African Collective', *Cultural Critique*, 6 (1987), 113–30.

LLOYD, DAVID, '"Pap for the Dispossessed": Seamus Heaney and the Poetics of Identity', *Boundary 2* (Winter/Spring 1985), 319–42.

—— *Nationalism and Minor Literature: James Clarence Mangan and the Emergence of Irish Cultural Nationalism.* (Berkeley, Calif.: University of California Press, 1988).

—— 'Writing in the Shit: Nationalism and the Colonial Subject', *Irish Review*, 4 (Spring 1988), 59–65.

—— 'The Poetics of Politics: Yeats and the Founding of the State', *Qui Parle*, 3:2 (1989).

LOFTUS, BELINDA, *Mirrors: William III and Mother Ireland* (Dundrum: Picture Press, 1990).

LONGLEY, EDNA, 'Stars and Horses, Pigs and Trees,' *Crane Bag*, 3:2 (1979), 54–60.

—— '"Inner Emigré" or "Artful Voyeur"? Seamus Heaney's North', in Tony Curtis (ed.) *The Art of Seamus Heaney*, (Bridgend: Poetry Wales Press, 1982).

—— 'Poetry and Politics in Northern Ireland,' *Crane Bag*, 9:1 (1985), 26–37.

—— 'A Reply [to Mark Patrick Hederman],' *Crane Bag*, 9:1 (1985), 120–2.

—— *Poetry in the Wars* (Newcastle upon Tyne: Bloodaxe Books, 1986).

—— *Culture in Ireland: Division or Diversity?* (Belfast: Institute of Irish Studies, 1991).

LONGLEY, MICHAEL, *Poems, 1963–83* (Edinburgh: Salamander, 1985).

LOTRINGER, SYLVERE, and MARAZZI, CHRISTIAN (eds.), *Autonomia: Post-Political Politics*, 3:3 (New York: Semiotext(e), 1980).

LYONS, F. S. L., *Ireland Since the Famine* (originally published 1971; London: Collins/Fontana, 1973).

—— *Culture and Anarchy in Ireland, 1890–1939* (Oxford: Oxford University Press, 1982).

MacCana, Proinsias, 'Women in Irish Mythology', *Crane Bag*, 4:2 (1980), 7–11.

McCurry, Jacqueline, '"S'crap": Colonialism Indicted in the Poetry of Paul Muldoon', *Eire–Ireland*, 27:3 (1992), 92–109.

MacCurtain, Margaret, 'Towards an Appraisal of the Religious Image of Women', *Crane Bag*, 4:1 (1980), 26–30.

—— and Ó Corráin, Donncha (eds.), *Women in Irish Society: The Historical Dimension* (Dublin: Arlen House, 1978).

McDiarmid, Lucy, 'From Signifump to Kierkegaard', rev. of Paul Muldoon, *Madoc—A Mystery*, in *New York Times* (28 July 1991), 14.

MacDonagh, Oliver, *States of Mind: A Study of Anglo-Irish Conflict, 1780–1980* (London: Allen and Unwin, 1983).

McGuckian, Medbh, *Portrait of Joanna* (Belfast: Ulsterman Publications, 1980).

—— *Single Ladies* (Budleigh Salterton: Interim Press, 1980).

—— 'Medbh McGuckian', in *Trio Poetry 2* (Belfast: Blackstaff, 1981), 24–44.

—— *The Flower Master* (Oxford: Oxford University Press, 1982).

—— *Venus and the Rain* (Oxford: Oxford University Press, 1984).

—— *On Ballycastle Beach* (Oxford: Oxford University Press, 1988).

—— *Marconi's Cottage* (Dublin: Gallery Press, 1991, and Newcastle upon Tyne: Bloodaxe Books, 1992).

—— (ed.), *The Big Striped Golfing Umbrella* (Belfast: Arts Council of Northern Ireland, 1985).

—— Personal interview (10 Jan. 1986).

—— Personal interview (20 Nov. 1986).

—— Personal interview (19 June 1988).

Mackinnon, Lachlan, 'A Dream Diffused in Words', rev. of Paul Muldoon, *Madoc—A Mystery*, in *Times Literary Supplement* (12–18 Oct. 1990), 1105.

Mahon, Derek, 'Poetry in Northern Ireland', *Twentieth Century Studies*, 4 (1970), 89–93.

—— *Lives* (Oxford: Oxford University Press, 1972).

Mahon, Evelyn, 'Women's Rights and Catholicism in Ireland', *New Left Review*, 166 (1987), 53–77.

Mandelstam, Osip, *Selected Essays*, ed. Sidney Monas (Austin, Tex.: University of Texas, 1977).

—— *Works in Two Volumes*, i, ed. P. M. Nerler (Moscow: Khudozhestvennaya Literatura, 1990).

Middleton, Peter, 'Language Poetry and Linguistic Activism', *Social Text*, 25/26 (1990), 242–53.

MILLER, KERBY A., *Emigrants and Exiles: Ireland and the Irish Exodus to North America* (Oxford: Oxford University Press, 1985).

MONTAGUE, JOHN, *The Rough Field* (Dublin: Dolmen, 1972).

MONTAGUE, JOHN, (ed.) *The Faber Book of Irish Verse* (London: Faber and Faber, 1974).

MOONEY, MARTIN, 'Body Logic: Some Notes on the Poetry of Medbh McGuckian', *Gown Literary Supplement* (1988), 16–18.

MORETTI, FRANCO, 'The Moment of Truth', in *Signs Taken For Wonders* (London: Verso, 1988), 249–61.

MORRISON, BLAKE, 'Tropical Storms', rev. of Medbh McGuckian, *Venus and the Rain*, in *London Review of Books* (6–19 Sept. 1984), 22–3.

—— and MOTION, ANDREW (eds.) *The Penguin Book of Contemporary British Poetry* (Harmondsworth: Penguin, 1982).

MULDOON, PAUL, *Knowing My Place* (Portrush: Ulsterman, 1971).

—— *New Weather* (London: Faber and Faber, 1973).

—— *Spirit of Dawn* (Belfast: Ulsterman, 1975).

—— *Mules* (London: Faber and Faber, 1977).

—— *Names and Addresses* (Belfast: Ulsterman, 1978).

—— *Why Brownlee Left* (London: Faber and Faber, 1980).

—— *The O-O's Party: New Year's Eve* (Dublin: Gallery, 1981).

—— *Ted Hughes and Paul Muldoon*, Faber Poetry Cassette (London: Faber, 1982).

—— *Quoof* (London: Faber and Faber, 1983).

——'Five Poems ["Bears", "Tibet", "Toxophilus", "Pandas", and "Wolves"]', *Times Literary Supplement* (10 Feb. 1984), 137.

—— *The Wishbone* (Dublin: Gallery, 1984).

—— *Selected Poems, 1968–83* (London: Faber and Faber, 1986).

—— *Meeting the British* (London: Faber and Faber, 1987).

—— *Madoc* (London: Faber and Faber, 1990).

—— (ed.), *The Scrake of Dawn* (Belfast: Arts Council of Northern Ireland, 1979).

—— (ed.), *The Faber Book of Contemporary Irish Verse* (London: Faber and Faber, 1986).

—— (ed.), *The Essential Byron* (New York: Ecco Press, 1989).

—— Interview with John Haffenden, in John Haffenden (ed.), *Viewpoints: Poets in Conversation with John Haffenden* (London: Faber and Faber, 1981), 130–42.

—— 'A Conversation with Paul Muldoon', with Michael Donaghy, in *Chicago Review*, 35:1 (1985), 76–85.

—— 'An Interview with Paul Muldoon', with Clair Wills, Nick Jenkins, and John Lanchester, in *Oxford Poetry*, 3:1 (Winter 1986/7), 14–20.

—— Personal interview (2 June 1987).

—— Interview, with Blake Morrison, 'Way Down Upon the Old Susquehanna', in *Independent on Sunday* (28 Oct. 1990), 37.

—— Interview with Kevin Smith, 'Lunch with Paul Muldoon', in *Rhinosceros*, 4 (1991), 75–94.

MULFORD, WENDY, '"Curved, Odd . . . Irregular". A Vision of Contemporary Poetry by Women', *Women: A Cultural Review*, 1:3 (1990), 261–74.

NAIRN, TOM, *The Enchanted Glass* (London: Radius Press, 1988).

NÍ CHUILLEANÁIN, EILÉAN (ed.), *Irish Women: Image and Achievement: Women in Irish Culture from Earliest Times* (Dublin: Arlen House, 1985).

—— *The Second Voyage* (Newcastle upon Tyne: Bloodaxe Books, 1986).

NÍ DHOMHNAILL, NUALA, *Selected Poems/Rogha Danta*, trans. Michael Hartnett (Dublin: Raven Arts Press, 1986).

NUSSBAUM, MARTHA, *The Fragility of Goodness: Luck and Ethics in Greek Tragedy and Philosophy* (Cambridge: Cambridge University Press, 1986).

O MAOLCHRAIBHE, PADRAIG, *The Role of Language in Ireland's Cultural Revival* (Belfast: Sinn Féin, 1984).

O'BRIEN, CONOR CRUISE, 'An Unhealthy Intersection', *New Review*, 2:16 (1975), 3–8.

—— 'A Tale of Two Nations', *New York Review of Books* (19 July 1990), 33–6.

O'BRIEN, SEAN, 'Unique Particulars', rev. of Paul Muldoon, *Selected Poems, 1968–1983*, in *Honest Ulsterman*, 83 (Summer 1987), 96–7.

O'DONOGHUE, BERNARD, rev. of Paul Muldoon, *Quoof*, in *Poetry Review*, 73:4 (Jan. 1984), 53–5.

—— 'Irish Plainstyle', rev. of Thomas Kinsella (ed.), *The New Oxford Book of Irish Verse*, and Paul Muldoon (ed.), *The Faber Book of Contemporary Irish Verse*, in *Poetry Review*, 76:3 (Oct. 1986) 51–3.

—— 'Voice-Shifts', rev. of Paul Muldoon, *Selected Poems, 1968–1983*, in *Irish Review*, 2 (1987), 121–5.

—— 'Involved Imaginings: Tom Paulin', in Neil Corcoran (ed.), *The Chosen Ground: Essays on the Contemporary Poetry of Northern Ireland* (Bridgend: Seren Books, 1992), 171–88.

O'DOWD, LIAM, 'Neglecting the Material Dimension: Irish Intellectuals and the Problem of Identity', *Irish Review*, 3 (1988), 8–17.

O'NEILL, MICHAEL, 'Bidding for Power', rev. of Medbh McGuckian, *Venus and the Rain*, in *Times Literary Supplement* (30 Nov. 1984), 1393.

O'ROURKE, BRIAN, 'The Long Walk of a Queen: The Representation of Ireland as a Woman in the Irish Literary Tradition', *Chiba Review*, 7 (1985), 1–49.

ORSMBY, FRANK (ed.), *Poets from the North of Ireland* (Belfast: Blackstaff, 1979).

OUTRAM, DORINDA, 'Holding the Future at Bay: The French Revolution and Modern Ireland', *Irish Review*, 6 (1989), 1–6.

Pasternak, Yevgeny, Pasternak, Yelena, and Azadovsky, Konstantin M. (eds.), *Letters Summer 1926: Correspondence between Pasternak, Tsvetayeva, Rilke* (Oxford: Oxford University Press, 1988).

Paulin, Tom, *A State of Justice* (London: Faber and Faber, 1977).

Paulin, Tom, *Thomas Hardy: The Poetry of Perception* (Basingstoke: Macmillan, 1977).

—— *The Strange Museum* (London: Faber and Faber, 1980).

—— *Liberty Tree* (London: Faber and Faber, 1983).

—— *Ireland and the English Crisis* (Newcastle upon Tyne: Bloodaxe Books, 1984).

—— *The Riot Act: A Version of Sophocles'* Antigone (London: Faber and Faber, 1985).

—— 'A New Look at the Language Question', *Ireland's Field Day*, ed. Field Day Theatre Company (London: Hutchinson, 1985).

—— 'Clare in Babylon', rev. of Mark Storey (ed.), *The Letters of John Clare*, in *Times Literary Supplement* (20 June 1986), 675–6.

—— *Fivemiletown* (London: Faber and Faber, 1987).

—— *The Hillsborough Script: A Dramatic Satire* (London: Faber and Faber, 1987).

—— *Minotaur: Poetry and the Nation State* (London: Faber and Faber, 1992).

—— (ed.), *The Faber Book of Political Verse* (London: Faber and Faber, 1986).

—— (ed.), *The Faber Book of Vernacular Verse* (London: Faber and Faber, 1990).

—— Interview with Eamonn Hughes, 'Q. & A. with Tom Paulin', *Irish Literary Supplement* (1988), 31–2.

—— Interview with John Haffenden, in John Haffenden (ed.), *Viewpoints: Poets in Conversation with John Haffenden* (London: Faber and Faber, 1981), 157–73.

—— Personal interview (20 Sept., 1991).

Rabinow, Paul (ed.), *The Foucault Reader* (Harmondsworth: Penguin, 1984).

Ramsey, Patrick, 'Quality and Quantity', rev. of Medbh McGuckian, *On Ballycastle Beach*, in *Irish Review*, 5 (Autumn 1988), 122–6.

Ricoeur, Paul, *Lectures on Ideology and Utopia*, ed. George H. Taylor (New York: Columbia University Press, 1986).

—— Interview with Richard Kearney, in Richard Kearney (ed.), *Dialogues with Contemporary Continental Thinkers: The Phenomenological Heritage* (Manchester: Manchester University Press, 1984), 36–45.

Robinson, Alan, *Instabilities in Contemporary British Poetry* (Basingstoke: Macmillan, 1988).

ROE, NICK, 'Cock and Bull Stories?', rev. of Paul Muldoon, *Quoof*, in *North Magazine*, 2 (1984), 44–5.

SAID, EDWARD, *The World, the Text and the Critic* (originally published 1983; London: Faber and Faber, 1984).

—— 'Permission to Narrate', *London Review of Books* (16–29 Feb. 1984), 13–17.

—— 'Representing the Colonized: Anthropology's Interlocuters', *Critical Inquiry*, 15:2 (1989), 205–25.

SARTRE, JEAN-PAUL, *What is Literature?*, trans. Bernard Frechtman (London: Methuen, 1950).

SCAMMELL, WILLIAM, 'Mid-air Street?', rev. of Paul Muldoon, *Meeting the British*, in *Irish Review*, 3 (1988), 144–6.

SMYTH, AILBHE, 'The Floozie in the Jacuzzi', *Irish Review*, 6 (1989), 7–24.

—— (ed.), *Women's Studies International Forum: Feminism in Ireland*, 2:4 (1988).

SPIVAK, GAYATRI CHAKRAVORTY, 'A Literary Representation of the Subaltern: A Woman's Text from the Third World', in *In Other Worlds* (London: Methuen, 1987).

STEVENSON, ANNE, 'With Eyes Open and Closed', rev. of Medbh McGuckian, *Portrait of Joanna*, in *Times Literary Supplement* (21 Aug. 1981), 952.

SWANN, CHARLES, 'Noah Webster: The Language of Politics/The Politics of Language', *Essays in Poetics*, 13:2 (Sept. 1988), 41–82.

TARROW, SIDNEY, *Democracy and Disorder* (Oxford: Oxford University Press, 1989).

TROTTER, DAVID, *The Making of the Reader: Language and Subjectivity in Modern American, English and Irish Poetry* (Basingstoke: Macmillan, 1984).

TYNYANOV, JURIJ, 'On Literary Evolution', in Ladislav Matejka and Krystyna Pomorska (eds.), *Readings in Russian Poetics* (Ann Arbor, Mich.: Michigan Slavic Publications, 1978).

VIRILIO, PAUL, and LOTRINGER, SYLVERE, *Pure War* (New York: Semiotext(e), 1983).

WALLACE, ANTHONY F. C., *The Death and Rebirth of the Seneca* (New York: Vintage Books, 1969).

WARD, MARGARET, and MCGIVERN, MARIE-THERESE, 'Images of Women in Northern Ireland', *Crane Bag*, 4:1 (1980), 66–72.

WARNER, MARINA, *Alone of All Her Sex: The Myth and Cult of the Virgin Mary* (originally published 1976; London: Pan, 1985).

WATSON, GEORGE, 'The Narrow Ground: Northern Poets and the Northern Irish Crisis', in Masaru Sekine (ed.), *Irish Writers and Society at Large* (Gerrards Cross: Colin Smythe, 1985).

WILLIAMS, GWYN, *Madoc: The Making of a Myth* (London: Eyre Methuen, 1979).

WILLIAMS, PATRICK, 'Spare that Tree!', rev. of Medbh McGuckian, *On Ballycastle Beach*, in *Honest Ulsterman*, 86 (1989), 49–52.

WILLS, CLAIR, 'Country Feelings', rev. of Medbh McGuckian, *On Ballycastle Beach*, in *Times Literary Supplement* (19–25 Aug. 1988), 915.

—— 'The Perfect Mother: Authority in the Poetry of Medbh McGuckian', *Text and Context*, 3 (1988), 91–111.

—— 'Upsetting the Public: Carnival, Hysteria, and Women's Texts', in David Shepherd and Ken Hirschkop (eds.), *Bakhtin and Cultural Theory* (Manchester: Manchester University Press, 1989), 130–51.

—— 'Contemporary Irish Women Poets: The Privatisation of Myth', in Harriet Jump (ed.), *Diverse Voices: Essays on Twentieth-Century Women Writers in English* (Hemel Hempstead: Harvester Wheatsheaf, 1991), 248–72.

—— 'The Lie of the Land: Language, Imperialism and Trade in Paul Muldoon's *Meeting the British*', in Neil Corcoran (ed.), *The Chosen Ground: Essays on the Contemporary Poetry of Northern Ireland* (Bridgend: Seren Books, 1992), 123–49.

—— 'Making Waves', rev. of Medbh McGuckian, in *Marconi's Cottage, Times Literary Supplement* (10 July 1992), 23.

—— 'Mothers and Other Strangers', rev. of Julia Kristeva, *Strangers to Ourselves*', in *Women: A Cultural Review*, 3:3 (1992), 281–91.

WILSON, WILLIAM A., 'Paul Muldoon and the Poetics of Sexual Difference', *Contemporary Literature*, 28:3 (1987), 317–31.

WITOSZEK, NINA, and SHEERAN, JO, 'From Explanations to Intervention', *Crane Bag*, 9:1 (1985), 83–6.

YEATS, W. B., *Collected Poems* (London: Macmillan, 1939).

—— *Collected Plays* (originally published 1934; London: Macmillan, 1953).

YOUNG, ROBERT, *White Mythologies: History, Writing and the West* (London: Routledge, 1990).

Index